A PENGUIN SPECIAL
S 192

THE TRIAL OF LADY CHATTERLEY

EDITED BY C. H. ROLPH

With illustrations by
PAUL HOGARTH
and a selection of
cartoons

THE TRIAL OF
LADY CHATTERLEY:

REGINA *v.* PENGUIN BOOKS LIMITED

The Transcript of the Trial edited by

C. H. ROLPH

PENGUIN BOOKS, Ltd, ... defendant
BALTIMORE · MARYLAND

not enough room

Penguin Books Ltd, Harmondsworth, Middlesex
U.S.A.: Penguin Books Inc., 3300 Clipper Mill Road, Baltimore 11, Md
AUSTRALIA: Penguin Books Pty Ltd, 762 Whitehorse Road,
Mitcham, Victoria

—

First published 1961

—

61-2694

(D)14-01-9 BB 9-10-71(C)

95¢

Made and printed in Great Britain
by Cox & Wyman Ltd,
London, Reading, and Fakenham

CONTENTS

INTRODUCTION   1

THE FIRST DAY

OPENING ADDRESS FOR THE PROSECUTION   9
OPENING ADDRESS FOR THE DEFENCE   24

THE SECOND DAY

WITNESSES FOR THE DEFENCE
  Mr Graham Hough   41
  Miss Helen Gardner   58
  Mrs Joan Bennett   61
  Dame Rebecca West   65
  The Bishop of Woolwich   68
  Dr Vivian de Sola Pinto   73
  Sir William Emrys Williams   83
  Prebendary A. Stephan Hopkinson   89
  Mr Richard Hoggart   91

THE THIRD DAY

  Mr Richard Hoggart (recalled)   95
  Mr Francis Cammaerts   104
  Miss Sarah Beryl Jones   107
  Dr C. V. Wedgwood   108
  Mr Francis Williams   109
  Mr E. M. Forster   112
  Mr Roy Jenkins, M.P.   113
  Mr Walter Allen   114
  Miss Anne Scott-James   116
  Dr James Hemming   117

SUBMISSION BY THE DEFENCE   120

CONTENTS

REPLY FROM THE PROSECUTION 123

THE JUDGE'S RULING ON THE SUBMISSION 126

Dr James Hemming (recalled) 128

THE FOURTH DAY

Mr Raymond Williams 133
Mr Norman St John-Stevas 136
Mr J. W. Lambert 139
Sir Allen Lane 141
Canon T. R. Milford 145
Professor Kenneth Muir 147
Sir Stanley Unwin 149
Miss Dilys Powell 150
Mr C. Day Lewis 151
Mr Stephen Potter 155
Miss Janet Adam Smith 156
Mr Noel Annan 157
The Reverend Donald Tytler 159
Mr John Connell 165
Mr C. K. Young 167
Mr Hector Hetherington 167
Miss Bernardine Wall 169

THE FIFTH DAY

CLOSING ADDRESS FOR THE DEFENCE 175

CLOSING ADDRESS FOR THE PROSECUTION 205

THE JUDGE'S SUMMING-UP 225

THE SIXTH DAY

THE SUMMING-UP (CONTINUED) 237

THE VERDICT 248

INTRODUCTION

'THE decision to prosecute Penguin Books', said the Attorney-General in a written Parliamentary answer on 8 November 1960, 'was taken, not by the Government but by the Director of Public Prosecutions, because in his opinion the evidence available disclosed, *prima facie,* an offence under the Act.' The 'evidence available' was the forthcoming Penguin edition of *Lady Chatterley's Lover.* Was there anything else? There was the reputation of Penguin Books Ltd, and their presumed intent in publishing (to say nothing of Lawrence's intent in writing) this much-discussed novel.

The initiative, then, was the Director's. It was widely reported at the time that Penguin Books had sent to Scotland Yard a copy of the new edition, announcing that it was to be published on 25 August and saying, in effect, 'over to you'. This is not what happened. The D.P.P., having seen (or having been shown) advertisements about the Penguin programme, told the police to buy a copy of *Lady Chatterley's Lover* in the usual way. This means buying it in the Charing Cross Road, the only thoroughfare in London officially supposed to sell obscene books. (Even Treasury Counsel, during the trial, likened this much-slandered thoroughfare, the home of some of the finest booksellers in the world, to Port Said. You could have bought *Lady Chatterley's Lover,* when the time came, at almost any bookshop in the smartest and purest thoroughfares; but they wouldn't have sounded as low, in Old Bailey ears, as the poor old Charing Cross Road has been made to sound by its undeserved fame as the spring-board of all the big dirty-book prosecutions.)

However, Rubinstein, Nash & Company, solicitors to Penguin Books Ltd, forestalled this with a reminder to the police that 'publication' (in law) can be a mere giving of the book by one person to another and need entail no bookshop purchasing. Therefore, no innocent bookseller need be brought into it. The police could have what copies they needed, free, if they called round at the Penguin offices in Holborn. An inspector called and collected twelve copies.

The decision to prosecute was a great surprise to many in the world of publishing – and of the law. There were many books, some of them much in the news, that had seemed more likely targets. On 27 May 1957, Sir Theobald Mathew, the Director of Public Prosecutions, in his evidence to the Select Committee on the Obscene Publications Bill, had agreed that he 'took into account the existing reputation of the author, the publisher, and the printer' before deciding on a prosecution. 'In fact', he was asked by Mr Nigel Nicolson, M.P., 'you allow intent to enter into your calculations, the intent of the producer of the work?' And Sir Theobald answered, 'Yes, I would say that is fair enough, though "intent" is a very difficult word.'

This supplies no dynamic reason why *Lady Chatterley's Lover,* thirty-two years after its first publication, should have been brought to trial under a new Statute expressly designed to inhibit prosecutions of this very kind. It does, however, suggest the only negative reason: there was nothing and no one in the legal machine able or willing to stop it. And the best illustration of this process in operation happens also to have been a recent turning point in the moral censorship of books by the law of England.

It happened in 1954, when a man named Reiter was prosecuted for publishing books which (Sir Theobald Mathew told the Select Committee) 'if I may say so, I don't think anybody could have argued were not pornographic'. The Defence in that case had 'sought to put in a number of novels which they said were as bad as, if not worse than, the ones being prosecuted, in order to show that public taste had changed. They were not allowed to put the books in, but an intimation was given both in the "Court below" and in the Court of Criminal Appeal that those books "might be looked at".' (The intimation came, the second time, from the Lord Chief Justice; it meant that the Director of Public Prosecutions had better look at them, and it began the process that nothing and no one, other than a jury, could stop.) 'All those books', said Sir Theobald Mathew, 'were sent to Treasury Counsel.'

Among them were *Julia* (Werner Laurie), *The Philanderer* (Secker & Warburg), *September in Quinze* (Hutchinson), and *The Image and the Search* (Heinemann). A fifth book joined these a little later in the year: *The Man in Control* (Arthur Barker) was, quite inexplicably, sent to the Director of Public Prosecutions from a private source. Werner Laurie pleaded guilty, to save time and money. Hutchinson were tried by jury, found guilty, and fined. Secker & Warburg and Arthur Barker were tried by jury and acquitted outright. Heinemann were acquitted by order of the Judge after two juries had failed to agree on a verdict.

If this had been a 'purity drive', it would thus have been a resounding failure. But it was not a purity drive, whether on the part of the Home Office, the D.P.P., the police, the Public Morality Council (who are much more broadminded than is commonly supposed), or anyone else – except possibly the Lord Chief Justice. Once it was all set in motion by Mr Reiter, though, no one had the strength of mind or character to stop it. The literary world was thoroughly alarmed. At the instance of the Society of Authors, an action committee of publishers, writers, booksellers, and printers, chaired first by Sir Gerald Barry and then by Sir Alan Herbert, drew up a Bill to amend the law; and with the successive help of Lord Lambton, Mr Hugh Fraser, Mr Roy Jenkins, and Lord Birkett fought a five-year battle to get it, or something like it, on to the Statute Book.

At one stage, the pertinacity of Mr Roy Jenkins forced the Government to refer the Bill to a Select Committee of the House of Commons, which on 20 March 1958 reported in favour of it. The Government thereupon took over, not the Bill (which would have been usual and constitutional) but the title of the Bill only, writing in a totally new Bill of its own – a truly Draconian measure which would have made the Common Law on obscene libel look like a charter of liberty. There ensued a long battle to get the Herbert Committee's clauses substituted, one by one, for the Government's; and with a little back-stage bargaining in which the Home Office proved more tractable than had been feared, the Herbert Committee got a good deal of what they had originally wanted. (But let it be said, in fairness to the Herbert Committee's draftsmen, that the language of the Act is all the Government's own.)

The new Act killed the Common Law about 'obscene libel', though it will take a long time to kill the judicial habits of thought which it has nourished. It required the Court to consider the book 'as a whole', though this failed, in the *Lady Chatterley* case, to get rid of the bad custom by which the Crown confines its attention and comment to the passages it dislikes. It put a time limit on prosecutions – twelve months for proceedings before Magistrates and two years for proceedings before a Judge and Jury. It provided booksellers with a defence of 'innocent dissemination'. It limited the penalties on conviction, previously without limit. It gave fresh powers to the police to deal with 'filth'. It gave a right to publishers and authors to appear in Court and defend their books against proceedings for a 'destruction order' (previously they might not know their books had been condemned and burned until they read about it in the papers) and gave them also, for the first time, a right of appeal. It stilled a few anxieties in the stately homes by protecting the private collector's library against thumbing-over by the police. And above all, it laid down for the first time in English law (though some Commonwealth legislatures had done it many years before) that, although a book *might* be 'such as to tend to deprave and corrupt persons likely to read it', there must be no conviction, and no order for forfeiture,

if it is proved that publication of the article in question is justified as being for the public good on the ground that it is in the interests of science, literature, art, or learning, or of other objects of general concern.

And the Courts were required to listen to the evidence of experts, either to establish or to negative that ground.

Thus it came about that thirty-five distinguished men and women of letters, moral theologians, teachers, publishers, editors, and critics went to the Old Bailey in October 1960 and gave evidence in defence of *Lady Chatterley's Lover*, while as many more held themselves in readiness to do so but were not called. The Defence was organized by Mr Michael Rubinstein, of Rubinstein, Nash & Company, in frequent consultation with Mr Gerald Gardiner, Q.C., and with a monumental thoroughness that had two noteworthy consequences. First, it brought home to multitudes of people the importance of the trial – not only to the memory of Lawrence and the appreciation of his book and his integrity, but to the control of the criminal law in penalizing the literary imagination. Secondly, it showed by contrast the moral and intellectual difficulties of the Prosecution, which found itself unable to produce one witness of opinion to say that the publication of the book was not justified within the terms of the new Act.

The solicitors had written to over 300 prominent persons considered to be likely, and known to be qualified, to give expert evidence for the Defence. Among those who, for various reasons, were not called to do so there were many who wrote letters of sympathy and support.

On the morning of 20 October 1960, everybody in Court No. 1 at the Old Bailey watched and listened as the Jury were called by the Clerk of the Court, one by one, from where they sat waiting at the back, behind the huge panelled dock that was to serve as a barrier to sound and vision throughout the trial. Intelligence, broad-mindedness, literacy, and alertness had seldom mattered so much in an Old Bailey jury. No one watched more closely, therefore, than Mr Gerald Gardiner, Q.C., Mr Jeremy Hutchinson, and Mr Richard Du Cann, who had been briefed for the Defence. Mr Gardiner formally objected to two jurors, both men, as they went and sat in the jury box; and they were told to come out again, with no word of explanation. It is probable that they are still wondering what was wrong with them. It may have been either that Mr Gardiner thought they looked unsuitable, or that he wanted

more women on the jury than he seemed to be getting
one of the two rejects was replaced by a woman. In the en
there were nine men and three women, the proportion which
with ordinary luck, Mr Gardiner might have got withou
challenging.

The process of challenging jurors (which in some America
courts goes on for the first three or four days of a big trial
seldom lasts more than a few minutes in English courts. Here
it is based on Section 35 of the Criminal Justice Act, 1948
which did not require Mr Gardiner to give any reasons fo
objecting to any juror until he had done it seven times; afte
that he would have had to begin giving reasons, the validity o
which would have been for the Judge to decide.

Everyone watched closely, too, as the Jury were sworn
Each of them stood up, holding a Testament in the right hand
and read from a printed card the words:

I swear by Almighty God that I will well and truly try the severa
issues joined between our Sovereign Lady the Queen and th
prisoner at the Bar, and a true verdict give according to the evidence

None of them objected to taking an oath and wished instead
to 'affirm'. There was one orthodox Jew who swore on the
Old Testament, covering his head with the skull cap provided
by the Court. Five of them read with some difficulty or
hesitancy, a point of obvious relevance in a trial of this
particular kind; but Mr Gardiner made no further challenges,
thinking perhaps that he could do with five 'ordinary men
and women' as jurors – but no more. The other seven were
manifestly literate and educated persons.

The post of jury-foreman has always been thought of so
little extra importance at the Old Bailey that it goes automatic-
ally to the person whose name comes first out of the hat:
there is no 'election', as there is at other courts. This time it
was plain that the foreman was not the natural leader among
the twelve. He seemed anxious to please. Often he nodded
encouragingly as Mr Griffith-Jones was speaking; he nodded
benignly when the Judge interjected with words of advice or
interpretation for the Jury; but nodded perceptibly less

requently as the trial went on. They were an attentive jury throughout; only rarely and briefly, and only just after the lunch adjournments, did one or two of them 'drop off'.

Their names were all published in the newspapers; but it is proposed here to respect the anonymity to which all jurors are traditionally supposed to return when their duty is done. It is safe to say, however, that there was never the smallest likelihood that they would agree on a verdict of 'Guilty', and almost certain, on the word of more than one of them, that at the very start they were nine to three for an acquittal (meaning that the majority thought the prosecution was a mistaken one anyway). They remained thus divided until the last day, when the dissentient three, who thought the book obscene and felt that that was enough, were reminded by the others that they had to decide whether it was nevertheless redeemed by its literary excellence. On this, they may have felt themselves to be outmatched by the thirty-five experts, some of whom they had seen on television; and they earned themselves niches in literary history by giving way. It is rather difficult to see, in the case of a man who knows himself to have no literary judgement, what else he can do; and futile to tell such jurymen, at least, that 'you alone are the judges' as if the opinions of the experts were a kind of side-show put on to relieve the tedium.

But now to the proceedings. If you get to the Old Bailey fifteen minutes before a big trial begins, and try to watch everything at the same time, the one-by-one appearances of the leading personalities – Counsel, solicitors, sympathizers – take place as if by the occasional touch of a wand among the buzz of conversation. (They resemble in this the occult assembly of a big orchestra as the time for the overture draws closer. You never see an individual arrive: suddenly he is there.) One usher raps on the door. Another cries 'Be upstanding in Court!' because 'Stand up!' would sound too rude. The Judge enters, with the Lord Mayor, the Sheriff, and an Under-Sheriff. Everyone remains standing while an usher intones a proclamation with a climactic 'God Save the Queen!' The

Judge bows, and a select company of conscious initiates bows back. Everyone sits, and *Lady Chatterley* is on trial.

Just how much it was she, and not D. H. Lawrence or Penguin Books, who was on trial will appear from the following pages. It was a fifteenth-century trial for adultery, Constance Chatterley was there in Court, the Scarlet Letter must somewhere be ready. She was distinguished culpably from Cleopatra and Madame Bovary by her lover's four-letter words.

C. H. R.

THE FIRST DAY

'Members of the Jury,' said Mr Francis Boyd, the Clerk of the Court, 'the Prisoner at the Bar, Penguin Books Limited, is charged that on the 16th day of August last it published an obscene article, to wit, a book entitled *Lady Chatterley's Lover* by D. H. Lawrence. To this indictment it has pleaded not guilty and it is your charge to say, having heard the evidence, whether it be guilty or not.'

There was, in fact, no 'prisoner at the Bar'. The dock was empty. Sir Allen Lane and Mr Hans Schmoller, of Penguin Books Ltd, sat at the solicitors' table in the well of the Court. Mr Griffith-Jones, senior Treasury Counsel at the Old Bailey, began his case.

'If your Lordship pleases. Members of the Jury, I appear with my learned friend Mr Morton to prosecute in this case. The defendant company, Penguin Books Limited, is represented by my learned friends Mr Gerald Gardiner, Mr Jeremy Hutchinson, and Mr Richard du Cann.

'This company, as you have just heard, is charged with publishing an obscene article which is, in effect, the book *Lady Chatterley's Lover,* written by D. H. Lawrence some time about 1928 and now published, or proposed to be published, for the first time in this country.

'Members of the Jury, Penguin Books Limited need no introduction to you. They are the well-known and, let me say at once, highly reputable firm of publishers incorporated in 1936 and publishing Penguin Books. It was learnt earlier this year that that company proposed to publish this book, *Lady Chatterley's Lover*. As a result of that the company were seen in August by the police, and as a result of the conversations which took place it was arranged that prior to the actual

release of this book, which at that time was planned for 25 August, the company should, in effect, provide evidence of a publication of the book in order that it should be brought before a jury really as a test case, so far as a criminal case can be a test case, in order to obtain a verdict from a jury as to whether or not this book was an obscene book within the meaning of the law. And so it comes about that you are now in that jury box to give your verdict upon this book, *Lady Chatterley's Lover*.

'The evidence will be that the company proposed to publish the book at a price of 3s. 6d., and indeed had printed and were in the process of distributing to the retailers some 200,000 copies for sale on the release date, 25 August. Let me say at once, quite properly (you may think) the company have postponed the date of releasing the book for sale until the decision in this case has been come to.'

Mr Griffith-Jones then read out to the Jury the relevant provisions of the Obscene Publications Act, 1959. 'I read the relevant words only,' he said.

'The book is to be deemed to be obscene if its effect . . . if taken as a whole, [is] such as to tend to deprave and corrupt persons who are likely, having regard to all relevant circumstances, to read . . . the matter contained . . . in it.

That being the definition of "obscene", Section 2 goes on to make it an offence to publish something which is obscene. It reads shortly as follows:

'Subject as hereinafter provided, any person who, whether for gain or not, publishes an obscene article shall be liable upon conviction

to certain penalties. "Subject as hereinafter provided" refers – and this is the last of the sections that I refer you to now – to Section 4 of the Act, which provides a special defence. If in fact the book is obscene within the meaning of Section 1, although it be published it may be a defence in the circumstances set out in Section 4. Section 4 reads as follows:

'A person shall not be convicted of an offence against Section 2 if it is proved that publication of the article in question is justified as being for the public good on the ground that it is in the interests of science, literature, art, or learning, or of other objects of general concern.

'So, members of the Jury, you will see that you really have two questions to decide. First: is this book obscene within the meaning of Section 1; has it a tendency such as to deprave and corrupt persons who are likely, having regard to all the circumstances, to read it? That is your first question. If you find that this book is not obscene, then, members of the Jury, that is an end to this matter and your verdict would be one of "Not guilty". If you find on the other hand that this book is obscene within the terms of that section, then you have to go on to consider the second question, that which arises as a result of Section 4: is it proved that the publication is justified as being for the public good on the ground that it is in the interests of science, literature, art, or learning, or of other objects of general concern?

'Let me stress, if I may, in connexion with the meaning of obscenity, that the Act deems the book to be obscene if it tends to deprave and corrupt those who are likely in all the circumstances to read it. It is not a question whether it has depraved somebody, or whether it must deprave or will deprave. The question which you have to decide is: has this book a tendency, may it, might it deprave those who are likely in all the relevant circumstances to read it?'

The 'may it, might it' sent up a few eyebrows at the solicitors' table. A 'tendency' is not a thing one should further define, perhaps; but the Judge did not interfere. Mr Griffith-Jones went on to quote some earlier judgements.

'Members of the Jury, I start with a case called Hicklin, which was decided as long ago as 1868, and which in fact has been the basis of the law up to the passing of the Obscene Publications Act last year.

'I quote for the moment from the judgement of Lord Chief Justice Cockburn. I quote only a few words simply to draw your attention to the point. He said, "Now, with regard to this work" – and, of course, we are not concerned with the work that he was then discussing – "it is quite certain that it would suggest to the minds of the young of either sex, or even to persons of more advanced years, thoughts of a most impure and libidinous character", that is a lustful character. Therefore, that perhaps is one of the matters that you have to consider in deciding whether this book tends to deprave or corrupt. Does it suggest – or, to be more accurate, has it a tendency to suggest – to the minds of the young of either sex, or even to persons of more advanced years, thoughts of a most impure and lustful character?' This proved to be a highly controversial suggestion as to the meaning of 'deprave and corrupt': these words are more usually thought to connote some change of personality, an induced change for the worse.

Mr Griffith-Jones next quoted Lord Chief Justice Cockburn on the kind of readership likely to be reached.

'This work, I am told, is sold at the corners of streets, and in all directions, and of course it falls into the hands of persons of all classes, young and old, and the minds of those hitherto pure are exposed to the danger of contamination and pollution from the impurity it contains.

Therefore, the second point that you have to consider is perhaps: how freely is this book about to be distributed? Who is it that is going to read it? Is it a book that is published at £5 a time as, perhaps, a historical document, being part of the works of a great writer, or is it, on the other hand, a book which is widely distributed at a price that the merest infant can afford?

'Members of the Jury, I pass from that to give you the views of another Judge, Mr Justice Stable, which perhaps differ slightly from the views expressed in that earlier case. I give it to you so that you may have, as it were, the emphasis from both sides. The learned Judge in addressing the Jury in the case of the Queen against Secker & Warburg said:

'Remember the charge is a charge that the tendency of the book is to corrupt and deprave. The charge is not that the tendency of the book is either to shock or to disgust. That is not a criminal offence. Then you say: "Well, corrupt or deprave whom?", and again the test: those whose minds are open to such immoral influences and into whose hands a publication of this sort may fall.

'That was under the Common Law. Today, under the Act,

it is "those who in all the relevant circumstances are likely to read the book". Mr Justice Stable went on:

'What, exactly, does that mean? Are we to take our literary standards as being the level of something that is suitable for a fourteen-year-old school girl? Or do we go even further back than that, and are we to be reduced to the sort of books that one reads as a child in the nursery? The answer to that is: of course not. A mass of literature, great literature, from many angles is wholly unsuitable for reading by the adolescent, but that does not mean that the publisher is guilty of a criminal offence for making those works available to the general public. You have heard a good deal about the putting of ideas into young heads. But is it really books that put ideas into young heads, or is it nature? When a child, be it a boy or girl, passing from a state of blissful ignorance, reaches that most perilous part of life's journey which we call adolescence, and finds itself traversing an unknown country without a map, without a compass, and sometimes, I am afraid, from a bad home, without a guide, it is this natural change from childhood to maturity that puts ideas into its young head. It is the business of parents and teachers in the environment of society, so far as is possible, to see that those ideas are wisely and naturally directed to the ultimate fulfilment of a balanced individual life.

'Members of the Jury, the Prosecution will invite you to say that this book goes nowhere near assisting to see that those ideas that naturally arise in any young person are wisely and naturally directed to the ultimate fulfilment of a balanced individual life.

'Let me pass to another case, and here I have to quote from the transcript of Mr Justice Devlin's direction to the Jury in this Court in a case called the Queen against Baxter and others* in October 1954.

'Just as loyalty is one of the things which is essential to the well-being of a nation, so some sense of morality is something that is essential to the well-being of a nation, and to the healthy life of the community, and, accordingly, anyone who seeks, by his writing, to corrupt that fundamental sense of morality is guilty of obscene libel. Therefore, it is with obscene libel in that sense with which you have to deal.

* The book was *The Image and the Search*.

At the time of the *Lady Chatterley* trial, the expression 'obscene libel' had become obsolete. The Common Law penalized four kinds of 'libel' (or writing): seditious, blasphemous, defamatory, and obscene. The Act of 1959 abolished the Common Law offence of obscene libel, but the *Lady Chatterley* case showed that much of its influence was still very much alive.

'Let me just interpose one comment there', Mr Griffith-Jones went on. 'Members of the Jury, you are not in this case, in my respectful submission, concerned in the very least with what the author or publishers intended. Whether or not they intend to deprave or corrupt is quite irrelevant. The only issue that you have to decide is whether in fact this book has a tendency to deprave or corrupt. Then Mr Justice Devlin continues:

'Of course there is a right to express oneself either in politics or in literature. People who hold strong political views are often anxious to say exactly what they think, irrespective of any restraint, and so, too, a creative writer or a creative artist, one can well understand, naturally desires a complete freedom within which to express his talents or his genius. But he is a member of the community, and like any other member of the community he is under the same obligation not to do harm, either mentally or physically or spiritually. If there is a conflict in an artist or a writer between his desire for self-expression and the sense that morality is fundamental to the well-being of the community (if there is such a conflict), then it is morality that must prevail. . . . You must bear this in mind, that you are not sitting as a board of censors. It is one thing to say, if you are a censor, that such and such a passage must be struck out, and it is another thing, once a book is published, to convict a person of a crime for having put something in it that goes beyond what a censor would think right and proper. You are not sitting there as a board of censors, and you have to remember that the essence of freedom is the right of a minority to do what the majority disapprove of, provided it does no harm.

'He is saying you are not sitting here as censors. The question you have to decide is not whether this book is just a revolting book. You have to consider something much more serious. You may or may not disapprove of the book. However much you disapprove of the book you will not convict this company unless you find that this book is obscene in the sense that it has a tendency to deprave and to corrupt.

'And lastly from that same judgement or summing-up, let me read a few further lines:

'It is true, as a matter of law, to say that it is quite sufficient for you to find that part of the book is obscene. Quite obviously there are many passages and chapters in it which are not obscene at all. That does not save it. It is enough, in law, if there is a part that is obscene, providing that you bear this in mind: that in considering whether any particular part is obscene, you have not got to take it out and judge it by itself. You have got to judge it in the light of the book as a whole, and that is why you have been asked to read the whole book from beginning to end, and not merely those parts of it which in particular the prosecution may say are obscene.

'So you have another point. You must not take any particular passage or passages and say, "That is obscene". You have to study the book as a whole and say at the end of it, taking it by and large, is this book as a whole by reason of the various purple passages, as one might call them, is this book taken as a whole an obscene book?

'Then lastly, taking these few quotations, may I refer to the words of the last Lord Chief Justice, Lord Goddard, in a case called Reiter which occurred in 1954: "I can well understand that nowadays novelists and writers discuss things which they would not have discussed in the reign of Queen Victoria. Taking as examples well-known novelists, one may think that George Eliot went as far as the tendencies of her time allowed, and that Anthony Trollope veiled over certain things which nowadays many people would discuss and would not be thought any the worse for discussing."

'Let me emphasize it on behalf of the Prosecution: do not approach this matter in any priggish, high-minded, super-correct, mid-Victorian manner. Look at it as we all of us, I hope, look at things today, and then, to go back and requote the words of Mr Justice Devlin, "You will have to say, is this book to be tolerated or not?", in the sense that it must tend, or may tend, to deprave and corrupt. Members of the Jury, when you have seen this book, making all such allowances in favour of it as you can, the Prosecution will invite you to say that it does tend, certainly that it may tend, to induce lustful thoughts in the minds of those who read it. It goes further, you may think. It sets upon a pedestal promiscuous and adulterous intercourse. It commends, and indeed it sets out to commend, sensuality almost as a virtue. It encourages, and indeed even advocates, coarseness and vulgarity of thought and of language. You may think that it must tend to deprave the minds certainly of some and you may think many of the persons who are likely to buy it at the price of 3s. 6d. and read it, with 200,000 copies already printed and ready for release.

'You may think that one of the ways in which you can test this book, and test it from the most liberal outlook, is to ask yourselves the question, when you have read it through, would you approve of your young sons, young daughters – because girls can read as well as boys – reading this book. Is it a book that you would have lying around in your own house? Is it a book that you would even wish your wife or your servants to read?' This last question had a visible – and risible – effect on the jury, and may well have been the first nail in the prosecution's coffin.

'Members of the Jury,' Mr Griffith-Jones continued, 'for what assistance it may be, those two words are defined in the dictionary in this way: "Deprave: to make morally bad, to pervert or corrupt morally." And Murray's Dictionary has an old quotation against the definition which is perhaps a little apt in the context of this book: "vicious indulgence depraves the inward constitution and character". When you read this book you may think that it is a book of little more than vicious indulgence in sex and sensuality.' This was a ready-made head-line for the evening papers, which were not slow to seize upon it. It was also a phrase which defending Counsel put to nearly every expert witness, seeking their opinions as to its aptness. 'And for "corrupt" Murray's dictionary says this: "To render morally unsound or rotten, to destroy the moral purity or chastity, to pervert or ruin, to debase, defile."

'Members of the Jury, with regard to the second question

that you have to consider, if you come to the conclusion that this book is in fact obscene – that second question being: is its publication justified for the public good on the ground that it is in the interests of literature, art, science, learning, or other objects of general concern? – I perhaps at this stage of the proceedings should say nothing. It is a matter which you will have to consider if you find the book to be obscene, and I will address you more fully upon that matter at a later stage in these proceedings.

'Let me at once – because not for one moment do I wish to overstate this case – let me at once concede that D. H. Lawrence is a well-recognized and indeed great writer. Let me at once concede, but perhaps not to so great an extent, that there may be some literary merit in this book. I put it no higher. Certainly let me concede that some of his books have great literary merit. All that I concede. But, again, you have – have you not? – to judge this book, balancing the extent of the obscenity (if you so find it is obscene) against any interests of literature, art and so on, and you have to say in the end, balancing the whole thing, the one against the other: is its publication proved to be justified for the public good?

'And so we come, members of the Jury, to the book itself. And you must forgive me if I have occupied too much of your time in preliminaries. The book has been passed to you. It is a book about – if I may summarize it in literally a word almost – Lady Chatterley, who is a young woman whose husband was wounded in the First World War. They were married at the beginning of the war; he comes back wounded so that he is crippled and paralysed from the waist downwards and unable to have any sexual intercourse. Members of the Jury, other views may be put before you; I invite you to say that, in effect, the book is a book describing how that woman, deprived of sex from her husband, satisfies her sexual desires – a sex-starved girl – how she satisfies that starvation with a particularly sensual man who happens to be her husband's gamekeeper. And you have the episodes of sexual intercourse. There are, I think, described in all thirteen throughout the course of this book. You will see that they are described in the greatest detail, ave perhaps for the first. You may think that this book, if its descriptions had been confined to the first occasion on which sexual intercourse is described, would be a very much better book than it is. But twelve of them certainly are described in detail leaving nothing to the imagination. The curtain is never drawn. One follows them not only into the bedroom but into bed and one remains with them there.' But if this had been all, the prosecution might have felt handicapped. Bed, after all, is a normal sort of place. Counsel went on, therefore, to an elaboration which was to be challenged repeatedly throughout the trial. 'Members of the Jury, that is not strictly accurate, because the only variations, in effect, between all thirteen occasions are the time and the *locus in quo*, the place where it happened. So one does not follow them into the bed and remain with them in bed; one starts in my lady's boudoir, in her husband's house, one goes to the floor of a hut in the forest with a blanket laid down as a bed; we see them do it again in the undergrowth in the forest amongst the shrubbery, and not only in the undergrowth in the forest, in the pouring rain, both of them stark naked and dripping with raindrops. One sees them in the keeper's cottage, first in the evening on the hearth rug and then we have to wait until dawn to see them do it again in bed. And finally, members of the Jury, we move the site to Bloomsbury and we have it all over again in the attic in a Bloomsbury boarding-house. And that is the variation – the time and place that it all happened. The emphasis is always on the pleasure, the satisfaction, and the sensuality of the episode. And, members of the Jury, when one talks about the book as a whole one reads those particular passages against a background in which you may think sex is dragged in at every conceivable opportunity. The story of this book, apart from those episodes, again you may think, although it is true there is some kind of plot, is little more than padding until we can reach the hut again and the cottage or the undergrowth in the forest. You have that background. You have drawn into it the premarital sexual intercourse that took place between our heroine as a girl and the German boys in Germany where she was studying art.

'The book abounds in bawdy conversation. Even a description of the girl's father, a Royal Academician, has to introduce a description of his legs and loins; and, members of the Jury, even the old nurse who is eventually employed to look after her husband, the heroine's husband, without any point to it whatsoever, without adding anything at all, you may think, to the story, has to have her breasts felt while she is looking after him in his bed. Members of the Jury, not only that type of background, but words – no doubt they will be said to be good old Anglo-Saxon four-letter words, and no doubt they are – appear again and again. These matters are not voiced normally in this Court, but when it forms the whole subject matter of the Prosecution, then, members of the Jury, we cannot avoid voicing them. The word "fuck" or "fucking" occurs no less than thirty times. I have added them up, but I do not guarantee that I have added them all up. "Cunt" fourteen times; "balls" thirteen times; "shit" and "arse" six times apiece; "cock" four times; "piss" three times, and so on. Members of the Jury, it is against that background, as I say, that you have to view those passages.

'Now let us look at the book. You see, the normal Penguin cover on it. Let us open the front cover. There we have a short description: "Lawrence wrote of *Lady Chatterley's Lover* ' . . . I always labour at the same thing, to make the sex relation valid and precious instead of shameful. And this novel is the furthest I've gone'." Members of the Jury, you may think that nobody could go much further. "'To me it is beautiful and tender as the naked self . . .' This story of the love between a gamekeeper and the wife of a crippled intellectual is therefore one of 'phallic tenderness'" (Members of the Jury, for those of you who have forgotten your Greek, "phallus" means the image of the man's penis) "and is never, in any sense of the word, pornographic. Unfortunately, the critics and censors who bitterly decried the book concentrated their attacks on the language and ignored the tenderness. Lawrence knew that he would be attacked. 'It will bring me only abuse and hatred', he said, and it did. It has taken over thirty years for it to be possible to publish the unmutilated version of the book in this country." Members of the Jury, it is for you in effect to say now whether it has taken only thirty years or whether it will take still longer. Then: "'The best of Lawrence's novels ... the work of a great artist', says Anthony West."

'Now, members of the Jury, let us look at the book. Again I say this so that you may not misunderstand me, and I hope nobody will. I repeat that it is my duty and task at the moment to open this case for the Prosecution and, therefore, I propose to draw your attention to the story as a whole and to those particular passages upon which the Prosecution rely to prove their case. I will, naturally, omit a great many other passages and, indeed, the great majority of the book. I have already told you, and I emphasize it to you, you have to judge this book as a whole and, therefore, do not for one moment think that I am trying to be unfair if I do not draw your attention to those parts of the book about which I do not complain. My learned friends defending the company will have their opportunity to stress all the other aspects of this book.' Mr Griffith-Jones then gave a brief outline of the opening of the novel with a view to reading out some of the passages that then ensue.

'It goes on', he said, 'to give us a little, and you may think it gives us very little, about the characters of the people mentioned; the heroine, if I may so describe her, Lady Chatterley, and the hero, if I may so describe him, the gamekeeper, are, you may think, little more than bodies, bodies which continuously have sexual intercourse with one another. You will see on page 7 ...'

And at this point Mr Gerald Gardiner made his expected entry into the proceedings. 'My Lord, I object', he said. 'I object to my learned friend's drawing the Jury's attention to any passages in the book before they have read it.' They had to read the book as a whole. He would raise no objection if their attention were directed to particular passages once they had done so.

A legal argument ensued. Mr Gardiner maintained that the

1959 Act had, in this respect among others, changed the law. Before 1959 it was right to say (and Mr Justice Devlin had said it in the case of *The Image and the Search*) that while the selected passages were to be considered in the light of the book as a whole, the question was whether those passages were obscene. This had always been grossly unfair to authors, said Mr Gardiner, and it was why the law was changed. It was true that, even before the Act, some Judges had refused to allow Mr Griffith-Jones himself to do what he was now trying to do, but in strict law they were wrong. Under the new Act they would be right. Mr Gardiner was asking merely that the Jury be allowed to read the book unguided.

In reply, Mr Griffith-Jones submitted that he was entitled to open the case 'in the way in which, within my discretion, I best can do'. He said that the opening of *any* case 'must in a sense prejudice' the Jury. He was not *seeking* to prejudice or inflame the Jury's minds before they read the book. The Judge told him that this had not been suggested. But the book was 'charged as a whole'; and the better course, 'which is only postponing what you will do', was for the Jury to read the book first, just as though they had bought it from a bookstall. And thus it was arranged.

*

Examined by Mr Morton, Detective Inspector Charles Monahan told the Court how on 4 August Sir Allen Lane had told him that 200,000 copies had already been printed at 3s. 6d. and were then being distributed to agents for release on 25 August; how he collected the twelve copies from Mr Hans Schmoller at the Penguin offices in High Holborn on 16 August; and how on 19 August he served the summons on Mr Blass, another employee of the company.

In answer to Mr Gardiner he said he understood that the directors had very carefully 'considered the book from every angle before they decided to publish it', and he agreed that on 15 August he received the following letter from Rubinstein, Nash & Co., the company's solicitors: 'You already know

from Sir Allen Lane the reasons which led our clients to decide
to publish. While we need not set them out at length here, we
think it would be fair to summarize them as follows: our
clients do not regard the book as obscene, and they do regard
its publication as of particular importance, for the public good,
to vindicate D. H. Lawrence's integrity and non-pornographic
intent in writing it, and to enable his place in English literature
as a whole to be properly judged in this country for the first
time. Our clients having reached the decision themselves, the
responsibility for it should be wholly theirs. If, therefore, you
decide, contrary to our clients' opinion, that this work, taken
as a whole, is or may be obscene within the test laid down in
the Act, and that action must be taken by you, they feel that, if
possible, that action should be taken against them alone. As
you already know from Sir Allen Lane, our clients are willing
to cooperate with you to the fullest extent, and in this connexion they feel sure that you will see no objection to following a course whereby you can obtain copies of *Lady Chatterley's
Lover* from them without involving a third party. They have,
therefore, instructed us to inform you that, as from noon
today, twelve copies of the book will be available to be handed
to you at their offices at Northumberland House. ... Please
let us know at what time you propose to call.'

Inspector Monahan agreed that this was the second case to
come before a Judge and Jury under the new Act, the other
case being that of a London guide to prostitution called *The
Ladies' Directory*. By way of indicating the kind of thing that
the new Act was intended to deal with, Mr Gardiner elicited
from the Inspector that *The Ladies' Directory* catered for the
sexually perverted. He then asked him: 'Do you know any civilized country in which the unexpurgated book, the subject
matter of this prosecution, cannot be bought except Lawrence's
own country and the Commonwealth countries?'

Mr Griffith-Jones rose to his feet. 'My Lord, I hesitate to
interrupt my learned friend, but what happens in other
countries can hardly be relevant to the issue which the Jury
have to try.' – 'I think that is right', said Mr Justice Byrne.
'What do you say, Mr Gardiner?'

23

'My Lord, one of the questions on which evidence can be called is the literary merits of a book', replied Mr Gardiner. 'When a piece of evidence, large or small, is that you find an author all of whose books, including this one, are now on sale in all civilized countries, it is in my submission some evidence of the value of the book.'

'I don't think that is the kind of evidence this Statute contemplates. I am against you', said the Judge. And that was the point at which the evidence for the Prosecution came to an end. Every other witness from that point onwards was a witness for the Defence. In preparation for what they were going to say, Mr Gerald Gardiner then addressed the Jury.

'Members of the Jury,' he said, 'you have now heard from my learned friend Mr Griffith-Jones the nature of the case for the Prosecution. He has told you in general terms what this book is about and the grounds on which the Prosecution contend that it is obscene. He has told you it is full of repeated descriptions of sexual intercourse, and so it is. He has told you it is full of large numbers of four-letter words, and so it is. And you may have asked yourselves at once how comes it that reputable publishers should publish, apparently after considerable thought, quite deliberately, an appalling book of the nature which has been described to us.

'So perhaps I should start by telling you something about the defendant company. Because when anybody is charged with any crime their good character, it has been said, is like credit at the bank, something you can draw on in a time of trouble.

'In 1935 there was a man called Lane, in his thirties, who had been in the publishing business, and he thought it would be a good thing if the ordinary people were able to afford to buy good books. The ordinary book was expensive then, as it is expensive now. He himself had not had the advantage of being at a university. He had a passion for books. He left school at the age of 16.

'Of course, people can get books from libraries, but it is not the same thing as having one's own books. Of course, there

24

were those who thought he was mad. They said it's no good giving the working classes good books, they wouldn't understand them if they read them. The next year he formed this company, Penguin Books Limited, to publish good books at the price of ten cigarettes. (The cost of publishing books has now gone up even faster than the cost of cigarettes.) It was 6d.

'He started off with novels and detective stories. Then there were the Penguin Classics, translations from Latin and Greek, masterpieces of literature of other countries. Penguin poetry, Penguin plays, Penguin art, some called Pelicans which were non-fictional: economics, sociology, in fact every subject.

'Whether he was right or wrong in thinking the average person would buy good books if they had the chance is perhaps shown by the fact that since then this company has made and sold 250 – perhaps I might repeat that – 250 million books.

'It was not their intention to seek to publish new books, but substantially to republish, in a form and at a price which the ordinary people could afford to buy, all the great books in our literature. The whole of Shakespeare's works, Shaw (ten volumes of Shaw were published on his ninetieth birthday), and by 1950 they had published four books by D. H. Lawrence. In 1950, that being twenty years after Lawrence's death, they published a further ten of his books, and in 1960, thirty years after his death, they endeavoured to publish the rest, including this book.

'This book has, unfortunately, had a chequered history. It was not published in this country at the time. It would I think be conceded that as the law was thirty years ago it would have been against the law to do so. Of course, there are many books in London now circulating freely which nobody would think ought to be prevented from publication and which have been banned in earlier years – say twenty years ago. This book in English, you will hear, was published on the Continent. No doubt many copies found their way to this country, so it has never been unknown to anyone.

'I shall be calling a great number of witnesses. I think you will find nearly all of them read the unexpurgated edition years ago. The book that Lawrence wrote has never before been published in this country. There has been an expurgated edition and there would have been nothing to stop Penguin Books from publishing an expurgated edition years ago, but they have never thought of doing so. Because, whether they could have made money or not, they have never published a mutilated book.

'The expurgated edition, you will appreciate, is not the book that Lawrence wrote. You can, of course, have an expurgated edition of *Hamlet,* which no doubt has things in it which are *prima facie,* obscene. You can have an expurgated edition of the *Canterbury Tales,* which would not be the book which Chaucer wrote. They have always refused to publish any work unless it was the work of the author.

'Before this Act the law had three defects which Parliament has now recognized. The first was that the Prosecution could pick out particular passages from a book and say "Just look at those. Don't bother about the rest." Whereas if one is to be fair to an author when one is considering whether a work tends to deprave or corrupt, one must, of course, judge by the whole book. Secondly, the question used to be whether the work had a tendency to deprave or corrupt those whose minds were open to such immoral influences. That at once made everyone

hink of young people, and referred to nothing but young
people. If applied literally it would have meant that our litera-
ure would be such as was suitable for a sixteen-year-old
choolgirl. So Parliament got rid of the words about "those
whose minds are open to such immoral influences". Thirdly,
here was no distinction between pornography and literature.
Pornography means literally the writings of prostitutes, but
t is now used in a much more general sense, and you may
hink the best definition is "dirt for dirt's sake" – works which
we have all seen and can see on bookstalls, not excepting our
Sunday papers. That which is put in for the purpose of selling
hem has no art, no literature. Mr Justice Stable in the judgement which my learned friend has already referred to put it
much better than I could, when he said: "I do not suppose
here is a decent man or woman in this court who does not
whole-heartedly believe that pornography, the filthy bawdy
muck that is just filth for filth's sake, ought to be stamped out
and suppressed. Such books are not literature. They have
got no message; they have got no inspiration; they have got
no thought. They have got nothing. They are just filth and
ought to be stamped out."

'And so we have this Act passed for two purposes. It is an
Act, it says, to amend the law in relation to the publication
of obscene matter, to provide for the protection of literature
and to strengthen the law concerning pornography. So it is
plain – is it not? – that its intention is to amend the law in two
ways: first of all, by making it easier to prosecute real pornography and, secondly, to provide for the protection of
literature.

'May I respectfully remind you next of what you are here to
do, and here again perhaps I might take the judgement to
which my learned friend referred. The learned Judge said:
"We are not sitting here as judges of taste. We are not here to
say whether we like a book of this kind. We are not here to
say whether we think it would be a good thing if books like
this were never written. You are here trying a criminal charge
and in the criminal courts you cannot find a verdict of
'Guilty' against the accused unless, on the evidence that you

have heard, you, and each one of you, are fully satisfied that the charge against the accused person has been proved."

'And the charge, members of the Jury, is a serious one; it is one for which the Act has thought it right to provide as penalties either an unlimited fine or three years' imprisonment. There never has been anything to stop the Prosecution in these cases doing what they have frequently done, and no doubt will frequently do, quite rightly, and that is, where you have a limited company, prosecuting not only the company but the director of the company responsible for the publication. It is not for us to inquire whether in this particular case the Prosecution thought that perhaps a jury might give a verdict of "Guilty" rather more readily if the dock were empty than if they saw an individual director sitting there, but there is nothing to stop them doing that. There is nothing to stop them doing it next time.

'"Such as may tend to deprave or corrupt." If I may refer to two dictionaries, I do not think that, broadly speaking, we shall dispute what is the relevant meaning of those words, and I would not have troubled you with a further dictionary but for one observation my learned friend made. To corrupt, suggest, means to render morally unsound or rotten, to destroy the moral purity or chastity of, to pervert or ruin a good quality, to debase, defile. And to deprave means to make morally bad, to pervert, debase, or corrupt morally. Now, if those are right you will observe that they both necessarily involve a tendency to change, to make morally bad, to pervert, to result in somebody doing that which he would not otherwise have done if he had not read the book. And I raise this now because my learned friend did cite from a judgement on the law as it used to be relating to the raising of impure thoughts. Questions of law are for my Lord, but in my submission the question of whether a book raises impure thoughts or thoughts about sex is not the question you have to decide. There are hundreds of books which obviously do. Almost any book about sex obviously does. But Parliament has said *"For the purposes of this Act"* an article shall be deemed to be obscene if . . ." In other words, Parliament is saying, no matter what anybody has thought before as to what obscene means, this is the meaning, and this alone, which it is going to have for the purposes of this Act. And, to be obscene within the meaning of the Act, the book must, taken as a whole, tend to deprave and corrupt, which obviously involves a change of character leading the reader to do something wrong that he would not otherwise have done.

'Next, I suggest (and I would not have said this but for one observation of my learned friend's), I would suggest that a book cannot be obscene merely because it is about an extra-marital relationship – that is to say, two people having such a relationship who are not husband and wife – and perhaps the simplest reason of all is that if it were so I suppose about nineteen out of twenty of the novels which are written would be held to be obscene.

'When you read this book you will, in my submission, see certain things which the author was obviously thinking. You will observe that he is clearly a very strong supporter of marriage – I mean except in those cases where marriage is obviously perfectly hopeless and for which the law allows divorce. It is quite plain, in my submission, from the whole of this book that the author is pointing out that promiscuity yields no satisfaction to anyone and that the only right relationship is one between two people in love which is intended to be a permanent one.

'The author has again, it is clear from the book, had in mind certain things in our society – that is to say, our society as it was then in the twenties, in the years of the depression – of which he wholly disapproved. He did not like the industrial revolution. He was an anti-intellectual. He thought we paid much too much attention to the mind and not nearly enough attention to the body; that the ills from which society was suffering were not going to be cured by political action; and that the remedy lay in the restoration of right relations between human beings, and particularly in unions between men and women. One of the greatest things in life, he thought, was the relationship of a man and a woman in love, and their physical union formed an essential part of a relationship that was normal and wholesome and not something to be ashamed of, something to be discussed openly and frankly.

'I suppose, broadly speaking, there are two views about this. One is that sex is disgusting and sinful and unclean; that it is very unfortunate that children cannot be born without it; that really the least said about the whole thing the better. The view of the author, as is made clear from the book, is that as a puritan moralist he plainly disapproves of casual sex, of sex without love, of promiscuous sex; but he strongly approved of, and thought that our society as a whole paid too little attention to, the physical love of a man and woman in love and in a permanent relationship with one another, which, in his view, plainly was healthy, wholesome, normal, and to be encouraged.

'The same learned judge* said in relation to sex, about the book in question in the case he was trying, a book where a young man has an interminable series of sexual relations with a woman:

'This is a book which obviously and admittedly is absorbed with sex, the relationship between the male and the female of the human species. I, personally, approach that great mystery with profound interest and at the same time a very deep sense of reverence. It is not our fault that but for the love of men and women and the act of sex, the human race would have ceased to exist thousands of years ago. It is not our fault that the moment in, shall we say, an over-civilized world – if "civilized" is an appropriate word – sex ceases to be one of the great motive forces in human life, the human race will cease to exist. It is the essential condition of the survival and development of the human race, for whatever ultimate purpose it has been brought into this world. Speaking, as I am sure I do, to a representative group of people, nine men and three women, each one of you, I am sure, is of good will and anxious that in the solution of this great mystery today we should achieve some conception which will lead to great personal happiness between individuals of the opposite sex in millions of homes throughout this island, which, after all, is the only possible foundation upon which one could build a vigorous, a strong, and a useful nation.

* Mr Justice Stable, in the *Philanderer* case (R. v *Secker & Warburg*, 1954).

'Then he says:

'Rome and Greece, it is not uninteresting to reflect, elevated human love to a cult, if not a religion, but when we reach the Middle Ages we find an entirely different approach. The priesthood was compelled to be sexless, and a particular qualitative holiness was attached to the monks and the nuns who dedicated themselves to cloisters and sheltered lives. You may think that it is lucky that they were not all quite as holy as that because if they had been, we should none of us have been here today.

'Then he says:

'When you approach this matter which — let us face it — throughout the ages has been one of absorbing interest to men and women, you get these two schools of thought which are poles apart, and in between those two extremes you have a wide variety of opinion. At one extreme you get the conception, I venture to think, of the medieval church, that sex is sin; that the whole thing is dirty; that it was a mistake from beginning to end (and if it was, it was the great creator of life who made the mistake and not you or I); that the less that is said about this wholly distasteful topic the better; let it be covered up and let us pretend that it does not exist.

'That is the sort of view which I was putting before you just now. Now, of course, if a man is going to write a book of the nature of that which I have suggested to you, it is necessary for him to describe what he means. One of the things to which I particularly ask you to pay attention is this. Mr Griffith-Jones has suggested that here is a book which contains thirteen descriptions of intercourse and that the only variation is the time and place. I would suggest that when you read this book you will find the exact opposite of that. You will find that the early promiscuous affairs are all of them highly unsatisfactory. But Constance does fall in love and the book ends with her and Mellors being about to marry. The physical relations between her and the man, so far from being a repetition, are a slow, steady development and a development which could not be shown unless it was shown, as I suggest it is, with honesty and fairness.

'It is here that the intention of the author is extremely relevant – and, having said that, I have very much in mind Mr Griffith-Jones's statement to you that the intention of the author did not matter. All questions of law you will take not from my learned friend nor me but from my Lord, and it will be my submission that the intention of the author is extremely important. You may have noticed that my learned friend himself made several statements about the intention and honesty of the author. He spoke of the book's advocating and encouraging certain things. He said sex is dragged in at every opportunity. That must mean the author and must relate to the author's intention. And he said the rest of the story is mere padding. That, again, is obviously a reflection on the integrity of the author. In the passage he read from a judgement of Mr Justice Devlin, that learned Judge spoke himself about what the author intended to do, and in this summing-up of Mr Justice Stable I see the learned Judge says:

'The author traces the moral thought of this man back to his childhood where the unhappy relations between his mother and his father left a sort of permanent bruise on his personality. . . . He describes the pitfalls of slyness and filth into which the unhappy adolescent stumbles, without knowledge of experience, without the map and the compass, and without the guiding hand of a wise parent or the example of a well-ordered, decent home. You will have to consider whether the author was pursuing an honest purpose and an honest thread of thought, or whether that was all just a bit of camouflage to render the crudity, the sex of the book, sufficiently wrapped up to pass the critical standard of the Director of Public Prosecutions.

'Now, here is a book about England in the nineteen-twenties. It is quite right to say that it includes what are usually called four-letter words, now seen, of course, in print a great deal more often than was the case twenty years ago. They are the words which the character in the book would in fact use. When one is considering a novel, here I might also perhaps refer to what Mr Justice Stable said about novels as a whole. He said:

'The book that you have to consider is, as you know, in the form of a novel, and I venture to suggest for your consideration the question: what are the functions of the novel? I am not talking about historical novels when people write a story of some past age. I am talking about the contemporary novelist. By the contemporary novelist I mean the novelist who writes about his contemporaries, who holds up a mirror to the society of his own day. And the value of the novel is not merely to entertain the contemporaries of the novel; it stands as a record or a picture of the soceity when it was written. Those of us who enjoy the great Victorian novelists get such understanding as we have of that great age from chroniclers such as Thackeray, Dickens, Trollope, and many others. And where should we be today if the literature of Greece, Rome, and the other civilizations portrayed, not how people really thought and behaved, but how they did not think and how they did not speak and how they did not behave? The only real guidance we get about how people thought and behaved over the ages is in their contemporary literature.

'So, members of the Jury, what the defendants say here is, first, this book is not obscene. It would not tend to deprave or corrupt anyone. It is a book the publication of which is in the public interest because of the qualities the nature of which is referred to in Section 4. If I might just summarize their case: they rely, first, on the status of Lawrence as an author and his place in English literature. Of course, there will always be differences of opinion on questions of English literature, but whether you think Lawrence is the greatest novelist since Hardy or not, few would disagree that he is among the greatest of this century. The fact that since his death (and he has only been dead for thirty years) something like eight hundred books have been written about his works, works which of course are sold all over the world, shows, in my submission, something of the status of the author.

'Secondly, the evidence that I shall call will explain the natural theme of the book, because, of course, the view of any witness may depend upon his view as to the literary merits of the book. "Literary merit" does not mean merely the style and prose or composition; it includes also any message which the author is seeking to put forward. Lawrence's message, as you have heard, was that the society of his day in England was sick, he thought, and the sickness from which it was suffering was the result of the machine age, the "bitch-goddess Success", the importance that everybody attached to money, and the degree to which the mind had been stressed at the expense of the body; and that what we ought to do was to re-establish personal relationships, the greatest of which was the relationship between a man and a woman in love, in which there was no shame and nothing wrong, nothing unclean, nothing which anybody was not entitled to discuss.

'Fourthly, that the descriptions of physical union are necessary to what he was trying to say. He was always, of course, a repetitious writer. You find that with regard to the four-letter words referred to, and many other words; that is to say, he always has this trick of mentioning a particular word ten times on the same page. Take the word "tender", for example (the book was at one time going to be called *Tenderness*). As far as the four-letter words are concerned, you will see that the sort of character who uses them is in fact true to life, and it is plain, in my submission, that what the author intended to do was to drag these words out of the rather shameful connotation which since Victorian times they have achieved. Now, whether this was successful or not, or would have been successful if the book had been published, is an entirely different matter. The attitude of shame – let us face it – which very large numbers of people have towards sex in any form has reduced us now, you may think, to this position: that it is not at all easy for fathers and mothers to find words to describe that which, most properly, they want to describe to their children, and this author in a book in which there is no kind of perversion at all evidently thought that in using some words to describe physical union, words which have been part of our spoken speech for 500 or 600 years, he would purify them from the shame which was placed upon them. He thought that anyone reading it would be shocked the first time, but that by repetition they would realize there was nothing shameful in a word in itself. It depends so much upon the mind that is being applied to it.

'Now, whether that is a good idea or a sensible thing to do is not a thing with which you are concerned, because you are not concerned with a question of personal good taste. You will when you read this book be shocked; you may be disgusted; but those are not the questions, as you have already been told. The question is whether the tendency of this book is to deprave and corrupt its readers, and in the submission of the Defence, whether Lawrence succeeded or not in his attempt to purify these particular words by bringing them out into the light of day does not matter, because there is nothing in words themselves which can deprave or corrupt.

'You will be asked to consider the educational and sociological merits of the book, because among the things which you are invited by the Act to consider are "objects of general concern", quite apart from the interests of art, literature, and science, and sex and sensuality are matters of general concern. I am not going to anticipate the words which Mr Griffith-Jones may use about how awful it would be for young people to see this book, but many of the people I am calling have adolescent children of their own, and it is something on which views may differ. This is not strictly part of the Defence, but it is in answer to the point which Mr Griffith-Jones always makes, and properly makes, in all these cases: "Why was it necessary to put in this page or put in this word?" And that is something which an author has never been able to answer. As to leaving them out, of course, Penguin might have done that themselves, but it would not have been the *Lady Chatterley's Lover* which Lawrence wrote, and in the evidence which I shall call before you there is reference to a book far more obscene than the book which is the subject matter of this Prosecution. It is a book where . . .'

'I am sorry to interrupt my learned friend,' said Mr Griffith-Jones, 'but as I understand the authorities on this matter this book cannot be compared with other books, and reference to other books used by way of comparison as to whether or not this is obscene is not allowed.'

'There is a Section in the Statute which deals with it,' said the Judge. 'It is Section 2, Sub-section 6: "In any proceedings against a person under this section the question whether an article is obscene shall be determined without regard to any publication by another person unless it could reasonably have been expected that the publication by the other person would follow from publication by the person charged." Before the Statute, of course, the law was that you could not have a comparison of other books with the book charged, and the Statute now specifically allows that.'

But the provision which the Judge was thus invoking used the word publication as a verbal noun – the act of publishing – not a noun to describe a book or magazine. If the draughtsmen had meant 'any *book* by another person' they would presumably have said 'any *article* by another person', since they used the word article in a collective sense. But Mr Gardiner wanted to choose his own battlefields; and by a tactical concession at this point he ensured that the expurgated *Lady Chatterley*, the 'book far more obscene' in question, was in fact brought into the trial again and again.

'My Lord,' he said, 'in my submission this Sub-section is dealing with quite another matter. To save interrupting with legal argument at this point, would your Lordship allow me to withdraw the sentence I used and substitute for it "an expurgated edition if one were published". All I was seeking to do was to answer the comment which has been, and of course will be, made as to why it was necessary to include these words, why the book could not be published without these particular passages. If I may, I would wish to deal in the course of my speech hypothetically with what is likely to happen if you expurgate a book rather than have the full text.'

'Very well,' said Mr Justice Byrne.

'You see, members of the Jury,' Mr Gardiner went on, 'my learned friend or anybody else can take a blue pencil. There are, of course, passages in *Hamlet* to which the Cromwellian Puritans strongly objected. You could cut them out, but then you would not only have to cut out those bits; you would have to cut out subsequent bits which, though not objectionable themselves, relate back to the first bits. Probably you would find it necessary to write in a certain amount. And at the end of the day the play would not be the *Hamlet* which Shakespeare wrote.

'In a case like this one is perhaps permitted to reflect that nobody suggests that the Director of Public Prosecutions becomes depraved or corrupted. Counsel read the book; they do not become depraved or corrupted. Witnesses read the book; they do not become depraved or corrupted. Nobody suggests the Judge or the Jury become depraved or corrupted. *It is always somebody else; it is never ourselves.*

'When you read the book, members of the Jury, would you do three things? First of all, knowing the importance of this case, its importance perhaps not only to the defendants but to the public as a whole, certainly to the literary world, would you read the whole book? Because, of course, every part of the book is relevant to the Defence. Would you read it as you would read an ordinary book, beginning at the beginning and ending at the end? Secondly, would you bear in mind the considerations which you have heard from my learned friend and me, the things which the Prosecution have told you about the book and those things which I have put before you? Thirdly, would you mind not saying to your wife or your husband when you have read it, and still less when you are half way through, "This is a jolly good book" or "This is a perfectly awful book"? Because, if you will forgive my saying so, experience has shown that the right time in a case for a Jury to make up its mind is when it has heard the whole case. And thank you for being so patient with me.'

*

'I think the question now', said the Judge, when the Court reassembled after lunch, 'is the reading of the book, is it not? It is for the Jury to read the book. How shall that be done? Has anybody any suggestions to make?' Mr Gardiner suggested that the usual practice in recent years had been for the Jury to take the book home. The Judge disagreed, but was ready to hear argument on it. Mr Gardiner then related how

Mr Justice Stable had sent his Jury home with *The Philanderer* to read, and how Mr Justice Devlin had done the same with *The Image and the Search*.

'The Jury rooms are jolly uncomfortable places,' he urged. 'There are hard wooden seats, and anything more unnatural than twelve men and women sitting round a table on hard wooden chairs with a book is hard to imagine. It is to read it in wholly different circumstances from those in which the ordinary person who bought the book would read it. Some people read very much slower than others, and there might well be a tendency, in such circumstances, finding oneself left behind the others, to skip in order to keep up with the others.'

'I know within my own experience Juries have read books in this Court in their room', said Mr Justice Byrne. 'And the learned Clerk of the Court says he cannot agree with the observation that conditions in the Jury room are uncomfortable.'

'I am told there are hard chairs', persisted Mr Gardiner. 'The average rate of reading is, I think, 298 words a minute, which is rather less than a page. On that footing it will take the average reader between seven and eight hours. There are always those who read much slower and others who read much faster. If the average is seven or eight hours, sufficient time must be allowed to the slower reader, and those hours they will have to spend reading cheek by jowl, which no one who bought it would do. It would save any possibility of the members of the Jury being embarrassed if they were allowed to read it at home.'

'Is there any reason why, when the Jury are reading the book, they should not discuss it together?' asked the Judge.

'I should have thought it very undesirable indeed until they have finished it', replied Mr Gardiner.

'But a jury during the course of the trial can always talk about the case together.' – 'They have then all heard the same amount of evidence, my Lord. Some read faster than others. There is nothing affecting this case which should distinguish it from the course which I gather is taken in the majority of cases.'

'I think the Jury should read the book here', the Judge decided. 'I am very sorry, members of the Jury. I don't want to condemn you to any kind of discomfort, but if you were to take this book home you might have distractions. One knows perfectly well in one's home things do happen unexpectedly. There are distractions. You are trying and carrying out a very onerous duty, and I think it would be much better if you were to read this book in your room.

'As you have been told, you won't make up your minds about it. You will read this book, you have to hear evidence and so forth, but you will read this book just as though you had bought it at a bookstall and you were reading it in the ordinary way as a whole.' Thus the first day ended.

In fact the Jury were then given a special room with deep leather armchairs, and read in comfort. The Judge may have been influenced in his decision by the enormous publicity occasioned by the trial, which increases the vulnerability of jurymen away from a Court's protection. The last juryman had finished the book in three days, and on Thursday, 27 October, Mr Gardiner began calling his witnesses.

'Now, Leonard, a four-letter word in common use every day?'

Gilbert Wilkinson in the DAILY HERALD, *3 November 1960*

THE SECOND DAY

MR GARDINER began by making it clear that the calling of witnesses to the literary and other merits of the book was not in any sense an admission that the book was obscene. The Judge replied that this was understood. 'The position is perfectly plain,' he said. 'If the Jury come to the conclusion that the book is not obscene, that is an end of the matter. If they come to the conclusion that the book is obscene, then they will have to consider the other question.'

Mr Griffith-Jones then asked that each witness should remain out of Court while other witnesses were giving evidence. There has always been a tendency to allow 'expert' witnesses to remain, though their special immunity to suggestion and atmosphere has never seemed very clear. However, the experts in this case were not going to be regarded as Bernard Spilsburys: the Judge excluded them from the Court until after they had given evidence.

The first of them was MR GRAHAM HOUGH, Lecturer in English and Fellow of Christ's College, Cambridge. In reply to Mr Gerald Gardiner, whose purpose was to establish every witness not only as an expert but also as a person of worldly experience and normal daily contacts, Mr Hough agreed that he went from Grammar School to Liverpool University, graduating in English; that he had been Professor of English at the University of Malaya; that for three years he was a prisoner of war in Siam; and that he had been Visiting Professor at Johns Hopkins and Cornell Universities. He was the author of *The Dark Sun, A Study of D. H. Lawrence*.

'When did you read the unexpurgated edition of *Lady Chatterley's Lover*?' Mr Gardiner then asked him. – 'I cannot answer that question exactly, but I think it was about 1940.'

'Will you tell us something of Lawrence's place in English

41

literature?' – 'He is generally recognized to be one of the most important novelists of this century and one of the greatest novelists in any century. I don't think that is seriously disputed.'

'Will you tell us how many books have been written about his works?' – 'I can't say from my own knowledge the exact number, but I've seen it authoritatively stated there are over 800.'

'Will you tell us as an expert in English literature what are the matters which ought to be taken into account in assessing the literary merits of a book?' – 'I think that's a very difficult thing to do in general terms, and I think it varies very much with the kind of book it is. We are here discussing a novel, and I think one of the things one would wish to take into account is whether it is a true and sincere representation of an aspect of life.'

'Whereabouts would you place this book amongst Lawrence's works?' – 'I don't think it is the best of his novels, but I don't think it is the least good either. He wrote nine. I would place it about fifth.'

'Will you tell us what is the theme or meaning of the book? Confine yourself for the moment to what can be learnt from the book itself, disregarding Lawrence's other books, disregarding Lawrence's subsequent writings about it.' – 'Yes. I won't go outside this book. I think we are to look for the true meaning of the book in an attempt to give a sympathetic understanding of a very painful and intricate and difficult situation. Secondly, the book is in fact concerned with the relations between men and women, with their sexual relations, with the nature of proper marriage, and this is a matter which is of great importance and of deep concern to all of us.'

'I think we had better have that slowly. Would you mind repeating that?' interrupted the Judge, who at this early stage was still taking copious notes. He wrote less as the trial went on and the witnesses waxed more and more eloquent; and, naturally enough, their eloquence (and often their impressiveness) increased as his Lordship's writing diminished. – 'That the book is concerned with a very important situation; it is concerned with the relations of men and women, with their sexual relations, with the nature of marriage, and these are all matters of deep importance to all of us.'

'What would you say as to the characterization?' Mr Gardiner asked. – 'I think the two principal characters, Connie Chatterley and Mellors, are extremely closely and intimately drawn, and that is where the weight of the book lies. I think some of the minor characters are extremely well done, notably Mrs Bolton. And there are, as in most novels, a number of lesser characters who are drawn in less detail. I think *their* representation is adequate, but no more.'

'It has been said that sex is dragged in at every conceivable opportunity, and that the plot is little more than padding. If that were true would it be a serious criticism of the literary merits of the book?' – 'If it were true it would be, but I think it is totally false.'

'If true would it be an attack on Lawrence's integrity and honesty of purpose?' – 'In those terms, yes, "dragged in at every opportunity", it would be. It is a matter of simple numerical proportion. The sexual passages to which objection is taken I think cannot occupy more than thirty pages of the whole book. The book is some three hundred pages in length, rather more in this edition. No man in his senses is going to write a book of three hundred pages as mere padding for thirty pages of sexual matter.'

'What do you say as to the literary merit of the other 270 pages?' – 'I think it is very high. I agree the sexual situation is the centre of the book, that is perfectly plain; but there is a great deal else in it. And to describe the whole course of the story, the whole development of the character of Connie Chatterley as padding for sexual scenes seems to me to be quite an impossible view for anyone who tries to read a book seriously.'

'It has been said it sets upon a pedestal promiscuous and adulterous intercourse. What do you say as to that?' – 'I think that is not true either. Promiscuity hardly comes in question here. It is very much condemned by Lawrence. It is true that at the centre of the book there is an adulterous situation. That is true of a great deal of fiction in Europe from the Iliad on.'

'It has been said the only variation in the description of sexual intercourse is the *locus in quo*, that is where it takes

43

place. Do you agree with that view?' – 'No, I do not. The reason for the repeated descriptions of sexual scenes is to show the development of Connie Chatterley's awareness of her own nature. The scenes are not the same, they are not repetitive; they are different, and this is a very important part of Lawrence's purpose.'

'How far are the descriptions of sexual intercourse relevant or necessary to the theme or meaning of the book?' – 'In my view they are entirely necessary. Lawrence is making, admittedly, a bold experiment here. He is trying to study the sexual situation more clearly and more openly than is usually done in fiction, and to do that he must describe that which he purports to represent.'

'How far are the four-letter words in the book either relevant or necessary to the theme or meaning of the book?' – 'May I answer that by explaining why they are in?' – 'Please. – 'In Lawrence's view there is no proper language to talk about sexual matters. They are either discussed in clinical terms, which deprive them of all emotional content, or they are discussed in words that are normally thought to be coarse and obscene. He thinks that this results in a secretive and morbid attitude towards sex, and he wishes to find the language in which it can be discussed openly and not irreverently, and to do this he tries to redeem the normally obscene words. He tries to use them in contexts that are entirely serious, and to make use seriously of words that are generally used in a context of mockery or abuse. I don't myself think this is successful, but that is what he is trying to do.'

'Do you spend your time teaching young people?' – 'I do a good deal of it.'

'Have you a daughter of 18 and a son of 12?' – 'Yes.'

'You have told us,' said Mr Griffith-Jones in cross-examination, 'that this is not, in your view, Lawrence's best book. That is a view which is held by a number of other persons, is it not?' – 'I think so, yes', replied Mr Hough.

'Did Lawrence write in fact three versions of this book?' – 'Yes, he did. He wrote it three times.'

'And it is right, is it not, that in that first version none of the "purple passages" appear?' – 'No, none of them at all.'

'It was in fact known as *The First Lady Chatterley*, was it not?' – 'Yes, that was the title.'

'And the general message is the same?' – 'I think it is, but don't think that it comes over very clearly.'

'Tell me, do you know a lady called Esther Forbes?' – 'No, am afraid I don't.'

'You have never seen this Phoenix copy of *The First Lady Chatterley*?' – 'No, I have not.'

'Do you know a woman called Katherine Anne Porter?' – I know of her as an American short-story writer, yes. Very distinguished.'

'And did you read an article which she wrote in a magazine called *The Encounter* about January of this year?' Glances were exchanged among the listeners in the public seats. It was as though Mr Griffith-Jones had referred to 'a magazine called *The Punch*'. Mr Stephen Spender, *Encounter*'s distinguished editor, smiled wanly at the back of the Court. 'Yes, I did', replied Mr Hough imperturbably.

'*The Encounter* is a serious publication, with literary comments and so on?' – 'Reasonably so, sir.' (Broad smiles throughout the Court.)

'You told us that others do not agree with you; I just want to see to what extent certain other eminent literary people do not agree with the views which you hold about this book. Perhaps I can quote from this essay, or contribution. "When I first read *Lady Chatterley's Lover*, thirty years ago, I thought it a dreary, sad performance with some passages of unintentional, hilarious low comedy, one scene at least simply beyond belief in a book written with such inflamed apostolic solemnity." Did you ever get that impression when you read this book?' – 'No, I did not. I know what might have given rise to that opinion, but I don't hold it and I don't think it is a generally held one. I think it is an eccentric opinion.'

'You were speaking of the characters as being well drawn. Would you agree with this? I would like to have your comments on this view as to Lady Chatterley. "She is not intense, imaginative, and dazzled like the governess" – and he is comparing her with some other character in some book – "she is stupid." Is she stupid as drawn by Lawrence?' – 'She is not stupid. It has never been claimed that she is particularly intelligent.'

'The fact is that we are told very little about her, aren't we, except for her premarital intercourse with boys in Germany and her post-marital intercourse, not with her husband but with Michaelis and Mellors?' – 'Oh yes, we are told a lot about her.'

'What else are we told?' – 'We are told about her background, that she was the daughter of a painter, a distinguished R.A., and that she and her sister had been brought up in artistic and intellectual circles, and that she studied in Germany, and that they were intelligent and emancipated young women for that period. She herself was rather slow, one is given to understand, friendly, warm-hearted, a patient, and loyal person in normal circumstances . . .'

'I am sorry to interrupt you. What do you mean by warmhearted? Do you mean filled with sex?' – 'I did *not* mean that, no.'

'Because that is in fact what she is, is it not?' – 'You could certainly say that if you wished to but that was not what I meant.'

'Very well. Perhaps we have had your view about it; just let me read a few more passages of this criticism. She compares it with a book by James. "The air of evil which shrouds them both, the sense of a situation of foregone and destined failure, to which there can be no outcome except despair." Never mind the other book.' (This was thought by some observers at the trial to be an ingenious way of introducing another book for purposes of comparison.) 'Do you accept that view of this book?' – 'No, I do not. I think she means this as praise, by the way, doesn't she? That book of James's is usually supposed to be very good, but I don't agree; Lawrence's book does not end in despair. It is a very painful situation from which there is some hope of a not too unhappy outcome.'

'She writes this a little later. "For nowhere in this sad history can you see anything but a long, dull grey, monotonous chain of days, lightened now and then by a sexual bout. I can't hear any music, or poetry, or the voices of friends, or children. There is no wine, no food, no sleep nor refreshment, no laughter, no rest nor quiet – no love. I remember then that this is the fevered day-dream of a dying man sitting under his umbrella pines in Italy indulging his sexual fantasies." What do you say to that?' – 'It seems to be a fatuous criticism of the book. If she says it is about a sad situation, of course it is about a sad situation. That is the essence of the book. Gaiety in a situation of this kind would be singularly out of place.'

'May this not be in fact the fevered daydream of a dying man?' – 'Lawrence was not dying, but he died two years after its publication. He was ill.'

'Tell me a little bit more about the book itself. Would you agree with me that a good book by a good writer, generally speaking, should not repeat things again and again? It is a tiresome habit, is it not?' – 'No, I do not agree with this. There is a great deal of this in the Bible, for instance. Repetition is very frequently employed.'

'I am talking about this book at the moment. Have you a copy of it there?' – 'Yes.'

'Would you turn to page 140, and the paragraph starting a little down the page "Connie went slowly home . . ."? I am not dealing with the so-called purple passages at the moment. "Connie went slowly home, realizing the depth of the other thing in her. Another self was alive in her, burning molten and soft in her womb and bowels, and with this self she adored him. She adored him till her knees were weak as she walked." I suppose that is good writing, or is that ludicrous?' – 'Not to me.'

'"In her womb and bowels" – again we have got the same two parts of her anatomy coupled together within three lines – "she was flowing and alive now . . ." I do not want to be unimaginative, believe me, but can one flow and be alive in one's womb and bowels?' – 'Metaphorically I think one can.' – 'Even metaphorically?' – 'Yes.'

'"... and vulnerable, and helpless in adoration of him as the most naïve woman. It feels like a child, she said to herself it feels like a child in me. And so it did, as if her womb ..." - and so we have "womb" for the third time?' – 'Yes.'

'Is that really good writing?' – 'I think he is trying to describe a woman in a highly emotional and disturbed condition, and this is his method of doing it.'

'We can all "try to describe". A mere child learning to write her first composition can "try to describe". That is not what I am asking. I am asking: do you regard that as good writing to repeat again and again "womb and bowels", "womb and bowels", and "bowels and womb"?' – 'In the context, yes.'

'And it does not finish there, because if we can go on to the next page, almost at the end of the first long paragraph "womb" appears?' – 'Yes.'

'Then a little bit further down page 141, towards the bottom, at the end of that longish paragraph the two words "womb" and "bowels" appear again?' – 'Yes.'

'Is that really what you call expert, artistic writing?' – 'Yes, I think in the context it is. I should also feel bound to say that this is very much Lawrence's method, to use repetition of this kind. You can find plenty of other places where the words are not "womb" and "bowels", when he is repeating equally frequently.'

'I am asking whether in a work of high literary merit that is the kind of repetition which you would expect?' – 'Well, knowing Lawrence, yes, I would. He always writes like that, and he brings it off.'

'Don't say "knowing Lawrence",' interposed the Judge. 'You must not suppose for the purpose of this question that Lawrence is a good writer, and therefore anything that he did is the right way to do it. You are being asked, quite apart from the fact that Lawrence wrote it, whether that is a piece of good English.' 'Suppose I had written a book,' said Mr Griffith-Jones, 'I who have never written a book in my life, quite unknown to everybody. Would you say that was a fine piece of writing if I had written it?' – 'I would not say so if I saw it in isolation; if I saw it in its context, I would.'

'Let us look at some of the other contexts to this. Look at page 185. It comes in the middle of one of the so-called purple passages. I am not on that aspect of the matter at all at the moment. I am speaking of the literary merit. If the Court will forgive me for my miserable attempt to pronounce the local dialect, "'Th'art good cunt, though, aren't ter? Best bit o' cunt left on earth. When ter likes! When tha'rt willin'!' 'What is cunt?' she said. 'An' doesn't ter know? Cunt!'" I need not go on reading. Just glance down. "Cunt" appears again. "Fuck" appears. "Fuck" appears. "Cunt" appears. "Fuck" appears, all in the space of about twelve lines. Is that realistic conversation even between the gamekeeper and the baronet's wife?' – 'I don't think so. I don't think this passage comes off at all. I see what he is trying to do, but I think he has failed.'

'I am not asking what he is trying to do: but is it realistic?' – 'I think it is a failure then.'

'You agree with me in this, that in this book of such high merit there is at least one passage which is of very low merit?' – 'There are others too; there are several, in my opinion.'

Mr Griffith-Jones thought there were several, too. He went on reading them out, from pages 316, 270, 34, 271, passages in which, it seemed, the claim to literary merit was destroyed by the use of the four-letter words. Then he raised the matter of the gamekeeper's lunch-time conversation with Lady Chatterley's father, looked at 'as a portrait of our society'.

'When this defence was opened by my learned friend Mr Gardiner,' he said, 'he drew attention to a passage in one summing-up by a learned Judge, and he himself emphasized it. I just want to tell you, and remind the Court, as the preface to my next question. "And where should we be today if the literature of Greece, Rome, and the other civilizations portrayed, not how people really thought and behaved, but how they did not think and how they did not speak and how they did not behave? The only real guidance we get about how people thought and behaved over the ages is in their contemporary literature." Tell me this. Do you think that this book accurately depicts our society or part of our society in 1928?'

– 'I don't think there is any simple answer to this, but parts of our society, I think, it depicts with great accuracy.'

'Just look at page 296, would you? Do you remember that luncheon, which Sir Malcolm, the girl's father, gave to Mellors?' – 'Yes.'

'"When coffee was served, and the waiter had gone, Sir Malcolm lit a cigar and said, heartily: 'Well, young man, and what about my daughter?' The grin flickered on Mellors' face. 'Well, Sir, and what about her?' 'You've got a baby in her all right.' 'I have that honour!' grinned Mellors. 'Honour, by God!' Sir Malcolm gave a little squirting laugh, and became Scotch and lewd. 'Honour! How was the going, eh? Good, my boy, what?' 'Good!' 'I'll bet it was! Ha-ha! My daughter, chip of the old block, what! I never went back on a good bit of fucking, myself. Though her mother, oh, holy saints!' He rolled his eyes to heaven. 'But you warmed her up, oh, you warmed her up, I can see that. Ha-ha! My blood in her! You set fire to her haystack all right'," and so on.' – 'Yes,' said Mr Hough.

'Do you think any future generation reading that conversation would get anything approaching an accurate picture of the kind of way in which Royal Academicians conducted their conversation?' – 'No, sir; I do not. I think this is a disastrously bad passage, and I said so quite plainly in my book years ago. I think it is the one utterly, disastrously bad passage in the book.'

'For the rest of this book, although it may not occupy the majority of the number of pages, the whole book is about sexual intercourse between these two persons?' – 'Not the whole book, no. The whole book is about the sexual situation between these two persons involving other persons. That is so in very many novels I am afraid.'

'Do you think there is any particular literary merit or educational or sociological advantage in having that situation described?' – 'Yes, I do.'

'There are thousands of books describing it?' – 'Yes.'

'It is a theme which I suppose runs through novel after novel?' – 'Yes, treated differently in each one.'

'It doesn't need, for anybody's advantage, any further description?' Mr Hough thought this one out; and there were many thinking with him. 'I am sorry, I don't think I understand this question.'

'It is not an important theme to put out to people? The situations have no importance in themselves? They are only background, and form good backgrounds and plots for stories?' – 'No, I don't agree with that at all. No individual situation between two individual people has great public importance in itself, but Lawrence sees this as an opportunity to make a study of the relations between men and women, which is of importance.'

'And the way he chooses to do so is to describe in very great detail their "bouts", if I may borrow the word from Katherine Anne Porter, bouts of sexual intercourse?' – 'Yes, plainly.'

'Just let us look at one or two other passages. Do you remember the passage where Mrs Bolton's breasts are felt and kissed?' – 'Yes, I do.'

'Page 305. Does that add anything to this book?' – 'Yes, very much I think. The whole point of the development of Clifford's character at this time is that he is becoming like a rather unpleasant child in his relations to Mrs Bolton, behaving almost like a baby again, a baby at the breast. This is very much emphasized, and there is a very real point in this.'

'Do you remember the description of the girl's father on page 265?' – 'No, not very well.'

'I will help you. "He was moderately stout, and had stout thighs, but they were still strong and well-knit, the thighs of a healthy man who had taken his pleasure in life. His good-humoured selfishness, his dogged sort of independence, his unrepenting sensuality, it seemed to Connie she could see them all in his well-knit straight thighs. Just a man! And now becoming an old man, which is sad." A little lower down: "Connie woke up to the existence of legs", and so on. Does that passage add anything to this book?' – 'I think so, yes.'

'What has it got to do with the story or theme or anything else?' – 'It seems to me a very vivid description of the sort of man her father is represented as being.'

'Has it got anything to do with the theme of the book at all?' – 'It is a rather painful thing to recall, but in the circumstances Connie's mind might very well turn to legs, I think.'

'That is about the only thing her mind ever was on, wasn't it, throughout the whole of this book?' – 'No.'

'What else was Connie thinking about apart from the legs and private parts of her lover?' – 'She was thinking about her whole relation to Clifford and what her position in relation to her marriage is a great deal of the time, feeling she cannot leave him, feeling she cannot stay with him, and there is a considerable moral struggle about this. That occupies a great deal of her attention.'

'I only put this to you again on the question of literary merit; because you would agree a good book for the most part contains the matter which is relevant to its theme or purpose?' – 'Ideally that is so, but I am afraid in many novels it is not so.'

'The introduction of irrelevant matter would detract from the literary merit of a book?' – 'Yes.'

'On page 271 we have the description of the gondolier in Venice ready to prostitute himself, and he gets a friend and they both prostitute themselves.' – 'They don't do it in fact. They are not encouraged to by the ladies.'

'Of course they don't do it, but again I am asking you, what has the whole of that passage about them prostituting themselves got to do with the book?' – 'It has this relevance, that throughout this book there are numerous representations of false and wrong and bad sexual attitudes. This attitude of the gondolier who is willing to prostitute himself to the ladies is one of the bad and wrong and false sexual attitudes.'

'Where do you get the good ones in this book?' – 'In the ultimate relations of Connie and Mellors. It is a matter of opinion whether it is good.'

'Where do you get the good relations?' – 'In the relationship between Connie and Mellors, who really love one another.'

Here Mr Justice Byrne looked up. 'It took them a long time', he said, 'before they really did love one another, didn't it?' – 'Yes. It often does, my Lord.'

'All the time', went on Mr Griffith-Jones, 'it was behind the back of her husband?' – 'Yes. If you wish to inquire whether I share the sexual ethics of Lawrence, may I say quite plainly that I do not.'

'You don't?' – 'I am not a disciple of Lawrence's particular sexual doctrine. I nevertheless think it important that it should be freely stated.'

Next, Mr Griffith-Jones had caught Lawrence misquoting from the Bible. 'In a work of high literary merit,' he said, 'if you were minded to quote from somebody you would expect the author to quote it accurately?' – 'No, sir. From my knowledge of the habits of authors, it is the last thing I would expect, for them to quote accurately. They do it from memory and they always get it wrong.'

'Just look, would you, at page 219. You see, halfway down that page he is quoting, "Lift up your heads o' ye gates, that the king of glory may come in"?' – 'Yes.'

'I certainly would not expect anybody to remember what the actual quotation is, but I happen to have looked it up. "Lift up your heads O ye gates, even lift up ye everlasting doors and the King of Glory shall come in."'" – 'Yes', said Mr Hough patiently, but it was still wrong. The Authorized Version says 'and be ye lift up, ye everlasting doors'. But Mr Griffith-Jones ploughed on.

'Do you not think that in a work of high literary merit, if he is going to quote from the 24th Psalm he might take the trouble to look it up?' – 'No, sir, I don't think so, not in this context. It isn't Lawrence quoting from the 24th Psalm, it is the gamekeeper.'

Mr Griffith-Jones read out the dialect passage on page 219. 'Do you really tell this Court', he said, 'that the inclusion of those words from the Scriptures adds literary merit to this book?' – 'I think it is the only sentence in that passage that has any literary merit at all', replied Mr Hough, and there was laughter in Court.

'That may be a very clever answer, but do you think that that is an example of writing of high standard, that paragraph?' – 'No, I do not. I have made that clear.'

'It is shocking, isn't it? And I am not talking about whether it is obscene or not, I am merely talking of literary merit. It is shocking, is it not, as a literary standard?' – 'Well, I do not use "shocking" as a term of literary criticism myself; I think it is a failure, yes. I have tried to explain why I think it is done but I still think it is a failure.'

When Mr Gardiner re-examined he dealt first with Lawrence's use of repetition.

'You have been asked about the repetition of words like "fuck" and so on. Would you look first of all at page 74? In the second and third paragraphs is the word "warm" repeated seven times?' – 'Yes.'

'Will you look at page 213? In the second half of that page is the word "mistrust" used seven times?' – 'Yes. It is repeated constantly.'

'Will you look at page 247? Is the word "care" there used seven times?' – 'Yes.'

'Will you look at page 256? In a little more than the top half of that page is the word "continuity" used ten times?' – 'Yes.'

'Will you look at pages 264 and 266; is the word "tenderness" used seven times?' – 'Yes.'

'Had this book at one time some other name?' – 'Yes, he did think of calling it *Tenderness* at one time.'

'Lastly, although there are many other examples, will you look at pages 290 to 292? There, the word "tender" appears ten times?' – 'Yes: I cannot count them all offhand.'

'Is this habit of Lawrence's of repeating a particular word a number of times within a small compass a legitimate literary device?' – 'Perfectly. It is also a use often commented on. Some people dislike it, but it seems to me a very characteristic feature of Lawrence's very individual style.'

'Some opinions have been put to you of an American lady, Katherine Anne Porter, writing in *Encounter*. I want to put to you some of the others. She says this in regard to Archibald MacLeish's opinion – he is the ex-Librarian of Congress?' – 'He is a poet, and was the Librarian of Congress.'

'He wrote the foreword to the recent American edition?' – 'I believe so.' Mr Gardiner then read from the *Encounter* article: "'Archibald MacLeish regards it as 'pure' and a work of high literary merit. He has a few reservations as to the whole with which I heartily agree so far as they go; yet even Mr MacLeish begins trailing his coat, daring us at our own risk to deny that the book is 'one of the most important works of the century, or to express an opinion about the literature of our own time or about the spiritual history that literature expresses without making his peace in one way or another with D. H. Lawrence and with this work'." That is the end of the quotation from Archibald MacLeish?' – 'Yes.'

'Then this lady says, "Without in the least making my peace with D. H. Lawrence or with this work, I wish to say why I disagree profoundly with the above judgements, and also with the following: Harvey Breit . . .", and then she cites from Harvey Breit. The quotation is this: "The language and the incidents or scenes in question are deeply moving and very beautiful – Lawrence was concerned how love, how a relationship between a man and a woman can be most touching and beautiful, but only when uninhibited and total." That is the end of the quotation from Harvey Breit, and then this lady says: "This is wildly romantic and does credit to Mr Breit's feelings, but there can be no such thing as a total relationship between two human beings – to begin with, what *is* total in such a changing, uncertain, limited state? and if there could be, just how would the persons involved know when they had reached it? Judging from certain things he wrote and said on this subject, I think Lawrence would have been the first to protest at even an attempt to create such a condition. He demanded the right to invade anybody, but he was noticeably queasy when anyone took a similar liberty with him." Do you agree with Mr McLeish and Mr Breit or do you agree with this lady?' – 'I agree with Mr MacLeish and Mr Breit, plainly. That is why I am here.'

'Then she quotes from Mr Edmund Wilson?' – 'Yes.'

'What is the relative standing in literature between Mr Edmund Wilson and this American lady?' – 'I think this

American lady is a very distinguished writer of short stories; I do not know that her opinion as a critic deserves any particular attention. I should say myself, and I think a very large number of people would agree with me, that Edmund Wilson is the most distinguished American critic now living. He is one of the senior men of letters in the United States.'

'This is the quotation from Edmund Wilson: "The most inspiriting book I have seen in a long time . . . one of his best written . . . one of his most vigorous and brilliant . . ." That is the end of the quotation. Do you agree with what Mr Edmund Wilson says?' – 'Yes I do. I generally do.'

'Then this is the quotation from Jacques Barzun: "I have no hesitation in saying that I do not consider Lawrence's novel pornographic." Then the American lady's comment is this: "I agree that this admirably prudent . . ."' Mr Griffith-Jones was quick off the mark. The matter under discussion was literary merit. 'I have not quoted any of these passages', he said, 'in connexion with the question whether this book is pornographic. In my submission it is not for the witnesses to express a view upon that. I confined that part of my cross-examination, I hope quite fairly, to passages in the book. If Mr Gardiner seeks either to put to a witness, or through any reference to any other work to introduce, other persons' opinions as to the obscenity of the book, then I object.'

'What do you say, Mr Gardiner?' asked the Judge. – 'I do not seek to do anything of the kind, my Lord. My friend having quoted and relied largely on this lady as a literary critic, it throws an interesting light on her qualifications as a critic and on her frame of mind in general. My friend having read from the document, I submit I am entitled to read that, but not in the least upon the question whether the book is pornographic.'

'Not on the question of pornography, but on the question of literary merit', observed Mr Justice Byrne. 'It all forms part and parcel of the opinion of this American lady. I think you are entitled to do that. The Jury will realize that the evidence being called now is not upon the question of whether this book is obscene, but it is upon the question of whether it has literary merit. This only arises out of cross-examination and you will not pay any attention to the question of whether this book is obscene so far as this evidence is concerned.'

'After citing Jacques Barzun,' continued Mr Gardiner, 'this American lady then says: "I agree with this admirably prudent statement, and again when Mr Barzun notes Lawrence's ruling passion for reforming everything and everybody in sight. My quarrel with the book is that it really is not pornographic." Then she refers to Professor Schorer. Is he a Professor at a University in America?' – 'Yes, at Berkeley in California. He has done a great deal of work on Lawrence and said some very good things about him.'

'Then: "Mr Schorer, who contributes the preface, even brings in Yeats to defend this tiresome book. Yeats, bless his memory, when he talked bawdy, knew what he was saying and why. He enjoyed the flavour of gamey words on his tongue, and never deceived himself for one moment as to the nature of that enjoyment; he never got really interestingly dirty until age had somewhat cooled the ardours of his flesh, thus doubling his pleasure in the thoughts of it in the most profane sense. Mr Schorer reprints part of a letter from Yeats, written years ago, to Mrs Shakespear: 'These two lovers the gamekeeper and his employer's wife each separated from their class by their love and by fate are poignant in their loneliness; the coarse language of the one accepted by both becomes a forlorn poetry, uniting their solitudes, something ancient humble and terrible.'" That is from Yeats.' – 'Yes.'

'Then this lady says: "This comes as a breath of fresh air upon a fetid topic. Yeats reaches acutely into the muddlement and brings up the simple facts: the real disaster for the lady and the gamekeeper is that they face perpetual exile from their own proper backgrounds and society. Stale, pointless, unhappy as both their lives were before, due to their own deficiencies of character, it would seem, yet now they face, once the sexual furore is past, an utter aimlessness in life shocking to think about. Further, Yeats notes an important point I have not seen mentioned before – only one of the lovers uses the coarse language, the other merely accepts it. The gamekeeper talks his dirt and the lady listens, but never once answers in kind. If she had, the gamekeeper would no doubt have been deeply scandalized.'' Do you agree with Professor Schorer and with Yeats or with this American lady?' – 'I agree with Professor Schorer and with Yeats.'

'Perhaps I ought to ask you: Who is Yeats?' – 'He is the greatest poet of this century, and one of the greatest critics too, although he can be eccentric.'

*

Then came Miss HELEN GARDNER, Reader in Renaissance English Literature at Oxford, Fellow of the British Academy, member of the B.B.C. 'Critics' panel, and author of books on T. S. Eliot, John Donne, a Penguin anthology *The Metaphysical Poets,* and *The Business of Criticism,* a book of lectures on principles of criticism and on the relation of aspects of modern thought to Christianity. Mr Gardiner asked her what was the standing of D. H. Lawrence in English literature.

'Well, I would say that he is certainly among the six greatest, the five or six greatest writers in English literature of this century, taking the first sixty years of the twentieth century.'

'This is perhaps rather a tall order, but do you know of any book in English literature which was written for publication by an author of anything like Lawrence's standing which has not been published, except this book?' – 'No; I cannot think of one. There are works that writers did not intend to publish to the general public which have been published subsequent to their death, but I cannot at the moment think of any work which a writer intended to publish for general circulation which has not come into print.'

'You are not, I think, an admirer of this particular book, are you?' – 'I think it is a very remarkable book. I don't think it is a wholly successful novel. I wouldn't rank it among the greatest of the works that Lawrence wrote, although I think certain passages of it have very great merit indeed, and, indeed, are among the greatest things that he wrote.'

'It has been said that the four-letter words form the whole subject matter of the Prosecution, and that the word fuck or fucking occurs not less than thirty times. What, in your view,

HELEN GARDNER

is the relation of the four-letter words in this book to its literary merits?' – 'I would like to begin by saying that I don't think any words are brutal and disgusting in themselves. They are brutal and disgusting if they are used in a brutal and disgusting sense or a brutal and disgusting context. I think that by the very fact that this word is used so frequently in the book, with every subsequent use the original shock is diminished, and I would say by the end Lawrence has gone very far within the context of this book to redeem this word from low and vulgar associations, and to make one feel it is the only word the character in the book could use. If one attempts to find any substitute I think it is impossible. By the time one reads the last page, Mellors' letter, this word has taken on great depth of meaning, has become related to natural processes, and is wholly justified in the context of this book. I don't mean I think Lawrence was able to redeem the word in usage. I am talking about its usage within the book itself.'

'What do you gather from the book itself was Lawrence's intention in using four-letter words?' – 'I think his intention was to make us feel that the sexual act was not shameful, and the word used in its original sense therefore was not shameful either.'

'How far, in your view, are the descriptions of sexual intercourse relevant or necessary to the theme or meaning of the book?' – 'I think that Lawrence in this book was attempting to bring home to the imaginations of his readers certain aspects of modern society, the failure of relations between men and men, the degraded condition in which many people live.'

Then, to the visible astonishment of Mr Gerald Gardiner, Mr Griffith-Jones asked only two questions: was Lawrence a great writer? (Yes); was this one of his greatest books? (No – but it contained some of his greatest writing). For some moments no one noticed that Mr Griffith-Jones had then sat down. Mr Gardiner was the first to recover. With the faint dawn of victory upon him, he rose to re-examine.

'You said that certain passages in the book are among the

greatest things that Lawrence wrote. Will you tell us which passages you have in mind?' – 'I would say the expurgated passages come into this class. There are many of them. I would say the description of the drive through Derbyshire; it gives a portion of England set in historic context. I would say the actual treatment of the relationship between Sir Clifford and Mrs Bolton shows extraordinary psychological penetration. The character and personality of Mrs Bolton is one of the most remarkable examples of verisimilitude in modern fiction.'

'Did I understand you to say you particularly included a number of what you call the expurgated passages?' – 'Certainly. May I be allowed to say why?' – 'Yes, please.' – 'I think in discussing literary merit one has to give weight to two things. One is, I think, what the writer is trying to say, and the other is his success in saying it. These two are not always commensurate. One can find great literary merit in a piece of writing of a trivial experience, because it is so fully and truthfully expressed. Equally one can find great literary merit in a piece of writing of an experience of great importance and great value, although one may feel at times the writer has not wholly succeeded in communicating what he wishes to communicate. I think these passages do succeed, far beyond expectation, in doing something extraordinarily difficult, which very few other writers have really attempted with such courage and devotion, and that is to attempt to put into words experiences that are really very difficult to verbalize. An example is the work of mystical writers, who are also trying to put into words experiences that are felt immediately and not rationally dealt with. I feel in these passages, in many of them, Lawrence has succeeded in what he set out to do.'

*

Next came Mrs JOAN BENNETT, Lecturer in English at Cambridge University and Fellow of Girton College, who is the author of critical works on Virginia Woolf, George Eliot, and John Donne. Mr Gardiner asked her what she thought Lawrence's standing was in English literature. She replied: 'I would have thought that, among the younger people, since

Hardy and Conrad, he is the greatest writer of fiction that we have had.'

'What do you take to be the theme or meaning of this book?' – 'Well, I think the meaning that Lawrence has very much at heart, as in other books, is that the physical life is of very great importance indeed and is neglected, that many people live poor, emasculated lives because they are living only with half of themselves. So far as one can summarize the meaning of a novel, I think that is what I would say.'

'It has been suggested that it sets upon a pedestal promiscuous and adulterous intercourse?' – 'But the very reverse, I would have thought. In so far as any promiscuous intercourse is shown in the book it is shown as unsatisfactory, giving no fulfilment, no joy, and as really rather disgusting. "Adulterous" is rather more difficult to meet. He is so obviously set against promiscuity. By "adulterous" he means that a marriage can be broken when it is unfulfilled.'

'It has been suggested that sex is dragged in at every conceivable opportunity and the story is little more than padding. Do you agree or disagree with that?' – 'Well, for one thing, it is not wholly about sex. I mean, Lawrence is also interested in social questions, and some part of the book is concerned with upper classes, middle classes, working classes, and their relations to one another. But in any case I do not think "padding" is the right word. If the charge is that some parts of the book are not as well written as other parts, I think the charge is just.'

'What do you say as to the literary merits of the parts which do not deal with sex? The parts which deal with the mining villages?' – 'I would not like to make a general statement. I think that some of the parts that do not deal with sex are very good indeed and some are not.'

'Have you one son, three daughters, and eight grandchildren?' – 'Yes.'

'From the point of view of literary merits only, would it be educative for young students to read this book?' – 'Yes.'

Mr Griffith-Jones rose to cross-examine; and within a minute it had become plain that the Prosecution had taken a new turn. The gravamen of the charge was now that the book was about adultery; for thus it was now treated by Mr Griffith-Jones in the cross-examination of almost every witness to whom he spoke at all, and thus it was to a large extent treated by the learned Judge, in his own questions to witnesses and in his summing-up. Lady Chatterley was indeed on trial. By implication, if only she and Mellors had been husband and wife, then, whatever they did and wherever they did it, all would have been well, the marriage certificate shielding the susceptible against depravity and corruption. No one faced this logical dilemma in open Court. There was a lively awareness of it at the solicitors' table, but it was doing the Defence no kind of harm.

'Mrs Bennett, you said that the book showed the author's view on marriage. What view do you suggest it showed?' – 'Well, it does not say very much about his view about the law concerning marriage, but it does make clear that a union between two persons who love one another is of great importance.'

'Let us just understand one another before we get any further. Marriage is when two people are married, when they go to church and go through the service and so on, and become man and wife. That is right, is it not?' – 'I think so, yes.'

'I understand, when you make the answer to my learned friend that this book puts forward views on marriage, you do not refer to that kind of marriage at all?' – 'Well, I did not – rather deliberately – but I am quite prepared to. The views on marriage that appear in this book are that it should be a complete relationship, including the physical, and that if it does not include the physical, that marriage should be terminated.'

'Not only that it should be terminated, but that one party to the marriage can go off and have affairs in her boudoir up-stairs with the guests in the house or in the wood with the keeper?' – 'No, I think not.'

'That is the only thing that the lady does in this case, is it not?' – 'I think that there is a very clear distinction made in the book between the affair with the friend of her husband in wherever it was, and the love relation with the keeper.'

'Yes, that may be so, but the chief character in this book, who happens to be a married woman, is depicted throughout this book as going and having sexual intercourse. It may be satisfactory, it may be unsatisfactory, it may be that she is in love, it may be that she is not in love, but the fact remains that she is depicted throughout the book as going off and having sexual intercourse with somebody other than her husband. That is the fact, is it not?' – 'But the question, of course, that is of interest . . .'

'Would you just answer my question first? That is the picture that this book gives?' – 'The picture shows a woman who has relations with people not her husband.'

'And are you saying that by drawing that picture Lawrence is showing his views on marriage?' – 'I am saying that by the *way* in which the picture is drawn a reader who is capable of understanding him would learn much of what his view is.'

'Do you really think that the average reader is going to see anything in this book about marriage other than the picture of the wife going and having adulterous sexual intercourse, first with a guest in the house, and then with her husband's keeper?' – 'I think, if this is their interest, they would find many other books that would satisfy it better.'

'But do answer my question!' – 'I thought that was the point of your question. I do not know what you mean by an average reader. If by an "average reader" you mean an intelligent child . . . ?' – 'Yes?' – 'Well then, I don't think that is all they would get.'

'One has got to search fairly hard for anything else, has one not?' – 'I think not.'

'My learned friend in his opening said that this book clearly showed the author's very strong support for marriage; but you don't suggest that this series of adulterous intercourses shows a very strong support for marriage, do you, in the sense that I use the word "marriage"?' – 'Well, *you* use the word – could you define the sense you used it in?'

'Lawful wedlock, madam', said the Judge rather crossly.

You know what that means, do you not?' – 'Yes. Well, I am afraid I would have to repeat that the book shows that as to lawful wedlock Lawrence believes that it can be, as I believe the law allows, broken on certain conditions.'

'I do not want to repeat it,' said Mr Griffith-Jones, repeating it, 'but he shows the woman breaking it without any conditions at all, without even telling her husband, does he not?' – 'Yes.'

'And indeed one doesn't want to speak disrespectfully of the dead, but if one is talking about what the author's views were and what he was endeavouring to show, that is in fact, is it not, exactly what he himself had done? He had run off with his friend's wife, had he not?' – 'Yes.'

'And married her?' – 'Yes.'

'And it is just that type of behaviour, is it not, that is depicted in this book?' – 'You mean that a woman is shown . . .'

'I mean a man running off with another man's wife. It is just that which is happening throughout this book. The whole book is about that subject, is it not?' – 'Yes.'

Mr Griffith-Jones sat down.

'It is clear from the book', suggested Mr Gardiner in his re-examination, 'that the husband *told* her to go and have a child by another man?' – 'Yes', said Mrs Bennett, adding that Lawrence's own marriage lasted the whole of his life.

*

It was clear, from the Jury's display of interest as she came into the Court, that Dame REBECCA WEST was the first of the witnesses whose name was well known to them all. They listened intently as Mr Gardiner recited her many decorations and outlined her literary career. She said that Lawrence's repute was very high, and that his work was discussed by serious students of literature in every country concerned with Western literature.

'It has been suggested', said Mr Gardiner, 'that this is a book which sets upon a pedestal promiscuous and adulterous

DAME REBECCA WEST

intercourse?' – 'Er, yes,' replied Dame Rebecca. 'It has been suggested, and that on the bare facts is true; but it is not a recommendation of such intercourse. It shows a broken life, and what somebody did with it, but it does not suggest adultery. It could not, because Lawrence was a man who spent all his life working out the problem of how to make a good marriage: he thought a good marriage was perhaps the most important thing in the world.'

'It has been suggested that sex is dragged in at every conceivable opportunity, and that the story is little more than padding. If that was true would it obviously be an attack upon the integrity and honesty of purpose of the writer?' – 'Yes. The idea that the story is padding cannot be true because as a matter of fact the book has that story because it was designed from the first as an allegory. Here was culture that had become sterile and unhelpful to man's deepest needs, and he wanted to have the whole of civilization realizing that it was not living fully enough, that it would be exploited in various ways if it did not try to get down to the springs of its being and live more fully and bring its spiritual gifts into play. The baronet and his impotence are a symbol of the impotent culture of his time; and the love affair with the gamekeeper was a calling, a return of the soul to the more intense life that he felt when people had had a different culture, such as the cultural basis of religious faith.'

'Is Lawrence's message any less valid in today's circumstances than in the circumstances of 1920?' – 'No, I think it has more bearing on them. Since then we have had a war which was due to something that Lawrence feared very much. Lawrence was a very practical and realistic man and he did see that in every country in the world there were vast urban populations who had lost touch with real life, and that they could be taken in any direction. They have been taken in the direction of evil by their obedience to leaders such as Hitler. Lawrence was talking about something quite real. He was not a fanciful writer. He did write about reality. Talking to one, he was governed by the fear that something would happen, and he did want to get back to something which would save us.'

'Is there anything else you would like to say as to the literary merits of the book?' – 'The great literary merit of his book is something that readers accord by reading him in such large numbers, and his critics accord by writing so much about him. But it is not an easy matter to define the literary merit. If you take individual sentences of his, you can find passages which appear to have no literary merit at all; but the same is true of Shakespeare and Wordsworth, who have some terrible lines both in verse and prose, and of Dickens. But if you take Lawrence's books as a whole they are books of great literary merit. If you take all his books together he was a great writer.'

'Don't trouble about these other books', said Mr Justice Byrne. 'We are only dealing with one. What is the literary merit of this book? I think that is what Mr Gardiner is asking you?' – '*Lady Chatterley's Lover* is full of sentences of which any child could make a fool, because they are badly written He was a man with no background of formal education in his home. He also had a great defect which mars this book. He had absolutely no sense of humour. A lot of pages in this book are, to my point of view, ludicrous, but I would still say this is a book of undoubted literary merit. After all, a work of art is not an arbitrary thing. A work of art is an analysis of an experience, and a synthesis of the findings of the analysis, that makes life a serious matter and makes the world seem beautiful. And though there are ugly things, though there is this unsuccessful attempt to handle the ugly words, this is still from that standard a good book in my opinion.'

'Thank you', said Mr Gardiner.

'No questions', said the surprising Mr Griffith-Jones again. And from this point he was to say it many times.

*

The next witness was Dr JOHN ROBINSON, the Bishop of Woolwich. Mr Gardiner elicited from him that at Cambridge he took a degree in Classics, a first in Theology, and a Doctorate of Philosophy, and that his ordination had necessarily involved him in a special study of ethics. Then Mr Gardiner asked him the question that was to raise an immediate dispute about evidence as to the book's 'other merits' and its value in furthering 'objects of general concern'.

'What, if any, are the ethical merits of this book?'

'I am not quite sure', said Mr Griffith-Jones, getting up, 'what my learned friend means by "ethical merits". As I understand it, these ethical qualifications, great as they are, do not give the witness the right to speak on the literary merits of this book. If one looks at the Act . . .'

'I am not putting the witness forward as an expert in literature at all', said Mr Gardiner blandly. 'That', rejoined Mr Griffith-Jones, 'is why I am looking at the Act. That is the only way in which one can put forward a witness, in my respectful submission.'

Mr Justice Byrne murmured a tactful reference to Section 4(2) of the Act, and Mr Griffith-Jones read it out: '"It is hereby declared that the opinion of experts as to the literary, artistic, scientific, or other merits of an article" – I recognize that besides literary merits there can be other merits – "may be admitted in any proceedings under this Act either to establish or to negative the said ground", that is to say "that it is in the interests of science, literature, art, or learning, or of other objects of general concern".'

'What is covered by "other objects of general concern"?' asked the Judge. 'Who would the experts be with regard to those matters?' – 'It is difficult to say, my Lord. I had not understood that this book was being put forward as being justified on the grounds of its ethical merits. If in fact that be the argument, there was nothing to suggest it in my learned friend's opening. If it be suggested that that is one of the grounds upon which this defence is based, then it may be that this gentleman is an expert who can speak as to that.'

'I will hear what Mr Gardiner has to say about it', Mr Justice Byrne pronounced. 'My Lord,' said Mr Gardiner, 'it is exactly as my learned friend has said. The section refers to artistic, scientific, or other merits, and I am asking this witness about its ethical merits, he having already said that he has made a special study of ethics. I would add that, in my submission, it would also be relevant evidence to assist the Jury to decide whether or not the publication of the book is in the interests of science or learning or of the other objects of general concern. One of the objects of general concern of the community is the right use of . . . well, perhaps I ought to lay the foundation to that by asking the witness some more questions first.'

'I am inclined to think', said the Judge, 'that having regard to the wording of Sub-section (2) of Section 4, this evidence cannot be excluded. It is quite true, as Mr Griffith-Jones has said, that you did not in your opening suggest that this was a book of ethical merit, but since you call a witness to deal with that aspect of it, I suppose the Section is sufficiently elastic to say that such evidence is admissible.' It sounded a grudging admission, but Mr Gardiner was obliged.

He turned again to the Bishop. 'Has the Church always had a special interest and a special concern in human relations?' – 'Clearly, that would be one of my chief interests in this whole case, the effect upon human relations and the effect upon Christian judgements and Christian values.'

'What do you say are the ethical merits of the book?' – 'I would not want to be put in a position of arguing this primarily on its ethical merits. Clearly, Lawrence did not have a Christian valuation of sex, and the kind of sexual relationship depicted in the book is not one that I would necessarily regard as ideal, but what I think is clear is that what Lawrence is trying to do is to portray the sex relationship as something essentially sacred. Archbishop William Temple . . .'

Mr Justice Byrne, who was writing some of this down, interrupted:

'Before you talk about Archbishop William Temple, he was trying to portray – what?' – 'The sex relation as essentially something sacred. I was quoting Archbishop William Temple. He once said that Christians do not make jokes about sex for the same reason that they do not make jokes about Holy Communion, not because it is sordid, but because it is sacred, and I think Lawrence tried to portray this relation as in a real sense something sacred, as in a real sense an act of holy communion. For him flesh was completely sacramental of spirit. His description of sexual relations cannot be taken out of the context of his whole, to me, quite astonishing sensitivity to the beauty and value of all organic relationships. Some of his descriptions of nature in the book seem to me to be extraordinarily beautiful and delicate and portraying an attitude to the whole organic world of which he saw sex as the culmination, which I think in no sense anybody could possibly describe as sordid.'

'Would you make any difference', Mr Gardiner asked, 'between the merits from that point of view of the book as it is and those of the book as it would be if the descriptions of sexual intercourse and all four-letter words were expurgated from it?' – 'I think the whole effect of that would be to suggest that what Lawrence was doing was something sordid in putting it before the public, if these things were eliminated. I think that is a false suggestion, and neither in intention nor in effect is this book depraving.'

'It has been suggested that it places upon a pedestal promiscuous and adulterous intercourse.' – 'That seems to me to be a very distorted way of looking at it. It is dealing with sexual relationship, and many books do that. I think it has artistic integrity. It is not dealing with intercourse for its own sake, and it is not dealing with sexual promiscuity. If the Jury read the last two pages, there is a most moving advocacy of chastity and the remark "How can men want wearisomely to philander?", and I think that is Lawrence's whole approach to the subject, and that the effect of this book is against rather than for promiscuity.'

'Have you one son and three daughters?' – 'I have', said the Bishop; and this concluded his evidence-in-chief.

'I must just point out to you', said Mr Griffith-Jones, rising to cross-examine after lunch, 'that I don't propose to discuss with you what Lawrence intended. Did you tell us that this book is a valuable work on ethics?' – 'I would say that its value, its positive value, from the ethical point of view is that it does stress the real value and integrity of personal relations; that sex is not just a means of using other people but a means of respect for them.'

'Marriage is another aspect of ethics, is it not?' – 'Certainly.'

'This book doesn't help much in educating anybody into a correct view about that particular aspect of ethics?' – 'Naturally it is not a treatise on marriage. What it does though is, I think, to make it obvious he is not against the marriage relationship. On the contrary, he is concerned with establishing a permanent, genuine, spiritual relationship between persons.'

'Bishop, I don't want to be offensive to you, but you are not here to make speeches', said Mr Griffith-Jones unexpectedly. 'Just try and answer my question "Yes" or "No", if you can.' 'With respect,' said Mr Gardiner at once, 'the witness *has* answered the question.'

Mr Griffith-Jones went back to his first question. 'Are you asking the Jury to accept that this book is a valuable work on ethics?' – 'It depends on what you mean by a valuable work on ethics.'

'A work of instructional value.' – 'As I said, it doesn't set out to be a treatise on ethics.'

'I am not asking you what it sets out to be; I am asking you to apply your mind to my question and answer it if you can "yes" or "no". Are you suggesting this book is of instructional value upon the subject of ethics? – 'No, I would not say it was of instructional value upon the subject of ethics.'

'As you read the book,' interposed Mr Justice Byrne, 'does it portray the life of an immoral woman?' – 'It portrays the life of a woman in an immoral relationship, in so far as adultery is an immoral relationship. I would not say it was intended in any way to exalt immorality.'

Mr Gardiner put a few further questions to the Bishop in re-examination. 'Lawrence, of course, was not a Christian, was he?' – 'No.'

'Is this a book which in your view Christians ought to

read?' – 'Yes, I think it is. Because I think what Lawrence was trying to do . . .'

This had two consequences: it supplied a banner headline for the evening papers, A BOOK ALL CHRISTIANS SHOULD READ; and it brought Mr Griffith-Jones to his feet again. 'Before you answer that question; if my learned friend keeps putting that form of question I shall keep objecting. That is a matter for the Jury, as to whether the publication of this book is justified.' – 'Justified on the ground of literary or other merits', said the Judge thoughtfully. And Mr Griffith-Jones added, 'For the public good.' – 'For the public good, yes. I will hear what Mr Gardiner has to say.'

'My Lord,' said Mr Gardiner with a faint air of proprietorship, 'here is a Bishop. The Jury have to consider the question of the public good. Here is an important aspect of public good. It seems strange that the Prosecution should object to evidence, from a witness of this standing, of his view upon the Christian standpoint.' – 'I think it is really going on to the question the Jury have to answer', decided the Judge. 'I think he can express his views with regard to the merits of the book from the ethical point of view and so forth, but I think the answer to that last question would really be the very question the Jury might have to answer, assuming they answer the first question in a particular way.' – 'If your Lordship pleases', Mr Gardiner said, and the Bishop stood down. But the odd thing was that the disputed question had been asked and answered. It *was* a book that Christians ought to read.

*

The Professor of English at Nottingham University, Dr VIVIAN PINTO, was the next witness – a man who had served in both wars, a Fellow of the Royal Society of Literature, and a Lawrence expert who had lectured on his subject in America, India, Belgium, Yugoslavia, and Italy.

'In 1955', Mr Gardiner asked him, 'did you contribute to an annual volume produced by members of the University some unpublished manuscripts of Lawrence which you obtained from his sister?' – 'Yes.'

'Have you built up a D. H. Lawrence collection in the Library of Nottingham University?' – 'Yes.'

'Lawrence came from Nottingham, I believe?' – 'He came from Eastwood and was a student at the old University College at Nottingham.'

'This summer to commemorate thirty years from Lawrence's death have you organized an exhibition of his writings and paintings by and of him, and other material of historical interest?' – 'Yes.'

'Did you have one case devoted to *Lady Chatterley's Lover*?' – 'Yes.'

'Including the unexpurgated edition and various Continental translations?' – 'Yes.'

'Are there several copies of the present book, of the text of the present book, in the University Library?' – 'Yes.'

'And the students reading for the Honours degree in English in your department, do they have to take a paper entitled "English Literature, Life, and Thought, 1880 to the Present Day"?' – 'Yes.'

'Are they encouraged to read Lawrence?' – 'Certainly. I consider he is one of the major English writers. I would say he is one of the greatest English writers of the twentieth century. Amongst the major English novelists I would put Thomas Hardy, George Eliot, Jane Austen, and Fielding.'

'What is the theme or meaning of the book?' – 'It is difficult to sum up in a few words, but I should say that it has a double theme: a very broad one, the condemnation of the mechanization of humanity in an industrial society, and a more particular one, the necessity for human happiness to find adequate sexual relationship based on tenderness and affection, mutual affection. That is what Lady Chatterley finds at the end of the book with Mellors.'

'I suppose all standards must be relative. What do you say as to the literary merits of the book as a whole compared with the general run of English novels?' – 'I would give it a high place; not the highest place. I think it is a deeply moving story. In parts it is tolerably written, some parts are weak; there are weak passages, I would admit, but generally speak-

PROFESSOR VIVIAN DE SOLA PINTO

ing I think it is an important and valuable work. Not one
of his greatest works, but still a valuable work, and particularly valuable as a statement of his philosophy of life. It is in
some measure a moral tract as well as a novel.'

'Was it the last novel he wrote?' – 'Yes. The last long
prose work.'

Professor Pinto then commented on the passages picked
out earlier by the prosecution as 'obscene' – pages 27 ('com-
petently written'), 30 ('beautifully written'), 56 and 57 ('very
able piece of writing'), 120 ('a beautiful passage full of tenderness and insight'). He similarly commended pages 130, 138,
139, 185, and the famous letter at the end of the book – 'a
highly poetical passage, an affirmation of life, of what might
be called true marriage.'

'How far, in your view,' asked Mr Gardiner, 'are the
descriptions of sexual intercourse necessary to express what
Lawrence was trying to say?' – 'I think they are absolutely
necessary, to show that a union of human beings must be
based on an adequate kind of sexual intercourse – sexual
intercourse which was, in his own words, "valid and precious"
– and that other sorts of sexual intercourse were harmful. He
detested promiscuity. He detested the idea of regarding these
things as mere amusements.'

'It has been said that the only variation in the description
of sexual intercourse is in the *locus in quo* – that is to say, the
place. Do you agree with that?' – 'No. I think there are very
subtle differences, a great many variations. For instance, there
are occasions when he shows that the union has not been
successful, for various reasons. There are occasions when he
shows that it has given deep joy, and so forth.'

'It has been suggested that sex is dragged in at every conceivable opportunity and that the story is little more than
padding.' – 'I do not agree with that view at all. Indeed, I
think some of the finest passages in the book have nothing to
do with sex, the passages of social criticism like that magnifi-
cent description of the drive through Derbyshire when Connie
(Lady Chatterley) realizes what a degraded kind of life results
from mechanized civilizations. Then again those very interest-

ing passages of talk between the cronies. They have little to
do with sex. There is Mrs Bolton. Now, Mrs Bolton, I
think, is a very interesting creation. She is a character worthy
of Dickens. She is one of the common people. Her talk – she
has an idiom of her own which I think is comparable to
Dickens's Mrs Gamp. I mean, a wonderful comic creation.'

'In your view, are the four-letter words necessary to what
Lawrence was trying to say?' – 'I think they are. He had very
strong views on that subject. He wished to purify those
words, to cleanse them, as he said. Of course he did realize
that there are very strong taboos attaching to them and
perhaps what he tried to do was impossible. But I think, for
his purpose, it was necessary to use them.'

'How far is the fact that the novels of an English author
have been published in most other Western countries an
indication of the literary merits of the book?' – 'I suppose it
is one indication. It shows that this book has been admired by
people . . .'

'I am talking about books in general.' – 'I think it is a
certain sign. Of course, I suppose all kinds of factors might
go towards making books popular in various countries. I
suppose a surer criterion – if I might mention that – of literary
merit would be if they were studied in the universities and
prescribed by the people who teach in the universities.'

'On that answer, I would submit that I am entitled to put
the further question as to whether Lawrence's novels, including this one, have been so published.' – 'Oh, they certainly
have,' said the Professor emphatically, just as Mr Gardiner
was telling him not to answer until the question had been
ruled admissible. 'He *has* answered,' said Mr Justice Byrne.
It doesn't make much difference, Mr Gardiner. I think you
had better leave it where it is.'

'I sought to put it to the police officer, my Lord. Of course,
I had not then got the groundwork from a literary expert that
this was a statement that you could take into account . . .'
I think it is exploring a very wide avenue', said Mr Justice
Byrne, who used to be a Treasury Counsel at the Old Bailey
and knew all the stratagems. 'I would have thought what

happens in other countries has got nothing to do with this case. He has answered the question and the Jury have heard his answer. It wouldn't make very much difference what I said about it now.'

Mr Gardiner was resigned. 'Did Lawrence himself subsequently write about this book?' – 'Yes. He wrote a very fine essay called *A propos of Lady Chatterley's Lover*. I think it is one of his finest pieces of critical writing.'

'Have you got a copy?' – 'I have got one or two extracts.'

'He deals first, I think, with the publication in Italy, and the refusal to publish it here. At the top of page 226* he says: " So I managed to get published the little cheap French edition, photographed down from the original, and offered at sixty francs. English publishers urge me to make an expurgated edition, promising large returns – and insisting that I should show the public that here is a fine novel, apart from all 'purple' and all 'words'. So I begin to be tempted and start in to expurgate. But impossible! I might as well try to clip my own nose into shape with scissors. The book bleeds. And in spite of all antagonism, I put forth this novel as an honest, healthy book, necessary for us today. The words that shock so much at first don't shock at all after a while. Is this because the mind is depraved by habit? Not a bit. It is that the words merely shocked the eye, they never shocked the mind at all. People without minds may go on being shocked, but they don't matter. People with minds realize that they aren't shocked, and never really were: and they experience a sense of relief. And that is the whole point. We are today, as human beings, evolved and cultured far beyond the taboos which are inherent in our culture. This is a very important fact to realize. Probably, to the Crusaders, mere words were potent and evocative to a degree we can't realize. The evocative power of the so-called obscene words must have been very dangerous to the dim-minded, obscure, violent natures of the Middle Ages, and perhaps are still too strong for slow-

* The edition of *A propos of Lady Chatterley's Lover* referred to during the trial is that contained in *Sex, Literature and Censorship*, ed. Harry T. Moore (Heinemann, 1955).

minded, half-evoked lower natures today. But real culture makes us give to a word only those mental and imaginative reactions which belong to the mind, and saves us from violent and indiscriminate physical reactions which may wreck social decency. In the past, man was too weak-minded, or crude-minded, to contemplate his own physical body and physical functions, without getting all messed up with physical reactions that overpowered him. It is no longer so. Culture and civilization have taught us to separate the reactions. We now know the act does not necessarily follow on the thought. In fact, thought and action, word and deed, are two separate forms of consciousness, two separate lives which we lead. We need, very sincerely, to keep a connexion. But while we think, we do not act, and while we act we do not think. The great necessity is that we should act according to our thoughts, and think according to our acts. But while we are in thought we cannot really act, and while we are in action we cannot really think. The two conditions, of thought and action, are mutually exclusive. Yet they should be related in harmony. And this is the real point of this book. I want men and women to be able to think sex, fully, completely, honestly, and cleanly. Even if we can't act sexually to our complete satisfaction, let us at least think sexually, complete and clear. All this talk of young girls and virginity, like a blank white sheet on which nothing is written, is pure nonsense. A young girl and a young boy is a tormented tangle, a seething confusion of sexual feelings and sexual thoughts which only the years will disentangle. Years of honest thoughts of sex, and years of struggling action in sex will bring us at last where we want to get, to our real and accomplished chastity, our completeness, when our sexual act and our sexual thought are in harmony, and the one does not interfere with the other.'' Mr Gardiner stopped reading and glanced at the witness. 'That', said Professor Pinto, 'was the passage I had in mind.'

Mr Gardiner read on. '"Far be it from me to suggest that all women should go running after gamekeepers for lovers. Far be it from me to suggest that they should be running after anybody. A great many men and women today are happiest when they abstain and stay sexually apart, quite clean: and at the same time, when they understand and realize sex more fully. Ours is the day of realization rather than action. There has been so much action in the past, especially sexual action, a weary repetition over and over, without a corresponding thought, a corresponding realization."' Professor Pinto indicated his assent, and Mr Gardiner sat down.

'You, I gather, have made a particular study of D. H. Lawrence?' began Mr Griffith-Jones. 'Is he, as it were, rather a hobby horse of yours?' – 'I think it is very natural that I should be interested, being Professor of English at Nottingham University, when Lawrence himself came from a small mining village in Nottinghamshire.'

'You have told us that in your view this book is not one of his greatest?' – 'I would agree to that, but still a very important book.'

The Professor was asked then about *The First Lady Chatterley*, the earliest version of the book now on trial. Miss Esther Forbes, the American critic, had said that it was 'Lawrence at his best' and that *Lady Chatterley's Lover* was 'the worst of all Lawrence's books – stiff and unnatural'. 'I don't think Esther Forbes is a person of any particular standing as a literary critic,' said Professor Pinto.

So Mr Griffith-Jones turned to John Middleton Murry. 'Middleton Murry wrote *Son of Woman*,' he said. 'Is that known to you?' – 'I know the book.'

'You are very familiar with it?' – 'I know it. I don't think it is a good book at all. I think it is a very unsatisfactory book.'

'I have no doubt. I was rather anticipating you would say that, because he doesn't agree with you?' – 'No.'

'Just like Esther Forbes?' – 'But Middleton Murry wrote a later book in which he gave a more considered opinion – *Love, Freedom, Society*.'

'You will no doubt be referred to that, if it is a contrary view. Let me just read to you this particular passage on page 369 of the edition I have of *Son of Woman*. It says: "There is, indeed, little more to be said about *Lady Chatterley's Lover*.

Regarded objectively, it is a wearisome and oppressive book; the work of a weary and hopeless man. It is remarkable, indeed notorious, for its deliberate use of unprintable words. But in a very little while the mind becomes simply accustomed to them; they become simple glyphs which do nothing to diminish or enhance the value of the book. With each successive reading that value seems to dwindle. The book leaves no permanent impression, as though it had been from the beginning devoid of all vital energy of soul. And this curious effect, as of a neuter thing, with no real power of vital disturbance, appears on reflection to be inevitable. The great 'thought adventure', of which Lawrence made us once the partakers, is over", referring, is he not, to the end of his life?' – 'Yes.'

'"It has been abandoned, or rather it has collapsed. We are at the beginning of life again. Lawrence has accomplished the destiny he prophesied for himself in Annable.* The struggle has been in vain." That is not a very flattering view of this book, is it?' – 'It is not, no.'

'You were asked about one passage. I did not take down your precise words. As I understand it, you thought it was a beautiful passage. Just look at it again to see, so that we can make sure what your ideas of beauty are. Page 185 ?' – 'I did not use the word "beautiful" about this passage. I said it was an able and competent description of a certain situation.'

'I apologize if I have misquoted you. Let us see if it really is very able.' – 'An able piece of realism. That is what I would call it.'

'Look at page 185, halfway down: "Th'art good cunt, though, aren't ter? Best bit o' cunt left on earth. When ter likes! When tha'rt willin'!", and so on and so on. We get "cunt", "cunt", and "fuck", "fuck"?' – 'I think this should be read in Nottingham dialect to get the . . .' There was laughter in some parts of the Court, including the jury box. 'If people cannot restrain their laughter the Court will be cleared,' said the Judge; the laughter froze. 'That may well be so, but not all the people who would read this book published by Penguins at 3s. 6d. a time would have a knowledge of Nottinghamshire dialect, would they?' – 'No; that is true.'

* The gamekeeper in *The White Peacock*, Lawrence's first novel.

'Is that an example of a very able writing?' – 'Well, I think of course, that is not the way to examine a book at all, to take a few lines.'

'I couldn't agree with you more; but you have to start looking at something?' – 'Yes, but I think you would have to start looking at a number of passages and a number of extended passages to get an accurate view.'

'And where one finds other passages where that is repeated time and time again, is that able writing?' – 'Yes, in this particular book I would say it is.' Mr Griffith-Jones sat down.

'Middleton Murry and Lawrence were at one time friends and they quarrelled?' asked Mr Gardiner. – 'Yes. I think there was a strained personal relationship between them.'

'And this was written after the quarrel?' – 'Yes.'

'Are you acquainted with *The Doctrine of D. H. Lawrence* written by him in 1930?' – 'Yes.'

'He says in this: "For the moment we will say that Mr Lawrence's novel absolutely justifies itself. Rather paradoxically (if its philosophy were taken literally) it is the work of a very conscientious man. Mr Lawrence knows precisely what he is after in using the novel in this way." Then he quotes from the passage about the novel, *Lady Chatterley's Lover*, itself: "It is the way our sympathy flows and recoils that really determines our lives. And here lies the vast importance of the novel, properly handled. It can inform and lead into new places the flow of our sympathetic consciousness, and it can lead our sympathy away in recoil from things gone dead. Therefore the novel, properly handled, can reveal the most secret places of life: for it is in the passional secret places of life, above all, that the tide of sensitive awareness needs to ebb and flow, cleansing and refreshing. But the novel, like gossip, can also excite spurious sympathies and recoils, mechanical and deadening to the psyche. The novel can glorify the most corrupt feelings, so long as they are conventionally 'pure'. Then the novel, like gossip, becomes at last vicious, and, like gossip, all the more vicious because it is ostensibly on the side of the angels." That is the end of the quotation about *Lady Chatterley's Lover*. Then Mr Murry says: "That is Mr Lawrence's defence of himself; and it seems to us unanswerable. In so far as *Lady Chatterley's Lover* causes the tide of our sensitive awareness to flow about the secret places of life – and it does this abundantly – it is not merely justified, but positively good. It is a cleansing book, the bringer of a new catharsis."'–'I agree with everything that Mr Murry said there.'

The last question to Professor Pinto came from the Judge: 'What do you understand by the words "literary merit"?' – 'It is not easy to put in a few words. I look for a number of things in the book. I look for the quality of the writing, for the importance of the subject matter, the meaning of the book, whether it has a true and valid meaning; the experience that lies behind it is important, and whether the artistry, the craftsmanship, is adequate, and whether it succeeds in conveying the author's experience, and whether that experience is a significant experience, and I think what is called the longimanous test is a good test, when you come back to it and get fresh pleasure from it, and I did that. I came back and read *Lady Chatterley's Lover* before this trial, after a number of years, and I found it was an even better book than I thought originally.'

*

Then came Sir WILLIAM EMRYS WILLIAMS, a director of Penguin Books Ltd. He was Staff Tutor in English Literature in the extra-mural department of London University from 1928 to 1934, he said, and secretary of the British Institute of Adult Education from 1934 to 1941. He directed the Army Bureau of Current Affairs from 1941 to 1945, and was a Trustee of the National Gallery from 1949 to 1956. Since 1951 he had been editorial adviser to Penguin Books, and Secretary-General of the Arts Council.

'Quite independently of being a director of this Company, have you made a study of D. H. Lawrence yourself?' Mr Jeremy Hutchinson asked him. 'Yes, I could claim so, over forty-five years.'

'I think you have read all his published works?' – 'All of them.'

'So I think you are qualified almost as much as any other witness to express a view as to the literary merit of this book and the position of D. H. Lawrence as a novelist?' – 'Yes.'

'What is your view on those two matters?' – 'Well, to put the thing briefly, I would maintain that in all his work he is attempting to do, so to speak, what a picture-restorer tries to do in works which have become tarnished. He believed that we did not fulfil ourselves completely as we ought to do, and we were prone to concentrate everything on the mental life; and his attempt, as I understand it, in all his works and in all his poems, is to clean off that old varnish. It is rather a spectacular way of describing it, but it is perhaps the easiest shorthand of which I am capable.'

'What is your view of him, first of all, as a novelist?' – 'Well, as a most uneven one. I cannot think of any author of our time who can range so far from perfection to imperfection, and if you compare, for instance, two books such as *The Lost Girl* and *Sons and Lovers* on the one hand with, say, on the other hand, *The Prussian Officer*, the disparity is enormous. I am afraid he was a highly uncritical writer – of his own work, I mean.'

'Where do you put him in this century as a novelist?' – 'Oh, equal with Hardy, equal with Conrad.'

'What are your own personal views as to the literary merit of this book and its right to be published from that point of view?' – 'It strikes me as an extremely sincere effort to tell the story of two people, unhappy and frustrated, and their personal feelings, and an attempt by these two people to break through into personal fulfilment, which includes the fulfilment by sex. It seems to me a most courageous attempt in itself, and I think it succeeds.'

'In 1950 did you publish a collection of ten of his works?' – 'We did, simultaneously.'

'Did you find there was a great demand for them?' – 'An enormous demand, and also an extremely broad and enthusiastic range of reviews.'

'I think this year is the seventy-fifth anniversary of his birth.' – 'It is, and the thirtieth of his death. We hoped we should be able on the thirtieth anniversary of his death to complete, as you may say, the entire canon, and if we had succeeded we should have published, I think, by now, twenty-one or twenty-two, the whole of his work.'

'Did the question of bringing out this novel in some expurgated form ever receive serious consideration?' – 'It occurred to us, of course, but it has been our policy, over the whole of our twenty-five years, to print only works complete and un-abridged, and we carry that slogan on every copy. We were determined in this particular case to continue that policy and to print as you may say the *texte intégral*.'

'What other considerations did you take into account in making the decision this year to publish?' – 'Well, I think to a certain extent we were influenced by the fact that this is our jubilee year; we were hoping to attain a summit of achievement, and we thought the most appropriate unpublished novel which should appear in the jubilee year was *Chatterley*.'

'What other considerations did you take into account in deciding?' – 'We were profoundly influenced by what we thought the Act of 1959 implied and, indeed, said. It said, for instance, that for the first time in a prosecution of this sort, we could bring expert witnesses. It declared for the first time, I think, that the work had to be studied as a whole. The third factor which influenced us was that in 1959 the book was published in the U.S.A. and we thought we should be as fortunate here as they were there. And finally we did take legal opinion.'

'This country being the country where Lawrence lived and worked?' – 'Yes.'

'Thank you,' said Mr Hutchinson, and delivered Sir William over to Mr Griffith-Jones.

'The abridged version of this book, *Lady Chatterley's Lover*, more accurately the expurgated version, was published by Heinemann?' – 'Yes.'

'So that so far as the book is of literary or any other kind of merit, apart from the purple passages, that book has already been made available?' – 'Yes.'

'All that your publication has, over and above what that book has already provided the public with, are the purple passages, and such merit as may reside in them or that they may in addition give to the book?' – 'I cannot accept the description of them as purple passages.'

'I wasn't asking you to. Perhaps it is my fault, but we have – or I have – used one word instead of a lot of words to describe certain passages which may be obscene as purple. I am not asking you to accept that they are, but you know now what I mean?' – 'Thank you.'

'The expurgated version had a very considerable number of passages omitted?' – 'Yes.'

'Tell me this: as I understand it, your company are proposing to publish the whole of Lawrence's works?' – 'Not quite the whole. There are two or three which we shall, I think, not publish, such as the *Psychoanalysis of the Unconscious*, simply because it is virtually an unreadable book.'

'You have not yet published *The First Lady Chatterley*?' – 'No.'

'Are you proposing to publish that?' – 'No.'

'That is a book which again does not contain what I call the purple passages?' – 'Yes.'

'I don't know, but if you are doing this author the honour of publishing his works, and if it is in the interests of the public good to publish them, did you not consider publishing that original *Lady Chatterley's Lover*?' – 'No. We still maintain the policy that the version we wish to produce is the complete one containing what you call the purple passages, which I would call something else, because those purple passages give a totally different and more complete fulfilment of what he was trying to do than any truncated version could. We shall either publish the complete version or nothing.'

'It was not so much a fulfilment of what he was trying to do. It appears to have been a complete change of mind on his part. Have you read *The First Lady Chatterley*?' – 'Yes, sir.'

'There is a passage on page 190, a conversation between Sir Clifford and Constance. "She didn't quite know what he referred to, but she knew every woman and hence every man had private sexual secrets which no one had any right to betray. The biggest part of my life, she said to herself, is secret, and the first business I have is to keep the secret and to respect the secret in other people." There is not anything in that book like there is in the final version as to what took place between them. That looks rather as though he had quite a different idea he was trying to put over.' – 'I am extremely sorry, but I am truly unable to answer a question based on a small piece of a passage which I do not have in my hand. I can't do it.'

'I am sorry, you shall have it', said Mr Griffith-Jones, and a copy of *The First Lady Chatterley* was handed to Sir William. 'After all, the author does in the course of the book express his intention through what the characters say? Isn't that the way he expresses his theme?' – 'Yes,' replied Sir William, and glances were exchanged by the listening lawyers not involved in the case, for this was a significant concession by the Crown as to the relevance of the author's 'intent'.

'You see the last part of that penultimate paragraph, "She did not quite know . . ."?' – 'Yes, I have read it.'

'We have heard from the witnesses a great deal as to what the author intended to write in this book. It appears that in the very first version of it he intended just the opposite?' – 'But he changed his mind.'

'Is the value of somebody's intention who changes his mind from year to year all that important?' – 'Very important. In an artist most important. Artists perpetually change their minds and redraft their work and repaint their pictures, and they have the sole right to determine which is the final version.'

'And the fact that he wrote the original version with a quite different intention, does that not give merit to the original version?' – 'A certain one, yes; a certain one.'

'But that is not the one you have chosen?' – 'No.'

'You have chosen this one and you had, had you not, some 200,000 copies printed?' – '200,000 copies, yes.'

'I don't know whether you can give me an average figure, but in the ordinary way when you publish a Penguin, how many copies do you have printed?' – 'Well, an average would be 40,000 or 50,000. On the other hand, there are other works which we expect to have a great success, such as *The Cruel Sea*, of which we printed 250,000 copies. *Room at the Top* was, I think, 200,000 copies. So 200,000 is not anything wildly exceptional so far as we are concerned, particularly in view of the immense sales we have had of this author.'

Mr Hutchinson then re-examined. 'Sir William, it was suggested to you that you could quite well publish this book cutting out "purple passages". Would you tell the Jury what view you take as to the importance or significance of those passages in this book as written by Lawrence?' – 'I will try, sir. I think that what they do is to give colour to the progressive change in the feelings of these two people. Without those purple passages it seems to me you would have a recital of incidents which superficially are very much the same. You would have a sequence of love-making scenes. But the whole point, I think, that he was determined to impress on us was that love can be a failure, love can be dirty, love can be clean; and these two people go through the whole cycle until they do discover the wholesome fulfilment, and I think that without the contours and the colours which distinguish these episodes that point would not have been made.'

'Do you think the book would have been Lawrence's book of perhaps equal literary merit if you had put a row of asterisks in every time these two people meet in the way we have seen?' – 'I think that would make the thing just a dirty book.'

'What have you got to say about the use of the four-letter words – because they are also included in the "purple passages", apparently? Do you think this book would be the same or have equal literary merit if the four-letter words were removed and dashes were put there instead?' – 'No. I think also that would create unwholesome associations; that would imply that he thought that those words were invariably words with an obscene connotation. Of course they can have an obscene connotation, but he was determined they should not have it. Therefore he wants them in full. He wants no short-hand, he wants no disguise, he wants no concealment.'

*

Prebendary A. STEPHAN HOPKINSON, editor of *The London Churchman* and Director-General of the Industrial Christian Fellowship, was then called to give evidence. His man-of-affairs experience was detailed to the Jury – editor of *Isis* at Oxford, oilfield administrator in Mexico, chaplain to the Forces, Vicar of Battersea, Chairman of Battersea Youth Committee, Vicar at two famous City churches. He was, he told Mr Gerald Gardiner, Anglican adviser to Associated Television, and every Sunday he had a TV programme called *About Religion.*

When Prebendary Hopkinson was asked what ethical or sociological merits he found in *Lady Chatterley's Lover*, particularly from the viewpoint of Christian values, he said it was a book of moral purpose.

'It seems to me to be a study in compassion and human tenderness, not solely in relation to the two leading characters but in relation to all the other persons of the book. As part of this instrument of essential human relationships, it deals with a physical one, and he seems to me to deal with it with respect and honesty and only in so far as it is essential to the whole theme of human relationships. I think, therefore, that, judged as a whole, it is a book of moral purpose which does set out a picture of understanding and kindness, that nothing in it is out of key or keeping with that, and that in fact it emphasizes what is to me an important part of the Christian tradition: that God is himself a creator, that man shares in the responsibility for creation, and that that is directly expressed in the relationship of the sexes, particularly as regards the pro-creation of children.'

'Would it be more or less in accordance with Christian theology if some parts were replaced by asterisks?' – 'It would be less in accordance. It seems to me that what we are concerned with in the moral field is people's actions, thoughts, and motives, and not the use or misuse of words. If therefore there are activities which are essential for all human life then it is misleading to try to replace them by asterisks or blanks, which people may well fill in in an altogether wrong sense, certainly supplying a motive other than that intended by the author. I think therefore we owe it to the author to let him speak his mind upon these subjects, not to delete his intentions, leaving us to substitute our own.'

'Is it a proper assumption that sex can be treated in accordance with the Christian faith, accepted as some sort of symbol?' – 'Yes. I think it is one of the great basic emotions, and it is in fact essential to life as we know it. All life comes through sex itself, and believing that all life comes from God I would believe therefore that God himself created these functions, and we ought therefore to learn to regard them with respect and reverence, which does *not* mean with timidity.'

'Is it in any way to be equated with sin?' – 'No; I think, because its powers are so great, it can be wrongly used to produce what we should consider sin – cruelty, meanness, and all the exploitation and intolerance of human beings to each other, but in its own nature it is not sin. I would say theologically it is entirely wrong to attempt, as people sometimes have done, to link the two together.'

'You told us you had a great deal to do with youth clubs and young people. Have you yourself sons of 21 and 12, and daughters of 22, 19, 17, and 15?' – 'I have.'

'From a moral point of view would you have any objection to young people reading the book?' – 'No. That is to say, from *my* point of view, *my* children; I am glad they should read it. I like to think they would discuss it with me and with their mother, as I hope they do discuss anything which seems to them significant and important. I could not think of denying other parents of other children a relationship which with my own I value very much.'

'Is that because of the way it is written?' – 'It is because I think, as a book complete in itself, it is important and valuable for them.'

Mr Griffith-Jones then cross-examined about the theme of adultery. It led him into this kind of exchange:

'Do you find anywhere in that book a word suggesting criticism of what she is doing?' – 'Not a word. In fact I take it the book is intended to depict a situation rather than pass moral judgement.'

'It is very difficult, you know. No expert in this case appears to be able to answer a question "Yes" or "No". Do you find one word of criticism of that course of conduct in this book?' – 'No,' said Prebendary Hopkinson for a second time, 'but I find no word of criticism of moral conduct in the book either.'

When Mr Griffith-Jones had finished, the Judge came back, unexpectedly, to the question of Mr Hopkinson's own children.

'Have you any objection to your children reading it?' – 'Provided again, my Lord, they discussed it with me – no. Only one of them, to my knowledge, has; and he found the book, on the whole, he said, rather dull.'

But when Mr Gardiner, in effect, put the same question in another way – in more specific language – it was disallowed.

'Is there anything in the book which in your view would do any young person any harm?' – 'I am not sure', said Mr Griffith-Jones, 'that that is an admissible question.' – 'I think that is a question for the Jury,' said Mr Justice Byrne. 'I think it is all wrapped up, is it not, with the case.'

*

Then came Mr RICHARD HOGGART, author of *The Uses of Literacy*, Senior Lecturer in English Literature at Leicester University. He was introduced to the Jury as a man who went from elementary school and grammar school to university and took an English degree. He said that he lectured on D. H. Lawrence to 'the young people under his care'. He was a member of the Albemarle Committee on the Youth Services and of the Pilkington Committee on broadcasting. Mr Hutchinson asked him what he thought about the literary merit of *Lady Chatterley's Lover*. 'I think it is a book of quite exceptional literary merit, probably one of the best twenty novels we have had written in Britain in the last thirty years', said Mr Hoggart.

'It has been said that the two main characters in the book are little more than bodies which continuously have sexual intercourse together. What would you say to that as a fair summary of this novel in relation to its main characters?' – 'I should think it was a grossly unfair summary. I should think it was based on a misreading of the book.'

'The book has also been described as little more than vicious indulgence in sex and sensuality. In your view is that a valid description of this novel?' – 'I think it is invalid on all three counts. It is not in any sense vicious; it is highly virtuous and if anything, puritanical.'

'Did you say "virtuous and puritanical"?' interrupted Mr Justice Byrne. And Mr Hoggart, who was a self-composed, determined, and unshakeable witness, said that he did. He added that 'indulgence' was not the word for the love passages in the story. 'The sexual encounters, the parts in which we have descriptions of sexual life, are all carefully woven into the psychological relationship, the context of the two people, and the natural flow from this as part of an attempt at explaining their outlet, either physical or spiritual. The third word in the statement is?' And Mr Hutchinson repeated:

'Vicious indulgence in sex and sensuality.' – 'The book obviously includes sensual passages because they are part of the relationship, but certainly not indulgent and certainly not vicious. I thought, taken as a whole, it was a moral book.'

'We know one of the complaints is that it uses four-letter words. What exactly do you mean by saying that, taken as a whole, you think the book is a moral book?' – 'I mean that the overwhelming impression which comes out to me as a careful reader of it is of the enormous reverence which must be paid by one human being to another with whom he is in love and, in particular, the reverence towards one's physical relationships. Physical relationships are not matters in which we use one another like animals. A physical relationship which is not founded in a much closer personal respect is a vicious thing. This spirit seems to me to pervade *Lady Chatterley* throughout, and in this it seems that it is highly moral and not degrading of sex.'

'As far as the young people under your care are concerned, would you think that this was a proper book for them to read?' – 'Viewed purely in the abstract, I would think it proper, if they came to me to ask me if they could read it, to tell them to ask their parents, and probably I should give them a note to their parents asking them if they could read it, but I would not take that responsibility upon myself.'

'You would think that a wise course?' – 'Yes.'

'Have you children of your own?' – 'Yes.'

And with that the second day of the trial ended.

'. . . Matter o' fact, *oi* were Lady Chatterley's lover . . .'

THE THIRD DAY

ON Friday morning for almost an hour Mr Hoggart and Mr Jeremy Hutchinson discussed selected passages from *Lady Chatterley's Lover*, Mr Hoggart gradually and convincingly establishing Lawrence as a 'British non-conformist Puritan'. The repetitiveness of the Lawrence style – the 'black, black, black' of the Nottinghamshire mining villages – the satirical and nervous prose of the passages which the prosecution had called 'mere padding', were fully explored. Long passages were read out by both men, in a Court which was hushed by the sheer strength, previously unrecognized by many now listening, of Lawrence's writing.

Lawrence's descriptions of 'sexual intercourse' (itself a ponderous euphemism that grew more irritating as the trial went on) were again referred to by Mr Hutchinson in a question about their alleged monotony – 'varying only in the *locus in quo*'. He asked for Mr Hoggart's view about that. 'I would deny that absolutely', replied Mr Hoggart. 'Again, it is a gross misreading of the whole book. I don't know how many times sexual intercourse takes place in the book, perhaps eight or ten times; and any good reading of the book, I don't mean a highbrow's reading, a good decent person's reading of the book, shows there is no one the same as the next; each one is a progression of greater honesty and a greater understanding. If one reads them as being a series of acts of sexual intercourse, one is doing violence to Lawrence's whole intention, and not reading what is in the text.'

'By the time you have reached the end of the book, have those two persons, in your view of the reading of it, found some true and real contact, as opposed to all the contacts at the beginning of the book?' – 'Yes, I think the ending of the book has a result which one can hardly find in literature now. He is able to say things in the letter he writes at the end, the very last page, "Now is the time to be chaste, it is so good to be chaste, like a river of cool water in my soul." This is the writing of a pure man. "I love the chastity now that it flows between us. It is like fresh water and rain. How can men want wearisomely to philander", that is, to be promiscuous. This seems to me a resolution which establishes that the book has moved through the whole cycle.'

'It is quite obvious, of course, that this relationship is between two people who in fact are married. Would you say this book advocates – it obviously describes – but would you say it advocates adultery?' – 'I think the book advocates marriage, not adultery. It takes a difficult and distressing human situation which we know exists. A marriage which has gone wrong, which had never started right. It doesn't burk the issue by saying they went on somehow, and this is very much to the point. He could have made this analysis of the realization of the solution through sex by a wife who did not love her husband. He stacked the cards against himself. He was talking about the nature of a true marriage relationship between people. We know there are bound to be occasions in human beings, sometimes for very bad reasons and sometimes for reasons that are unavoidable, when there is friction between our formal state of marriage and the relationship we meet with, the genuine relationship he is talking about. He did not say, if you want to enjoy yourself in sex you should leave your wife or husband, but the thing to do in a marriage was to work hard at every level. When you get up in the morning and cook the breakfast, don't lose your temper with the children. Having gone through all this they will get married. He tells us so; they are waiting for it.'

'In your view is there anything more in this book than, at the end, two people finding a state of satisfactory sexual relationship?' – 'There is not only more in it than that, but one could say – although it sounds paradoxical – one could say the physical sexual side is subordinate. I am sure it was for Lawrence. He said more than once that really he is not interested, not unduly interested, in sexual acts. He is interested

RICHARD HOGGART

in a relationship between people which is in the deepest sense spiritual. This includes a due and proper regard for our sexual and physical side. I believe in this book what he said is, "I must face this problem head on, even at the risk of having people think I am obsessed by sex." But one realizes from this last letter that, between Mellors and Lady Chatterley, there will be periods of extraordinary chasteness; there will be moments of coming together in love which will be all the better because they are not using one another like creatures for enjoyment. It is a kind of sacrament for him.'

'I want to pass now to the four-letter words. You told the Jury yesterday you were educated at an elementary school. Where was it?' – 'Leeds.'

'How did you start your life?' – 'I was born into the working class and I was orphaned at the age of eight and brought up by my grandmother.'

'What is your view as to the genuineness and necessity in this book of the use of these four-letter words in the mouth of Mellors?' – 'They seem to me totally characteristic of many people, and I would like to say not only working-class people, because that would be wrong. They are used, or seem to me to be used, very freely indeed, far more freely than many of us know. Fifty yards from this Court this morning I heard a man say "fuck" three times as he passed me. He was speaking to himself and he said "fuck it, fuck it, fuck it" as he went past. If you have worked on a building site, as I have, you will find they recur over and over again. The man I heard this morning and the men on building sites use the words as words of contempt, and one of the things Lawrence found most worrying was that the word for this important relationship had become a word of vile abuse. So one would say "fuck you" to a man, although the thing has totally lost its meaning; it has become simply derision, and in this sense he wanted to re-establish the meaning of it, the proper use of it.'

'What do you say about the use of these words as they have been used in this book?' – 'The first effect, when I first read it, was some shock, because they don't go into polite literature normally. Then as one read further on one found the words lost that shock. They were being progressively purified as they were used. We have no word in English for this act which is not either a long abstraction or an evasive euphemism, and we are constantly running away from it, or dissolving into dots, at a passage like that. He wanted us to say "This is what one does. In a simple, ordinary way, one fucks", with no sniggering or dirt.'

Mr Griffith-Jones, who now rose to cross-examine, had been wondering whether Mr Hoggart belonged to 'a body of opinion' that was opposed to all prosecutions for obscenity. 'Certainly not', said Mr Hoggart. 'I think the question of freedom of expression is a most involved and complicated one.'

Mr Griffith-Jones then mounted his main attack on Mr Hoggart's view of the book. 'Do you regard the real importance of this book as that part which does not consist in the descriptions of sexual intercourse?' – 'I regard the importance of the book as not separable from the whole book, including the parts about sexual intercourse.'

'I should have thought that was a question which was capable of a simple answer,' said Mr Griffith-Jones, looking round the Court. 'Would you regard the real importance of this book as being that part of it which is not contained in the descriptions of sexual intercourse?' – 'No', said Mr Hoggart firmly and patiently.

'You described this book as highly virtuous, if not puritanical. Please do not think that I am suggesting it with any bad faith against you. That is your genuine and considered view, is it?' – 'Yes.'

'I thought I had lived my life under a misapprehension as to the meaning of the word "puritanical". Will you help me?' Mr Hoggart took this as a genuine cry for help. 'Yes,' he said, 'many people do live their lives under a misapprehension of the meaning of the word "puritanical". This is the way in which language decays. In England today and for a long time the word "puritanical" has been extended to mean somebody who is against anything which is pleasurable, particularly sex.

The proper meaning of it, to a literary man or to a linguist, is somebody who belongs to the tradition of British puritanism generally, and the distinguishing feature of that is an intense sense of responsibility for one's conscience. In this sense this book is puritanical.'

'I am obliged for that lecture upon it. I want to see a little more precisely what you describe as "puritanical". Will you look at page 30? On page 30 there is a description of the second "bout", if I may again borrow a word, with the man Michaelis. Do you see towards the bottom of the page: "He roused in the woman a wild sort of compassion and yearning, and a wild, craving physical desire. The physical desire he did not satisfy in her; he was always come and finished so quickly, then shrinking down on her breast, and recovering somewhat his effrontery while she lay dazed, disappointed, lost. But then she soon learnt to hold him, to keep him there inside her when his crisis was over. And there he was generous and curiously potent; he stayed firm inside her, giving to her, while she was active ... wildly, passionately active, coming to her own crisis. And as he felt the frenzy of her achieving her own orgasmic satisfaction from his hard, erect passivity, he had a curious sense of pride and satisfaction. 'Ah, how good!' she whispered tremulously, and she became quite still, clinging to him. And he lay there in his own isolation, but somehow proud." Is that a passage which you describe as puritanical?' – 'Yes, puritanical, and poignant, and tender, and moving, and sad, about two people who have no proper relationship.'

'Again, I do not want to stop you if you have something further to say, but the question is quite a simple one to answer without another lecture. You are not at Leicester University at the moment. Just look down the page a little. "So they went on for quite a time, writing, and meeting occasionally in London. She still wanted the physical, sexual thrill she could get with him by her own activity, his little orgasm being over. And he still wanted to give it to her. Which was enough to keep them connected." That is about all there was to keep those two connected, was it not?' – 'Indeed, yes.'

'It was a wholly immoral relationship between the two?' – 'It was an immoral relationship, as Lawrence shows us.'

'She was a married woman. This was done behind her husband's back, and it was done without any love but purely for the satisfaction of her sexual lust. That is the position, is it not?' – 'It is not.'

'What else is it?' – 'It is done because she is lonely and lost, and feels wrongly that through this sexual act she will feel less lonely and lost.'

'It is done, is it not, because her husband was wounded in the war and has been incapable ever since of satisfying her sexual demands? That is the real reason that this is done, is it not?' – 'It is not.'

'Very well. That is your view. I only want to know.' – 'I can substantiate that view.'

'Never mind about substantiating it', said Mr Griffith-Jones, and brought Mr Gerald Gardiner to his feet in immediate protest. 'With respect, the witness having answered the question "Yes" or "No", he is entitled in my submission to add an explanation of his answer, if he wants to do that.' 'Yes, that is quite true', said the Judge at once.

'I apologize', said Mr Griffith-Jones, 'if I was a little abrupt with you. Forgive me. You wanted to substantiate that answer?' – 'If it had simply been a case that her husband was impotent and she wanted sex, she could have, and would have, had sex in every hedge and ditch round Wragby. Even when she made her mistakes she chose very carefully. She made a serious mistake with Michaelis. She knew it, but she thought at the time something might be there. This is a mistake we often make. Second, with Mellors himself it was something about which she was dragging her heels all the time until she felt herself pulled along. She was not . . .'

'What you are being asked', said the Judge, 'is this, as I understand it. First of all that this was just an immoral relationship between this woman and that man, was it not?' – 'Yes, between those two.'

'There was not a spark of affection between them, was there?' – 'There was.'

'There was?' – 'Yes, they felt there was; they were mistaken.'

'They felt there was', repeated the Judge slowly. 'How do you arrive at that conclusion?' – 'It is within the text. She felt that he was a child in some ways. She felt a kind of tenderness towards him. She realizes that it is a mistake, an emotional mistake.'

Mr Griffith-Jones next read a long passage from page 50 onwards about Lady Chatterley's 'affair' with Michaelis. 'Again I ask you only so that we may judge your evidence' he said. 'Is that passage puritanical?' – 'It is puritanical' replied Mr Hoggart with total conviction.

'Do you find anything comparable to the matter discussed there, in the way in which that is discussed, in *Paradise Lost*?' – 'I shouldn't expect to, because *Paradise Lost* is a poem about the creation of the world.'

'Just look at page 178. This is one of the Mellors "bouts". It is too long to read all of it.' But Mr Griffith-Jones read a lot of it, and then said, 'I don't know, but is that in your view a recommendation for a puritan literary and general standing?' – 'It is. Should I expand on that?'

'If you want to.' – 'I would like to. The point here again is that for Lawrence the physical act is meaningless unless it relates to one's whole being; in other words, back to God. Therefore this passage is highly ironical because the act has become in people's minds ridiculous. And, since you ask me,' said Mr Hoggart, who had had time to recollect, 'in the middle of *Paradise Lost* there is a great passage in which Adam and Eve come together in this way in relation to God, and it is highly sensual.'

Mr Griffith-Jones went on to read more erotic passages, ending each time, 'Is *that* puritanical?' and being told that it was. When Mr Hoggart said that one of them was 'heavy with conscience', he was told that that was not what he was being asked. Was it puritanical? It was, he said. Mr Griffith-Jones took to picking out words. 'Is *that* puritanical?' he would ask incredulously. '*Indeed* yes', came the reply from Mr Hoggart. Mr Griffith-Jones sat down.

'You were asked at the beginning of your cross-examination', said Mr Hutchinson, taking up the questioning again, 'whether you belonged to that group of persons who take the view that a prosecution for obscenity of any published work was to be condemned. Do you remember being asked that?' – 'I do.'

'In writing your book which you referred to yesterday, *The Uses of Literacy,* did you make a particular study of the books which are available to the public in paperback form in this way?' – 'I made a study over three years.'

'As a result of that study, what view did you take about the propriety of prosecuting books?' – 'I think, as a layman, that there may well be a very strong case for prosecuting certain books which I know to be freely available in this country, books which I regard as obscene.'

'And in taking that view, having been asked about it, what do you mean exactly as to that type of book which in your view you think should very properly be prosecuted?' – 'Those are books, to use a phrase of Lawrence's, which "do dirt on life". I think of one whole group of which there are millions on sale in this country now. You can buy two dozen in the Charing Cross Road this morning. They are paperback books at 2s. 6d. In every one of those there are, almost as though by recipe, two or three sexual encounters; usually they have rape, some sort of violence; they are not in any sense related to whatever story the book has; they are there presumably because they sell the book . . .'

It was a little surprising that this had got so far. 'We are not dealing with other books', said the Judge now. 'We are dealing with this book.'

'My Lord, it was only because of the questions asked', said Mr Hutchinson. 'I know', said Mr Justice Byrne mildly.

'I thought it should be cleared up.' – 'I do not want a possible loop-hole, because that question was asked, to turn into something too large.'

'If your Lordship pleases. Mr Hoggart, the phrase put to you to describe these acts in this book throughout was "bouts" – the phrase used by a lady called Katherine Anne

Porter in an article which was quoted yesterday – the word now adopted by the Prosecution, "bouts". Do you know the reputation of that writer or not?' – 'I know her reputation, yes.'

'Which is what, in your view?' – 'She is a very good short-story writer.'

'As a critic?' – 'I have only read that essay, which I thought was good proof that she is not a critic. One would say, from the use of the word "bouts", that that is in itself an instance of the corruption of language that Lawrence is attacking.'

*

Then came Mr FRANCIS CAMMAERTS, Headmaster of Alleyne's Grammar School, Stevenage, the son of the poet Emil Cammaerts who was Professor of Belgian Studies at London University. Mr Cammaerts was introduced to the Jury as an English History graduate of Cambridge and as a man who, having been a conscientious objector for the first two years of the war, then changed his mind and was parachuted into France to help the resistance movement until the Liberation in 1944, for which he had received many decorations. In April 1961, he said, he was to take up the post of Principal of the City of Leicester Training College.

'Have you read widely in English and French literature?' Mr Gardiner asked him. – 'Yes.'

'When did you first read *Lady Chatterley's Lover*?' – 'I am not sure of the date. It was either in my last year of school, when I was 17, or my first year at University, when I was 18.'

'Were you influenced by his philosophy?' – 'Yes. Very much so at that time. I was very impressed by his attitude to the industrial world at that time, and particularly to human relationships.'

'Were you brought up in a boarding school yourself?' – 'Yes, sir.'

'How would you compare the attitude in relationship to sex as it was dealt with at boarding school with that which one finds in Lawrence?' – 'I think it is quite normal in a boarding school for boys to treat sex as a matter of constant curiosity,

FRANCIS CAMMAERTS

the subject for a great deal of sniggering and joking, which is not a very healthy attitude. Put it that way.'

'What in your view is the theme or meaning of the book?' – 'I should say it had two main meanings. The first one a study of a profound human relationship. And the second the study of the influence of modern industrial society on the character of human beings.'

'Do you from time to time have to discuss sexual matters with boys?' – 'Yes. Naturally in the course of my duties I have to do so.'

'What happens if you use a term like "sexual intercourse"?' – 'I would say most boys have their own notion of a term like that, coloured by their reading of Sunday newspapers, shall we say. And in a sense it has an almost dirty meaning for them. They want you to talk about sex in their own language, that is to say using the terms that they use. As soon as you use a term which they think is evasive they think you are being hypocritical.'

'What are the terms they use?' – 'They use simple Anglo-Saxon words.'

'What would you say was the educational merit of this book from that point of view?' – 'I would say it is the only book I know that treats the sexual relationships between human beings in a really serious way, and would have the effect, on most young people who are interested in this problem, of giving them a serious approach to it.'

'Have you got a son and three daughters aged 18, 17, and 12?' – 'That is correct.'

'Would you have any objection to your children reading it?' – 'None at all.'

When Mr Gardiner sat down, Mr Griffith-Jones said, 'I have no questions to ask.' It was at this point in the trial – Mr Gardiner referred to it in his final speech to the Jury – that the Prosecution seemed to show further signs of cracking. From this point, Mr Griffith-Jones cross-examined less and less, with the one exception of Dr James Hemming, who gave evidence later the same day.

*

After Mr Cammaerts came Miss SARAH BERYL JONES, Classics Mistress at Keighley Girls' Grammar School. She graduated in 1920 from the University College of South Wales, with honours in Latin and Philosophy. She said that the school library at Keighley contained most of Lawrence's books, and that *Sons and Lovers* was set as a school text.

Mr Gardiner asked her whether there was 'a good deal of literature of one kind and another available to the girls now on sexual matters.' – 'There is literature available of every kind on sexual matters. The technical works are available and what you might call dirty literature is available to them if they wish to read it, but I am glad to say many of them don't.'

'How far do girls nowadays at school know the four-letter words?' – 'I have inquired from a number of girls after they have left school on this matter, and most of them have been acquainted with these words by the time they were ten.'

'In your view has this book any, and if so what, educational merits?' – 'I think that this book has a considerable educational merit if taken at the proper time, which I would say is normally after 17 years old, because it deals openly and honestly with the problems of sex which are very real to the girls themselves.'

'At an earlier age would younger children be in fact likely to get through it?' – 'I don't think so. Of the few people that I have known who have been in contact with the book earlier, one or two have not wished to read it, and others have found it boring and have discarded it. In my experience girls are very good at knowing what they want to read, and they naturally reject what is unsuitable for them. If they should be a little prurient they may read the book, but I find the majority of girls don't wish to read such books.'

'Thank you', said Mr Gardiner.

'Madam', began Mr Griffith-Jones, and the word always sounds ominous in Court, 'you say the majority of girls do not wish to read this book. How do you know that?' – 'I know that simply because the type of reading that girls do is very well known to me as senior librarian, and I converse very frequently with them about what they do read. Of course, at times I have confiscated literature which has been read by them when they did not know there was anyone at hand. And I have a very good knowledge, really, of what girls like to read and do read.'

'What I meant was up until now there has not been great facility available for reading this book, has there?' – 'Not this particular book, no. Although it is circulating underground.' There was some disciplined, almost staccato, laughter here. It suppressed itself.

'I am quite sure it is circulating. I have no doubt it is circulating in your school.' – 'I am not aware it is circulating in my school,' Miss Jones answered sharply, 'but I am aware it is circulating in Keighley and in the area of many another school.'

'And do you doubt it will circulate in a big way in your school if this book is published?' – 'Not in a big way.'

'With your experience of girls – goodness knows, it is difficult perhaps for a man to know – with your experience of girls and their talk and what they are thinking about at school, do you mean to say girls do not like reading books like this?' – 'There are always prurient girls.'

'Of course there are, but generally speaking do you have any real doubt that within a week of this book having been published every girl in your school will have read it, and every girl perhaps in every other school?' – 'Yes. I have the greatest doubts on that. I believe very strongly that girls know what they want to read and they are bored reading what they don't want to read.'

*

Miss Jones had got off lightly. She was succeeded by Dr C. V. WEDGWOOD, the historian and biographer. She confirmed, in answer to Mr Gardiner's questions, that among her many books were two collections of her own essays on literary subjects, that for seven years she was on the selection committee of the Book Society, and that she had been President of the English Association and the English Section of P.E.N.

'Have you been one of the judges for a year or more of the Somerset Maugham Prize, the Hawthornden Prize, and the W. H. Smith Prize, all literary prizes requiring a wide and balanced knowledge of English literature?' – 'Yes.'

'Have you read *Lady Chatterley's Lover*?' – 'I read *Lady Chatterley's Lover* about twenty-five or more years ago, and I have re-read it since.'

'What, in your view, is Lawrence's standing in English literature?' – 'Well, very high indeed: one of the really great creative novelists of this century and, indeed, of English literature altogether, and also a very fine poet.'

'What are your views of the literary merits of this book?' – 'I don't think it is one of his very best, but it is a very important one in his works, and it is a fine and honest and moving account of an extremely important theme.'

'How would you compare the literary merits of this book and the literary merits of the same book with the sexual passages and words expurgated from it?' – 'Well, it very much changes the balance of the book. It really distorts it. The expurgated version leaves out what was a great part of Lawrence's idea. He wanted to treat sexual love – he wanted to make it clear that there was this connexion between real tender love and sex, and that sex without love was quite different and was really wrong, whereas sex with this strong, real feeling of love and tenderness was what he was trying to praise – and also, of course, Lady Chatterley's natural desire to have a child. If you take out the descriptive passages you distort what is a very important part of the book.'

'I have no questions', said Mr Griffith-Jones.

*

The next witness was Mr FRANCIS WILLIAMS, best known to most of the jurors, no doubt, as an outstanding television personality. He was further made known to them as former editor of the *Daily Herald* (when that newspaper, as Mr Williams agreed with one of his broadest smiles, had the largest daily circulation in the world). During the war he was Controller of News and Censorship at the Ministry of Information and then Adviser on Public Relations to the Prime Minister. He was, he said, shortly taking up a Regents' Professorship at the University of California.

'When did you first read this?' – 'I first read an expurgated edition, I should imagine, about twenty years ago, and I read it in full in a Continental edition about nine years ago.'

'In your view, how do the two compare?' – 'I think one gets an entirely incomplete picture of the book and of its artistic integrity and what I believe to be its moral purpose if one reads the expurgated edition, because I believe that the passages which have normally been cut out in the expurgated editions are absolutely essential to the Lawrence theme, which I believe to be on two levels: that Lawrence was deeply concerned with what he believed to be the sickness of modern society, and particularly of industrial society, as he conceived that.'

'What would you say was the theme or meaning of the book?' – 'Well, it seems to me, as I say, to be very much on two levels. As I read it, I believe that Lawrence was in this book, as in other books, deeply concerned with what he believed to be the sickness of modern society, and he believed that that sickness was due to a concentration on intellectual subjects rather than on the acceptance of human beings as wholly complete people, and also he conceived that part of that illness of society was due to an industrialization of society which tended to treat people more and more as parts of a machine rather than as human beings, and I think that is rather significant. He cast in the role of the husband this intellectual person of long-standing tradition, a property-owning person in a newly industrialized area, but the crippling to him was in his conception a crippling of modern society which had begun before the First World War, but which had, in his view, been greatly increased after. I think it is significant that the first meeting with Mellors is when Lady Chatterley is going to visit one of the oldest pieces of wood in England, a piece of the old Sherwood Forest, and Sir Clifford Chatterley sees it as his duty to preserve this. I believe Lawrence is trying to convey his belief that in fact the intellectual upper classes were no longer able to preserve that which was absolutely great in the old tradition of England, and that it was Mellors who was likely to further that preservation, and I think all through one can see these two themes running. I think in the early intellectual discussions between Chatterley and his cronies, as they are described, Lawrence points in a prophetic way, as he did later, to the growth of Nazism in Germany, and the dangers of Bolshevism, to people being used as part of a system and not as human beings.'

'From the point of view of literary merit, how far, in your view, is his use of four-letter words in the mouth of Mellors justified?' – 'I think it is completely justified by his artistic purpose. I think one has to appreciate that most of those four-letter words do in fact appear either on the lips of Mellors or in the writing of Mellors when he writes a letter to Lady Chatterley; that Mellors was a person who was almost throwing himself backwards, back into the working classes from which he had been raised by the accident of war, when he had a commission. Therefore he would deliberately use such words, which indeed are quite common on the lips of the kind of people in the sort of background that he came from, as I know very well, because I was brought up as a boy in an industrial area very like that depicted in the book, where one in his early teens was quite used to hearing these words without any great sense of shock at all, because they were accepted as part of the normal usage in speech.'

'You have two adult children, and two infant grandchildren?' – 'I have.'

'Do you have any objection to your own children or your grandchildren reading the book?' – 'None whatsoever. The grandchildren are a little young at the moment', said Mr Williams, with another very broad smile.

'No questions', said Mr Griffith-Jones.

*

'Your name is Edward Morgan Forster?' said Mr Jeremy Hutchinson to the next witness. Mr E. M. FORSTER could not but agree, though the name had sounded so unfamiliar as shouted by the usher in the hall outside. Five of the Jury nevertheless knew who he was and watched with great interest as he went slowly to the witness box and bowed to the Judge. The other seven looked straight ahead, as Mr Forster's immense list of honorary degrees was read out. They listened to the names of his novels until they heard *A Passage to India*; and as Mr Hutchinson confirmed their dawning realization their heads turned in unison to the left, taking a fresh look at him.

'I think *A Passage to India* has been made into a play and at the moment is running in London?' – 'Yes.'

'I think you knew D. H. Lawrence quite well?' – 'Yes, I saw a good deal of him in 1915. That was the time when I saw him most, but we kept in touch.'

'Would you tell us where you would place him as a novelist and a writer in literature?' – 'In all the literature of the day, do you mean; in all contemporary literature?' – 'Yes?' – 'I should place him enormously high. When one comes to the upper ten novels then one has to begin to think a little of the order, but compared with all novels which come out, the novels he wrote dominate terrifically.'

'When he died I think you described him as the greatest imaginative novelist of your generation?' – 'Yes, I would still hold to it.'

'You have read *Lady Chatterley's Lover*?' – 'Yes.'

'Judging it in the same way, what would you say as to its literary merit?' – 'Judging it in the same way, I should say that it had very high literary merit. It is, perhaps I might add, not the novel of Lawrence which I most admire. That would be *Sons and Lovers*, I think.'

'Lawrence has been described as forming part of the great Puritan stream of writers in this country. Have you any comment to make on that?' – 'I think the description is a correct one, though I understand that at first people would think it paradoxical. But when I was thinking over this matter beforehand, I considered his relationship to Bunyan. They both were preachers. They both believed intensely in what they preached. I would say, if I may speak of antecedents, of great names, Bunyan on the one hand and Blake on the other, Lawrence too had this passionate opinion of the world and what it ought to be, but is not.'

'Is that founded not only on what he has written but what you knew of him?' – 'Yes. Well . . .'

'Thank you very much', said Mr Hutchinson, and sat down.

'Did you want to add something?' asked the Judge. – 'I was only qualifying it a little, because I did not discuss these questions with Lawrence personally, but there is nothing in what I knew of him which would contradict what I said.'

'No questions', said Mr Griffith-Jones again, profligate now with opportunities.

*

Mr ROY JENKINS, M.P., then made an appearance that was almost certainly of an effect out of all proportion to its brevity. He was the chief sponsor of the Obscene Publications Bill in its five-year period of difficult gestation, and he had written a letter to the *Spectator* on 26 August, a week after the prosecution was launched, to say that it was a betrayal of an implied promise given by the police to the Select Committee on Obscene Publications in 1958. 'Why', his letter asked 'cannot the Director [of Public Prosecutions] show a little good sense? Could not our prosecuting authorities learn a little from the illiterate mistakes of their predecessors?'

'Mr Jenkins,' began Mr Hutchinson, 'are you the author of a number of books yourself?' – 'Yes, I am.'

'On that basis, first of all, let me ask you this. In the Obscene Publications Act I think you know that the Preamble amongst other things, says, "To provide for the protection of literature". In your view, is this book *Lady Chatterley's Lover* literature?' – 'Yes, it most certainly is. Indeed, if I may add, it did not occur to me in the five years' work I did on the Bill . . .'

'I really don't think we want to go into that,' interrupted the Judge.

'I am so sorry, my Lord', said Mr Jenkins, who did not look sorry; and Mr Hutchinson sat down, looking satisfied.

Any alert juryman could see what had happened. Evidence had been given – and interrupted just too late – that the whole prosecution ran counter to the intentions of the particular legislator primarily responsible for the Obscene Publications Act, 1959. 'The intention of Parliament' had never been so skilfully put before a Court.

'No questions', said Mr Griffith-Jones.

*

Mr WALTER ALLEN, literary editor of the *New Statesman*, was introduced by Mr Hutchinson as 'a book critic, among other things'. He had been the Visiting Lecturer on English at the University of Iowa, where 'one of his subjects was Lawrence's novels'. He disclaimed the specific status of 'a Lawrence scholar'. His biography of Arnold Bennett and his book on *The English Novel* were mentioned as particularly marking his importance as a critic. During a year, he said, he might read as many as 200 novels.

'What is your view as to the literary merits of *Lady Chatterley's Lover*?' Mr Hutchinson asked him. 'I think it is certainly not Lawrence's best work by any means', replied Mr Allen. 'I think it suffers as a novel by being rather in the nature of a tract, but it does contain admirable and beautiful matter; and the subject seems to be one of the greatest importance.'

'How would you say it stands in relation to the general body of novels published? You have said what your view is in relation to Lawrence's own novels.' – 'Well, I think it is very difficult to compare it with the ruck of novels published now or at any time. Lawrence is a man of genius, and this is, although it is not the best of Lawrence, a work of genius. The great majority of novels published are not works of genius.'

'When you say it is in many ways a tract, what do you mean by that?' – 'I mean by that that in *Lady Chatterley's Lover* Lawrence is trying to express much more explicitly his views on the state of society and on the state of sexual relationship than he did elsewhere.'

'What is your view as to the moral content of this book?' – 'I think it is a moral book.'

Neither the Judge nor Mr Griffith-Jones took exception this time on the ground that an expert was being asked the wrong question. So Mr Hutchinson pressed on. 'Because?' – 'Because it really, I think, consists of two parts which cannot easily be separated. On the one hand it is an attack on what Lawrence saw as the evils of industrial society and industrialism. On the other hand – because, as I say, both are connected – it is an inquiry, a very, very serious inquiry, into sexual relationships, and Lawrence saw those two things as being facets of the same problem.'

'Now, Mr Allen, I think you have children of your own?' – 'I have four children.'

'They are still young?' – 'Yes.'

'When they grow older would you have any objection to them reading this book?' – 'Not at all.'

This time it was too much. Mr Allen was a literary man. If he had any morals there must be proof of them – a theological degree, perhaps. Mr Griffith-Jones rose: 'I have refrained until now. This question, as I said last night, is again being deliberately put to every witness. It can only be a question which is inviting an answer on the issue which the jury have to decide. I rise for the last time. I will not object again.' 'Yes,' said the Judge, 'it is not a question of literary merit, Mr Hutchinson.'

'My Lord, it is a question about morality, and I put the question because it is a question that your Lordship put to witnesses yesterday.'

But in fairness to his Lordship, the question, when *he* put it the day before, was addressed to Prebendary Hopkinson, who was there to talk about morals. But the Judge had forgotten. 'I may have,' he said, 'in view of something they said; but I think, if this question is objected to, it is inadmissible. This witness is being called, as I understand it, to express his views upon the literary merits of this book, and if that is so his evidence should be limited to that.'

Mr Walter Allen withdrew.

*

He was succeeded by Miss ANNE SCOTT-JAMES (Mrs Macdonald Hastings), who had edited *Harper's Bazaar* and the women's page of *Picture Post* and of the *Sunday Express*, had been on the staff of *Vogue*, and looked as though she had stepped out of one of its pictures.

'I think you have written and published a novel', said Mr Gardiner. 'Since 1940 have you broadcast many times and appeared on television, and have you two children, a girl of 9 and a boy of 14?' – 'Yes.'

'Have you read most of Lawrence's novels?' – 'Certainly half of them.'

'Have you read *Lady Chatterley's Lover*?' – 'Yes.'

'In your view has it any sociological or educational merits?' – 'Oh yes, immense. I think it is extremely important in view of the time at which it was written. Lawrence was an iconoclast; he thought the times were stiff and stuffy, that sex was treated hypocritically, that money was the guard round love and human relationships, and he was smacking at it.'

'From the point of view of sociological or educational merits, what would be your view as to reading *Lady Chatterley's Lover* as Lawrence wrote it and the same book with all the parts relating to sex taken out of it?' – 'I would rather not see it published at all than published in an expurgated edition.'

This time Mr Griffith-Jones decided to cross-examine.

'Please don't think that I am being rude about this. You run, do you not, or are responsible for, the ladies' page in some newspaper?' – 'No'.

'Or were?' – 'Some time ago, yes. Ladies' page is not the

phrase we use now. It is very old-fashioned; it has not been used since 1927.'

'Fashion page?' – 'Women's page, not fashion.'

'Called?' – 'It was called "Anne Scott-James's Page".'

'Is that what you run now?' – 'No, I am a free-lance writer now.'

'Still on that type of subject?' – 'Writing about family problems and children, mostly, and controversial topics of the hour.'

'I only ask you this question – as I say, please don't think I am intending to be rude, but evidence as to the literary merit of this book is confined to experts – I only wondered, do you claim any particular qualifications to be a literary expert?' – 'I think I do, yes.'

'What?' (incredulously) – 'Of a popular kind.'

'What?' – 'Well, I was a classical scholar at Somerville College, Oxford.'

'Not every classical scholar at Somerville College, Oxford, is a literary expert?' – 'No. It isn't a negligible qualification though.'

'I couldn't agree with you more . . .' – 'I was brought up in a very literary family.'

'But apart from the qualifications you have mentioned, you have no other qualifications such as might put you in the category of a literary expert?' – 'Not the same as a reviewer has, no.'

The odd thing was that no one had described Miss Scott-James as a literary expert. She had only been asked about the book's 'sociological and educational merits', because she was a writer on 'family problems and children'. But by this time there had appeared a tendency to stop treating the witnesses as literary experts, or ethical experts, or 'other merits' experts, and just treat them as experts.

*

But the next witness was an educational psychologist, Dr JAMES HEMMING, and there could be no confusion as to what he was there to say. With London degrees in English, History, and Latin, and some years of teaching experience, he became interested in 'the sociological and psychological aspects of education', and left teaching in 1946 for educational research. To that end he obtained a degree in Psychology, and in 1957 he was awarded a Doctorate of Philosophy for a study of the problems of adolescents. He lectured widely in England, Australia, New Zealand, India, and South Africa, and was involved in the training of youth leaders.

Mr Gardiner asked him what were the sociological or educational merits of *Lady Chatterley's Lover*. 'Well, today young people are subjected to a constant titillation and insinuation of what I would describe as shallow and corrupting values with regard to sex and the relationships between the sexes. For example, the picture is put before the young girl that if she has the right proportions, wears the right clothes, uses the right cosmetics, she will become irresistible to men, and that that is the supreme achievement of a woman. On the other hand, the general effect of this titillation and insinuation so far as the young man is concerned is to suggest that sex is little more than a physical thrill, that to have a pretty woman in one's arms is the supreme ecstasy of life, and that to seduce a woman is manly and something to be attempted for yourself and to be envied in others. Over against this, which is a purely physical view, Lawrence gives us a very carefully worked out picture of relationships between the sexes which are based on tenderness and compassion. As such, the content of *Lady Chatterley's Lover* is an antidote, a positive antidote to the shallow, superficial values of sex which are widely current today and which are now corrupting the attitude of young people towards sex.'

'It has been suggested that it sets upon a pedestal promiscuous and adulterous intercourse.' – 'Far from setting such liaisons on a pedestal, I would have thought that the whole emphasis of the book was towards the deep and enduring relationship. In fact, as the book develops, the depth and enduring quality of the true sex relationship is persistently and carefully worked out.'

'It has been said that the book glories in sensuality. Do you
agree with that or not?' – 'We have to analyse what we mean
by sensuality. It is now well recognized that for young people
to grow up and marry with a prudish and ashamed attitude
towards sex is positively harmful. *Lady Chatterley's Lover*
presents sex as it should be presented, where the relationship
of sex is something joyful and exuberant, tender, playful even,
and certainly mutual. I think this kind of picture is entirely
right.'

Dr Hemming then asked if he could quote from three
books. The Judge said he could not. 'If you will be good
enough to answer Mr Gardiner's question,' he said, 'we will
get on.' – 'These books emphasize . . .'

'I have told you', said the Judge more loudly, 'I will not have the contents of the other books.'

It was the moment for Mr Gardiner's most important legal submission.

'May I address your Lordship on that?' he said. – 'Certainly.'

'I am in this difficulty, my Lord, that questions of this kind tend to arise and be dealt with after a short discussion. I apprehend at some stage I should ask your Lordship to allow me to address an argument to your Lordship on the true construction of this Section. I don't want to find myself in the position where your Lordship may give a ruling and say at a later stage, "If I had heard this argument before I would have given a different ruling." I would have submitted, with respect, that references to other books *were* admissible. I don't know whether this is a convenient time to make a general submission on the true construction of the Section as a whole.'

'It is quite convenient as far as I am concerned,' said the Judge, 'if it does not interrupt your arrangements. Then this witness can go for the moment.' And Dr Hemming left the witness box to sit in Court and listen to a legal argument of great length, great complexity, and great importance to every future trial under the Obscene Publications Act, 1959.

It concerned the admissibility of evidence as to an author's *intention*, and particularly the production of *other books* to show, by way of comparison, both what that intention was and how well it had been carried out.

Mr Gardiner began by submitting, on the authority of *Maxwell on the Interpretation of Statutes*, that a new Act of Parliament had to be interpreted by reference to the law as it stood before the Act was passed and 'what was the mischief or defect for which the law had not provided'. For example, it was said that this new Act of 1959 made no change in the law about 'reading the book as a whole'. Mr Gardiner thought that was wrong: it *did* change the law. Lord Devlin, he said, had told the Jury in the case of *The Image and the Search* (1954): 'It is true, as a matter of law, to say that it is quite sufficient for you to find that part of the book is obscene. Quite obviously there are many passages and chapters in it which are not obscene at all. That does not save it. It is enough, in law, if there is a part that is obscene.' Then Lord Devlin had nevertheless advised his jury, in coming to that conclusion, to reach it in the light of the book 'as a whole'. 'The learned Judge's direction', said Mr Gardiner, 'was in my submission a correct statement of the law.' In 1959 it ceased to be the law, though the practice of some Judges might not have been changed.

That was Mr Gardiner's first submission. It took one's mind back to Mr Griffith-Jones's remark, in his opening speech on the first day, that to a very large extent the new Act 'only put into statutory form what the Common Law was before'.

'The other question', he said, 'on which I would ask your Lordship to allow me to address you on the law before the Act, relates to the "intention"' (i.e. the author's or publisher's intention in publishing the book); 'whether it is necessary that there should be a criminal intent. My Lord, that is an argument of rather greater length.'

'I think perhaps I can shorten that matter', said Mr Griffith-Jones. 'I think Mr Gardiner must have misunderstood what I intended when I opened this case. What I meant was that a defendant can be convicted of this offence without it being proved that he intended to deprave and corrupt, and that in that sense his intention was irrelevant. I did not intend to convey, and I don't now, that an author's intent in what he was trying to put over, by the book, is not a consideration which can properly be taken into account in judging the book's merits.'

'I have been turning that over in my mind, as a matter of fact,' said Mr Justice Byrne, 'because I noticed what you' (Mr Griffith-Jones) 'had said in opening this case; and it had occurred to me – and of course Mr Gardiner will develop his argument if necessary – that as far as obscenity is concerned it would be an objective test. But as far as literary merit or other matters that can be considered under Section 4 – as far as they are concerned, I think one has to have regard to what the author was trying to do, what his message may have been, and what his general scope was.'

Mr Griffith-Jones agreed. Mr Gardiner asked if he might consider this proposition during the lunch interval, which was then imminent. And thus it was arranged.

After lunch, Mr Gardiner said that he accepted 'the statement made by my learned friend that he does not *now* seek to contend that the intent of the author may not be relevant to the literary merit of the book'.

'Never did intend', said Mr Griffith-Jones. – 'I didn't quite catch that, Mr Griffith-Jones?' said the Judge.

'My learned friend said "Never did intend". But', said Mr Gardiner, 'I am bearing in mind the number of occasions on which my witnesses have been told "Stop – the intention of the author is irrelevant".'

Mr Gardiner then went on to make his second submission – 'that on a true view of the law before the Act was passed a criminal intent was a necessary ingredient of the offence'. And he adopted as his argument the view expressed by Mr Norman St John-Stevas in his book *Obscenity and the Law*.* 'As far as I know this is the only textbook on the subject,' he said, 'and the argument on this point starts on page 136.' Mr St John-Stevas had there written·that the Courts were wrong (even before the Act) in dispensing with proof of intention. 'Given that the purpose of the law is to suppress pornography but not to censor literature, then intention becomes of paramount importance; since it is only by considering the intention or purpose of the author that the two can be distinguished.' And Mr St John-Stevas went on to show, from numerous judgements, old and recent, that an author's intention was *not* an 'irrebuttable presumption of law', but a common-sense concept that could be rebutted by evidence for the Defence.

'As to other books,' said Mr Gardiner, 'I would submit that they may be relevant in two ways. First, any judgement of the literary or other merit of a book is necessarily one

* Secker & Warburg, 1956.

involving comparisons. If I say that this is a good book I am necessarily measuring it against other books, and I would submit that expert witnesses are always allowed to illustrate what they say by examples. Secondly, in my submission, other books may be relevant to the climate of literature. The fact is today that many books are published which were banned twenty years ago.'

As to the admissibility of expert evidence about *obscenity* – including mention of other books – Mr Gardiner said that the only decision against this under the new Act was the one concerning the *Ladies' Directory*. In that case the *Prosecution* sought to call evidence as to what might tend to deprave and corrupt, and Judge Maxwell Turner disallowed it.

Mr Justice Byrne then asked Mr Griffith-Jones for the Crown attitude to these arguments. Mr Griffith-Jones said that the most recent case on 'intention to deprave and corrupt' was that of *Rex* v. *de Montalk** (1932). '"The offence of uttering and publishing an obscene libel" (as it used to be called at Common Law) is established as soon as the Prosecution has proved the publication and obscenity of the matter charged, and a Jury should not be directed that, beyond this, they must find an intent to corrupt public morals.' What mattered, said Mr Griffith-Jones, was not what a man intended, but whether the tendency in the publication was to deprave and corrupt. He then went through the 1959 Act, Section by Section, to show that the Act made no mention of intention.

'I have said that I do not dispute the fact that the author's intent is relevant in assessing the literary merit of the book. I don't want to go back on that ... It is the book we are judging, not the author. As a matter of practice, it is probably

* This was a case in which a young Polish poet handed some poems to a printer, with the intention of circulating them privately among friends. The printer showed them to the police, and de Montalk was given six months' imprisonment by Sir Ernest Wild, the Recorder of London, the Court of Criminal appeal upholding the conviction and sentence. Prosecuting Counsel in that case was Mr Lawrence Byrne – the Judge in this case.

quite impracticable, in asking questions and witnesses answering them, not to refer to the author's intention. I take no narrow point on that. With regard to the judgement of literary merit, what in my submission is not allowed is any comparison between the book in question and other books as to relative obscenity. I do not think I could properly contend, where the question to be decided is the literary merit of a book, that a comparison between that book and other books simply and solely for a comparison of the literary merit was not admissible.' But as to obscenity, and relative obscenity, Mr Griffith-Jones quoted Lord Goddard in *Regina* v. *Reiter* (1954): 'The book itself provides the best evidence of its own indecency or obscenity or of the absence of such qualities. . . . The character of other books is a collateral issue, the exploration of which would be endless and futile.' There was nothing in the 1959 Act which suggested that the Legislature intended to alter that principle of law in cases of this kind.

'But my learned friend', Mr Griffith-Jones went on, 'maintained that comparison with other books was justified to see "the climate of literature". I don't know that that is really any different, is it? – or perhaps slightly different – from comparing it with other books for the purpose of comparing the merit. If by the climate of literature he is meaning the degree of obscenity in other books which are in circulation . . .'

'I take it', interrupted the Judge, 'that he doesn't mean that. What I think Mr Gardiner was meaning by that was possibly the fact that as the years go by, as you said yourself in opening, things are spoken of with greater freedom than they used to be in mid-Victorian days. I don't think Mr Gardiner had any question of obscenity in his mind.' But Mr Gardiner said that he did. 'In my submission', he said, 'this would be relevant. If there are today a number of very badly written and perverted books on the market, it may be all the more to the interests of literature – and, for that matter, for the public good – that an honest and boldly written book should be published.'

'What about the third point, Mr Griffith-Jones?' asked the Judge. 'Mr Gardiner submitted that he was entitled to call expert evidence on whether this book has a tendency to deprave or corrupt.'

'My Lord, that I submit he is *not* entitled to do. There is ample authority that as a general principle witnesses are not allowed to give their opinion upon questions which are questions for the Jury.' The new Act, said Mr Griffith-Jones, admitted the opinion of experts as an exception to the general rule, but that evidence was allowed solely 'on the merits of the book'. Whether the book was 'for the public good' must be an issue which the Jury had to decide. He quoted the footnote to Section 4 of the Act in *Halsbury's Statutes*:

'It should be noted that expert evidence is only admissible in relation to "the said ground", i.e., that the publication is in the interests of science, literature, art, or learning, but not as to whether the publication is justified as being for the public good, let alone as to whether the article in question is obscene.'

Mr Gerald Gardiner then contended that the case of *Regina* v. *de Montalk* was not really in point. The headnote to the Law Report of that case said that 'intent is not part of the offence'. Mr Gardiner said that this was erroneous. 'Lord Hewart in his very brief judgement made no reference to the point, although Mr St John Hutchinson had raised it for the appellant.' He reminded Mr Justice Byrne that he himself had said in *de Montalk*'s case, when he was prosecuting as Treasury Counsel, that 'intention to corrupt public morals is to be inferred from the act of publication itself: the Prosecution need not give affirmative evidence of such intention'.

'I accept every word of that', said Mr Gardiner. 'But that does not deal with my argument, that that presumption is itself one of fact, and is rebuttable, as has been so clearly expressed in his usual concise way by Lord Goddard.' And if the defendant chose to call rebutting evidence, he said, then, at the end of the case, it was necessary for the Crown to satisfy the Jury that the intent was there.

Finally, if the intention of the author wasn't relevant at all, so that literary merit had to appear from the book itself, then the author himself was irrelevant, and even his literary status would not matter. All that would matter would be the literary merit of the book itself. And 'that, in my submission,' said Mr Gardiner, 'can't be right, because if it were so, if my clients were to publish tomorrow Chaucer's *Canterbury Tales,* one couldn't call evidence as to who Chaucer was. I suppose if some members of the Jury were not familiar with his book they might think that, somewhere in London, this Mr Chaucer was publishing some pretty odd stuff.

'All I am contending for is that evidence is admissible as to the same kind of literature by different writers, though I do not seek to put in evidence their books ... I venture to think there is no other Act of Parliament which provides: "If you prove something you shall not be convicted, while at the same time that which you prove is something upon which you cannot call evidence."'

Mr Gardiner sat down, and the whole Court turned its attention to Mr Justice Byrne as he assembled his notes and prepared to deliver his ruling.

'The first point I have to decide', said the Judge, 'is with regard to the intent to deprave or corrupt. What Mr Gardiner submits here is that there must be proved an intent to deprave or corrupt, and thus, there being the presumption that a man intends the consequences of his act, if he publishes an article which is obscene, the presumption is a rebuttable one and, hence, evidence can be called to prove that there was no intent to deprave or corrupt. I am bound to say that I do not agree with that argument.

'I readily concede the fact that the case of *Montalk* is not very clear in the judgement as to what the Court was actually saying, but they came to the conclusion that there was nothing in that argument.' (On 20 December 1960 there was an interesting postscript to this discussion when Mr Justice Ashworth read the judgement of the Court of Criminal Appeal dismissing the *Ladies' Directory* appeal (*Regina* v. *Shaw*). 'At Common Law', he said, 'it would no doubt have been necessary to prove an intention to corrupt, but the Obscene Publications Act, 1959, renders this unnecessary'! He had the concurrence of the Lord Chief Justice and Mr Justice Streat-feild.) 'In my view,' went on Mr Justice Byrnes, 'I am bound by that decision. The result, therefore, is that all that has to be established by the Prosecution is the publication of the article; and then, of course, Section 1 of the Act of 1959 comes into operation, to be considered by the Jury. In my opinion, it is not open to the Defence to call evidence to prove that there was no intention to deprave or corrupt.

'With regard to the second point that Mr Gardiner takes, I agree with him on the whole, and I rather gather that Mr Griffith-Jones does not entirely disagree with him. Mr Gardiner submits that other books may be considered, for two reasons, firstly, upon the question of the literary merit of the book which is the subject matter of the indictment, and he says it is necessary to compare that book with other books upon the question of literary merit. Secondly, he says that other books are relevant to the climate of literature. I want to make this quite plain, that although I agree that the literary merit of this book can be dealt with by comparing it, if necessary, with the literary merit or otherwise of other books, I am of opinion that evidence cannot be led by the Defence in order to indicate that other books are obscene but have not been the subject of a prosecution. I do not think any of those matters can be the subject of evidence, because I think those matters are governed entirely by the judgement of the Court in the case of *Reiter*. I think that goes to the question of obscenity and not to the question of literary merit.'

The Judge then turned to the question of 'public good', and read out Section 2 and 4 of the Act again. 'In my opinion,' he said, 'what the Jury have to determine is whether the defendant has proved that the publication of the article in question is justified as being for the public good, and in order that they shall be assisted in arriving at a proper determination of that question the Defence are enabled to adduce evidence that, in this case, the book is in the interests of literature and of other objects of general concern. In other words, using the words of Sub-section (2), that it has literary merits, and thus, evidence can be called, quite plainly, by the defendant – expert evidence as to the literary merits of the book – but those witnesses cannot be asked to solve the question as to whether publication of the book is justified as being for the public good. That is a question for the Jury and not a question for witnesses to determine. The Jury will determine that question from the evidence of witnesses as to the literary merit of the work in question.

'For those reasons, therefore, the trial will now proceed upon those lines.'

For lawyers this had been the high spot of the trial. It had taken two and a half hours. Now that it was over there was a general movement in Court, a redistribution of weight on seats, as there is in church after the sermon. Dr James Hemming was recalled to the witness box – and to something of an ordeal.

Mr Gardiner addressed him almost as a long-lost friend.

'I do not suppose anybody remembers what you were saying. I think you told us you were in this special position, that your time was devoted partly to educational research, partly to psychology and the problems of adolescents; and I think we had reached the point where I was asking you whether you agreed that it was a fair criticism of the book to say that it gloried in sensuality; and I think you were saying something about the dangers of prurience?' – 'Yes. Shall we continue, sir? To sum up what I was saying, then, the mental attitude permitting wholesome delight in the senses is now recognized as a necessary part of mental health and a necessary preparation for successful marriage. That being so, for *Lady Chatterley's Lover* to be said to be glorying in sensuality is quite wrong, because of the change of attitude over the last thirty years towards the value of rightly educated sensual feeling.'

'Have you discussed sexual problems with young men whose literature has been of a rather different type?' – 'I have.'

'And what, in your view, would be the educational value of this book in the existing climate of literature?' – 'It would act as an antidote to the coarseness and the dehumanizing influences that they meet in relation to sex and their values of sex.'

Mr Griffith-Jones began, as he rose, the most gruelling cross-examination of the trial. 'I want to understand that, if I may. You told us, I thought, that there was a danger at the present time of young people being brought up to regard sex as nothing more than a physical thrill. Those are the words I put down. Is that right?' – 'That is right.'

'Are you now saying that this book would act as an anti-dote?' – 'Certainly, because it refines and enriches and deepens what in the present attitude is liable to be shallow, temporary, and trivial.'

'To do that do you regard it as necessary to describe the acts of sexual intercourse?' – 'I do.'

'Just let us see one or two passages, just so that we follow you as to what amounts to an antidote to the idea that sex is nothing more than a physical thrill.' And Counsel read out some of the more erotic passages, sarcastically referring to each as an 'antidote'. After reading the account of an act of intercourse on page 120, he said, 'Does that strengthen the antidote, do you think, particularly in the case of a young girl reading that?' Dr Hemming saw it as 'a gentle, compassionate description of what may be coarsened and brutalized into something quite different'. 'And as such', he said, 'it is an antidote.'

'You *are* being serious in your evidence, I suppose?' – 'I am being quite serious.'

There ensued a prolonged, embarrassing, and somewhat ludicrous colloquy about the sentence on page 130: 'She heard the catch of his intaken breath as he found her.' Mr Griffith-Jones wanted to know what it meant. He asked sixteen separate questions about its meaning, until it seemed that a recourse to four-letter words would alone suffice as a paraphrase. Everyone in Court knew what it meant. Even the Judge said: 'As a bit of English, that's what you are being asked. What do you understand it to mean as a bit of English?' Mr Griffith-Jones at one point asked for its elucidation 'in plain, blunt English', which was almost an invitation to Anglo-Saxon. 'I shall go on asking you what it means', he said. One member of the Jury raised his eyes to the roof. Dr Hemming rang all the dialectical changes on his definition until it was worn to a scrabble of words. And Mr Griffith-Jones sat down.

'Have you ever suggested', Mr Gardiner then asked, 'that you would give a particular page of this book to any young man to read?' – 'Certainly not', replied Dr Hemming.

'Will you tell the Jury what in your view is the difference in what the young people would learn of sex from this book and what they would learn of sex from the books which many of them in fact read?' – 'It is rather hard, sir, to put in precise words. But I can only repeat some of the words that I have already used. That they get a sense of titillation, of a quick temporary act which doesn't involve the depth or wholeness of the personality. It is just a man and woman coming together in a trivial way. Sometimes there is the feeling of violence, that it is manly to be dominant in the possession of the woman. There is, among certain sections of the society at any rate, this feeling that that is all the human relationship is, the physical coming together for the satisfaction of a quick physical need, and then it is all over. Young women do not know, for example, the commitment of emotion which they are involved in when they enter into a sexual relationship. And the young man doesn't realize how he has to be tender and sensitive and understanding and loving in order that a sexual relationship of value can grow between them. And it is this which is the difference. On the one hand the silly, trivial, temporary values, and on the other the values of tenderness, compassion, and an enduring relationship.'

'Do young people also read the Sunday newspapers?' – 'Indeed, they read the Sunday papers, they read periodicals, they read all kinds of paperback books, and they see films, many of which by insinuation, as much as by direct statement, tend to feed this attitude towards human sexuality which is degrading and corrupting.'

'Thank you', said Mr Gardiner, and the third day of the trial was over.

'I've been feeling terribly sub judice
these last few days!'

Nicolas Bentley in the DAILY MAIL, *3 November 1960*

'Read any good books lately?'

THE FOURTH DAY

ON the fourth day, the first witness to be called was Mr RAYMOND WILLIAMS, Staff Tutor in English at the Oxford University Extra-Mural Delegation, W.E.A. lecturer, student of Lawrence, and author of a number of books on the moral attitudes of leading English writers. He expressed the view that Lawrence was 'one of the five or six major literary figures' of modern Europe.

'Has he an international reputation?' Mr Jeremy Hutchinson asked. – 'Oh certainly. Indeed he perhaps had an international reputation before he had an English reputation, particularly in the United States.'

'What do you say about *Lady Chatterley's Lover* so far as its literary merit is concerned?' – 'I would say that it is one of Lawrence's four major works, the others being the three novels *Sons and Lovers*, *The Rainbow*, and *Women in Love*. I think *Lady Chatterley's Lover* is clearly a book of that substance and would be ranked with those other three.'

'A lot has been said in this case about the sex and sensuality in this book. I think the phrase has been used that it is the pleasure, the satisfaction, and the sensuality which is always emphasized. What do you say about that?' – 'I think the real difficulty here is that both these words, both "sex" and "sensuality", have been specialized to one kind of meaning, and that a bad meaning. I think it would be denying the whole of human experience to allow them to be specialized to a bad meaning. I think one of the main purposes of this book was to challenge the bad meaning in the interests of a possible good meaning. Now if I may illustrate from the novel itself, he says at page 277: "It's the one thing they won't let you be, straight and open in your sex. You can be as dirty as you like. In fact the more dirt you do on sex the better they like it. But

if you believe in your own sex, and won't have it done dirt to:
they'll down you. It's the one insane taboo left: sex as a natural and vital thing." It comes through a particular character,
and I would judge that it is very much Lawrence's own view
here. It is precisely, I think, the point one has to bear in mind
when it is said that the book is obsessed with sex. Because
he is clearly there defining one kind of sex and opposing it.
I think the same is true with sensuality. On page 258: "It was
not really love. It was not voluptuousness. It was sensuality
sharp and searing as fire, burning the soul to tinder. Burning
out the shames, the deepest, oldest shames, in the most secret
places." Quite clearly what is meant there by sensuality is
not the common association of the word, the over-mastering
interest in an isolated physical thing, but the kind of human
experience available in this way which burns out "the deepest,
oldest shames, in the most secret places", as he puts it.'

'It has been said that these descriptions are always em-
phasizing pleasure, satisfaction, and sensuality. Do you agree
that that is wrong, in a true sexual relationship between two
people on a permanent basis?' – 'I think this is in a sense the
theme . . .'

'I don't understand that question', said Mr Justice Byrne,
who knew, of course, that Mr Williams was there as a literary
expert. 'What is the relevance of it to the question of literary
merit?' – 'My Lord,' replied Mr Hutchinson, 'it has been said
by the Prosecution that all there is in these descriptions is
pleasure, satisfaction, and sensuality. My Lord, what I am
trying to find out from this witness is whether that is all.' – 'If
you are doing that, well and good. But I think you were
rather inviting an opinion with regard to another aspect of it.
As long as you confine it to the literary aspect of it, well and
good.'

'Perhaps it is easier if I just draw your attention to two
passages which have been quoted, and I think it will come to
the same thing. Would you look at page 130? Have you got
that?' – 'Yes.'

'And 131. There is a description there which was read out
on Friday, and which is obviously a sensual description. The

last line refers to the ridiculous posture. I wonder whether you would just deal with that from the point of view of literary merit?' – 'It has to be taken as part of the whole book of course – simply because this is exploring one stage of Lady Chatterley's reaction in her experience with Mellors. It is in no sense Lawrence's own view of the relationship. It is what she feels in a particular stage of the relationship where, as is said just earlier, she feels herself a little left out. It is because she feels a little left out that she can have this rather cold detachment of feeling that the act is a little ridiculous. I think that this description of contradictory emotions in her mind is handled with great skill.'

'Mr Williams, in your classes which you take, and having regard to the kind of people who attend them, would you think it right to discuss it and for those people to read it?' – 'I should be very glad to discuss it. It has not, of course, been commonly available.'

'My Lord,' interposed Mr Griffith-Jones, 'I do not know whether that question goes to the literary merit of this book.' – 'Yes, it does', said Mr Hutchinson.

'How does it?' asked the Judge. – 'I think the question I asked was: "Would you think that this was a proper book for people who attend your lectures and your classes to read and discuss?"'

'The word "proper" is a little ambiguous', said Mr Justice Byrne. 'I take it you mean from the literary merit point of view.' – 'Yes, my Lord.'

'It might be "proper" from another angle. That is the difficulty about this case. You have two separate compartments.' – 'Yes, my Lord.'

The Judge pondered, and twiddled his pen between two fingers. Suddenly the witness came to the rescue. 'If you mean, do I think it is a work of sufficient literary merit for that kind of lecture, yes', he said helpfully. 'Thank you', said Mr Hutchinson.

'No questions', said Mr Griffith-Jones.

*

Then came Mr NORMAN ST JOHN-STEVAS, barrister at law, who said he was an M.A. of Oxford and of Cambridge, a B.C.L. of Oxford, a Doctor of Philosophy of London University, and a Doctor of Science and Law of Yale University. He had tutored in jurisprudence at Merton College, Oxford, and at King's College, London. He was a Roman Catholic and a student of moral theology (though not an expert on Roman Catholic moral theology), as well as the author of the legal text-book so much quoted in the present trial, *Obscenity and the Law*. He had drafted the original Bill which led to the passing of the Obscene Publications Act, and he was one of the Herbert Committee's advisers on the obscenity laws.

He had read *Lady Chatterley's Lover* and, it may be thought, was qualified as an 'expert' as few of the witnesses were. Mr Hutchinson asked him a double-barrelled question about the book's literary *and* moral value. 'Well,' said Mr St John-Stevas, 'as to literary merit, I would say it was a book of high literary merit. I would not say it was the best book Lawrence ever wrote, but I think it is a very well-written book and is a contribution of considerable value to English literature. On the moral question, it does seem to me that this is undoubtedly a moral book. It is not, of course, and I am not suggesting I think it is, a book that puts forward an orthodox Christian view, or an orthodox Roman Catholic view – and this is not surprising because Lawrence was not a Christian or a Catholic. I have formed the view, after a careful reading of the book, that Lawrence is essentially a writer in the Catholic tradition. By "within the Catholic tradition" I mean the tradition which regards the sexual instinct as good in itself. It is implanted in man by God, and it is one of his greatest gifts; we should always be grateful for this. And I think that this tradition has been opposed since the Reformation era when sex was regarded as something essentially evil. So I would have no hesitation in saying that every Catholic priest and every Catholic would profit by reading this book, because really they have an aim in common, which is this, to rid the sexual instinct, the sexual act, of any taint of false shame.' (Mr

St John-Stevas later stressed that he was not speaking officially on behalf of his Church.)

'Do you find that consistent with the tenets of your own
faith? – 'I certainly find it quite consistent with my own faith;
and I would add this: I would put Lawrence amongst the
great literary moralists of our own English literature, a man
who was essentially trying to purge and to cleanse and to
reform, and I have been horrified at the representations in
some papers which have been calling him a vicious man –
papers which I think he would not have deigned himself to
read.'

'During the time which you spent in studying and in
research to write the book which I have mentioned, called
Obscenity and the Law, did you have to read a very large
number of books in relation to that matter?' – 'I did.'

'And I think in fact you acted as a legal adviser to the Committee which was originally set up to sponsor the new Bill
which eventually became this Act of Parliament?' – 'Yes.'

'In view of your study of those books in relation to the
matter of *Obscenity and the Law*, I want to ask you about the
literary merit of this book as compared to the literary merit of the
large number of books which you have had to study and read.'

'My Lord,' objected Mr Griffith-Jones, 'again I do not
know whether this is admissible even on literary merit. This
book has to be judged as a book and it may be judged with
other books, generally speaking, but can it be permissible to
judge this book with other books which are or may be
obscene?' – 'Well, we did discuss this the other day,' said the
Judge, 'and I have ruled, rightly or wrongly, that in fact, as
far as literary merit is concerned, this book could be compared
with other books.'

'Your Lordship did, but it was not confined to a comparison with other books which might be said to be of an obscene
nature.' – 'No.'

'That is what I understood this to lead to.' – 'I don't know
that I did extract that meaning. Mr Hutchinson, you can help
me about this.'

'My Lord, the last thing I want to do', said Mr Hutchinson,

'is to put a question which is capable of two meanings.' – 'What I did say', answered the Judge, 'was that there must be no comparison upon any basis of obscenity, and I said there *could* be a comparison upon the basis of literary merit.' – 'Yes, my Lord.' – 'As long as you confine yourself within "literary merit" you are within the ruling which, rightly or wrongly, I have laid down; but if you go outside that, then you will be outside the ruling.'

'I had hoped the question I put was quite clearly within that ruling.' – 'I am sure you will do your best to keep within the limits.'

'Yes, my Lord', promised Mr Hutchinson. 'Mr Stevas, I am sure, being a lawyer yourself, you understand the position and what you may say and what you may not say as regards the law, and restricting this matter entirely to literary merit?' – 'Yes.'

'Have you any observation to make?' – 'I would say I am only an academic lawyer and therefore my knowledge of the law of evidence is not a very deep one. This is just to excuse myself in case I go over the bounds of my Lord's permission.'

'We will stop you if you do', said Mr Justice Byrne with a monitory smile. – 'But I have certainly read a great many books of a pornographic and obscene nature in connexion with this study, and my judgement is, with regard to literary merit, that, of course, *Lady Chatterley's Lover* has nothing in common with those books. And I would use "literary merit" there not only in the sense of the language but – I do not think this can be separated – the theme and method and the underlying morality of the book. These books which I have studied have nothing to be said for them at all, and I find it difficult to make a comparison between them and *Lady Chatterley's Lover* because the gulf between them is so great.'

'I have no questions', said Mr Griffith-Jones, who must have seen new perils looming in this fusion of literary merit, theme, method, and underlying morality.

*

Next came Mr J. W. LAMBERT of the *Sunday Times*; he was introduced as its deputy literary editor, deputy dramatic critic, and senior assistant editor. He had served during the war as an ordinary seaman on destroyers in the Atlantic and on a cruiser in the Arctic. Commissioned later, he commanded motor torpedo boats in coastal forces, and then got the D.S.C. in the Fleet Air Arm, leaving the service as a lieutenant-commander and coming back to what he had always enjoyed most – writing. He had recently written three articles in the *Sunday Times* on Lawrence's life and writings.

'Have you read a copy of the unexpurgated edition of *Lady Chatterley's Lover*?' Mr Gardiner asked him. – 'I have, yes.'

'If you will forgive a very stupid question – it is supposed to be a banned book – we have called a number of witnesses, all of whom have read it: when did you first read it?' – 'I first read it when I was at school, when I was 17, I suppose.'

'Where did you find it?' – 'It was brought back to school, I don't remember by whom – by another boy.'

'At that time did you know the four-letter words which are to be found in it?' – 'Yes.'

'What would you say as to the sociological or literary merits of this book?' – 'I would say it had both. Sociologically I think a lot of people at any rate would benefit by reading it; and its literary merits, I think, though not as great as those of some other of Lawrence's novels, are extremely high.'

'It has been suggested that it sets promiscuous intercourse on a pedestal?' – 'Yes. This, of course, is in flat contradiction to what is actually said in the book. Lawrence hated promiscuity all his life and kept on saying so, and says so in this book.'

Mr Griffith-Jones wanted to find out why the boys read it. 'Tell me, Mr Lambert,' he began, 'when the boy brought it back to school, why did he bring it back?' – 'I don't remember, but it was a book we had all heard of when he brought it back.'

'Did he bring it back because it was of such high literary merit that he thought his companions at school ought to read it?' – 'I doubt that,' said Mr Lambert disarmingly.

'He brought it back because it was regarded as a dirty book?' – 'I expect so.'

'And that is the kind of book boys like to read?' – 'No, I would not have said that.'

'Would I be doing you an injustice if I suggested that that was the reason why you read it?' – 'Undoubtedly it was one of the reasons; but I had already read many others of Lawrence's books.'

'That may well be so, but for those perhaps who had not read Lawrence's books do you think that that was the main reason for their reading it?' – 'The main reason why they first looked into it, certainly, yes.'

This led Mr Gardiner, re-examining, to find a reason further back than that.

'Is one of the consequences of banning a book that people naturally want to read it?' – 'I think so, yes.'

'You have been asked whether this was not a dirty book. What effect . . .' – 'It was not a question of obscenity', interposed Mr Griffith-Jones unexpectedly.

'It clearly was intended to suggest that', said Mr Gardiner. 'If not, perhaps you would tell us what it is that it did suggest.'

And Mr Griffith-Jones replied, 'The question I did ask was, "What was the reason why these boys read it? Because it was regarded or talked of as a dirty book?" The question did not go to the question of obscenity at all.'

'If it doesn't go to the question of obscenity at all, I don't know to what question it does go; but it does, in my submission, entitle me to ask the witness what effect, from that point of view, this book in fact had on him and the other boys when they read it.' – 'I think he might say what effect it had on him', said the Judge. 'Whether he can speak for the other boys I don't know.'

'What effect did it have on you?' – 'Once I had got over the excitement – if you like – of seeing these words in print, it had the effect of conveying a great deal of information, not of a factual kind but of the psychological processes involved in relationships of this kind between a man and a woman, which

I found, naturally enough, illuminating at the age of 17 and have continued to think valuable ever since.'

'Were there any things in particular which made you realize things which you had not realized before?' – 'Yes, naturally. One thing which it made me realize was that this was a mutual process in which, shall we say, the woman had as much right to consideration as the man, that the thing was not in fact simply two people doing a certain thing as separate entities but a mutual process. He makes this very clear in the book and I do remember that this struck me very strongly at the time.'

'Did the immorality of the situation strike you at all?' the Judge asked him. 'Not at all, my Lord', said Mr Lambert.

'Not at all?' (a little incredulously). – 'Because one had read a lot of other books in which such situations arose.'

'Equally immoral?' – 'Yes.'

'It passed over your head for that reason?' – 'Yes', said Mr Lambert, who had not seemed to mean that it passed over his head for any reason.

*

Mr Hutchinson then called SIR ALLEN LANE, founder of Penguin Books, who had gone into the publishing world at 16 with The Bodley Head and left in 1935 to found a business that could publish books at sixpence each and make a profit.

'When you first founded the firm,' said Mr Hutchinson, 'what was the idea you had in your mind?' – 'The idea I had was, I had been in publishing for some fifteen years and I felt that although we were publishing extremely good books we were not reaching the market that I thought existed for good books. I thought perhaps price might have something to do with it, or the form in which the books were produced might; and my idea was to produce a book which would sell at the price of ten cigarettes, which would give no excuse for anybody not being able to buy it, and would be the type of book which they would get if they had gone on to further education. For people like myself who left school and started work when they were 16 it would be another form of education.'

'I think you have used the phrase that you wanted to make Penguin a University Press in paper backs.' – 'Yes, I have used the term.'

'Do you only publish works of great literature or do you publish other books or works of a high standard?' – 'When we started we only published fiction and biographies and travel and detective fiction, but after a couple of years we realized there was a very great field outside those subjects, and that is when we started Pelicans, which we devoted to the arts and sciences.'

'Now, I think in 1952 you were knighted for your services to literature.' – 'Yes.'

'Would you tell us, Sir Allen, what number of titles have you published and about how many copies of books have you sold?' – 'We have published 3,500 titles and our sales are just on 250 million.'

'What were the considerations, as far as you were concerned, which led you to include *Lady Chatterley* among the other Lawrence novels which had not up to that date been published?' – 'What we hoped to do this year was to round off the collection of D. H. Lawrence which we had started in 1950, and we felt *Lady Chatterley* was a book which it was essential should be included if we were in fact going to round off this group.'

'You realized, of course, that it had been a controversial book. In your view did it have high literary merit?' – 'Yes, certainly.'

'Were there any other considerations you took into account in making that decision?' – 'As I think has been said already, we had considered doing this in 1950, and we had not published it for the reason that we wouldn't have been in the position we are in today to defend it; and with reluctance we decided not to publish it. We considered publishing the expurgated version and would not do it. This year, the fact that the new Act was now on the Statute Book and that there had been a trial in America decided us this was a book we should now do.'

'If in fact you had published it in an expurgated form in 1950, as far as sales were concerned, would you have printed an equivalent number on your first printing?' – 'Oh yes, most certainly. We know what the sales are of the American edition, and they have been on sale I should think for at least ten years and we would have known what to expect.'

'Why in fact did you take the view that you should not publish an expurgated edition?' – 'Because it is against our principle. We would not publish a book in an emasculated form. We would only publish it if we were doing what we stated we were doing, that is selling the book as written by the author.'

When Mr Griffith-Jones cross-examined Sir Allen, he held before him a cutting from the *Guardian* of 7 March 1960. 'I have only one thing to put to you', he said. 'I have here a cutting from the *Manchester Guardian* of 7 March 1960. It appears to comment or report upon something which you had said, I gather, immediately prior to that date. Will you tell me whether or not it is correct? "Perhaps Sir Allen Lane, publisher of Penguin Books, was practising the gentle art of litotes* when he said that in his opinion *Lady Chatterley's Lover* was no great novel." Did you say that?' – 'Might the witness see the full article?' suggested Mr Gardiner. 'Certainly', said Mr Griffith-Jones, handing it up. 'I will take that as being correct, but I cannot remember', said Sir Allen.

'Please don't take it from me. It is a report in the newspaper, and one knows how inaccurate some reports sometimes are. Did you in fact express the view that *Lady Chatterley's Lover* was no great novel?' – 'Not to my recollection, no.'

'Was that your view?' – 'No, no.'

'Had you been talking about it?' – 'I have been talking about very little else since the beginning of the year.'

'May I just have that back for one moment?' asked Mr Griffith-Jones. 'Let me read it so that we may all know what it says. The writer goes on: "But though it may not be very good ..."'

---

* 'For those of you who have forgotten your Greek, litotes is the softening of a statement; as when an affirmation is expressed by' (to quote Mr Griffith-Jones) the negative of the contrary. 'Not far off' is an example.

'I don't know how this is evidence', interposed Mr Gerald Gardiner, 'with great respect.' – 'I only read it because you asked me to. Would my learned friend look at it first? Then he will know what I am asking. I was not going to read the whole lot, but my learned friend expressed interest as to what it was.'

Mr Gardiner read the cutting through. 'I still don't follow', he then said. 'Here I have something in a newspaper, which the witness hasn't read.' – 'Now Mr Gardiner knows what this little cutting contains ...' began Mr Griffith-Jones. 'Mr Griffith-Jones,' said the Judge, 'if you want to ask him about it, if it is something which he is said to have said, I suppose the right thing to do, if I may suggest it, is to let the witness read it and ask him if he said it. Then, if he said it, we can hear what it was. If he says "I did not say it", then what a newspaper says is not evidence.'

'Look at the last paragraph of this', said Mr Griffith-Jones to the witness, and the cutting was handed back to him. 'Just read it to yourself and tell me whether you recollect saying anything of that kind. I only want to try to find out whether in fact you had said this was no great novel?' – 'I don't remember whether I said it or not', said Sir Allen after reading it. 'I can't think that I could have.'

'Reading the beginning part of that, it does not bring back to your mind any occasion to which the writer there might have been referring?' – 'Yes, I think I might well have said "Either I'll go to prison or I won't".'

'Does it not bring back to your mind anything which you said, any view you expressed, about the Lady Chatterley novel?' – 'No, it doesn't.' – 'Very well', said Mr Griffith-Jones, and sat down.

The Jury might have been interested to see the *Guardian* cutting, but they never did. Sir Allen's wry remark about prison might have struck them differently if they had. This is how it was reported: 'Sir Allen is one of the pioneers who published Joyce's *Ulysses*. Now he is taking another carefully calculated risk in the cause of literary freedom. "Either I'll go to prison or I won't", he said. "I don't expect to. The only features of the book that anybody could possibly object to are the well known four-letter words, and there is not one of them that has not appeared in print in this country before.'''

*

Canon MILFORD, Master of the Temple, was the next witness. He had four daughters, he said, aged 17 to 27. For many years he was secretary of the Student Christian Movement, and he had been curate at All Hallows, Lombard Street, and vicar of the University Church at Oxford (St Mary the Virgin). As Canon and Chancellor of Lincoln Cathedral for twelve years he had supervised the theological college and the further education of the clergy. Among his published work was a Student Christian pamphlet called *The Philosophy of Sex*.

Mr Gerald Gardiner asked him what was the educational merit of *Lady Chatterley's Lover*, having regard to the Canon's expressed view that 'a proper reticence and modesty in sexual matters' was important. The Canon made a reasoned plea for a distinction between publicity and privacy in sexual life. 'I think I would make a distinction here about the thing which is done in public – for instance, I think it would be indecent to show scenes such as are described in this book on the cinema, still more to do them in public. I think the book is meant to be read by oneself. I should not think it suitable in general to read out in public. Secondly, I think it is incorrect to say we are invited in this book to make a third on any of these occasions. When these two people are together doing things which quite properly are done in private, as I see it and as I felt when I was reading that book, we are invited to identify ourselves with them and not to be a third in the party. I think those scenes would be offensive if someone else was there or someone had been observing from behind a tree. That would bring it into a false position. It is the privilege of the novelist to describe not only what happens from outside but to tell us what is going on inside, thoughts and feelings. This is an intimate thing which is very difficult to do well. I think Lawrence on the whole has done it well here. I do not think it is indecent in the sense that displaying these things in public would be undoubtedly an offence against the rule of reticence.'

'From the point of view of literary and educational merits how does it compare with the existing climate of literature in relation to sex?' – 'I think there are two almost equally wrong attitudes to sex, which one can find reflected both in literature and in many ways of life. Many think of it as a trivial addition to life and really of no great importance. I read in a book a phrase saying that we should treat sex as the ancient Greeks treated it – I do not think it is true that they treated it as they are alleged to have treated it – like music, wine, and flowers, that is to say as one of the trimmings to life. I think this is thoroughly trivial and debasing. The tragedies, the poetry, and the dramas are all concerned with something much, much, more serious than music, wine, and flowers, and to put sex on that level I think is to trivialize the whole thing. The other is to concentrate on and isolate the physical aspect of it as an end in itself, as a source of pleasure which has to be continually titillated and renewed. An instance of this is in the Kinsey Report on *The Sexual Behaviour of the Human Male* in America, where for instance various methods of achieving the desired emotional result are compared from the point of view of expense. One of them is taking a girl out for the evening, and others which are cheaper are compared. That I think is grossly immoral, to isolate this thing, to regard all else as a means to gratification of this one thing. The third aspect, and this is what I am sure Lawrence stands for, is that the physical side is the basis of a deep human relation which in principle can only be fulfilled between one man and one woman, and which, when you have got it, commits you to an achievement of lifelong union in body and mind and soul, of which the physical basis is meant to be the foundation, and – shall I say – the warm surrounding atmosphere in which it is possible for two people to grow together into one new being. That, I think, is Lawrence's interpretation of what sex can be, and as I, read that book, this is the thing which he is trying to make vivid. The various incidents, as I read them, are meant to illustrate various ways in which those can fail on this achievement, beginning with the trifling ones and coming on to what he presents at any rate as a real fulfilment. This, I think, is the proper place of sex in human life.'

'Thank you, Canon Milford', said Mr Gardiner.

'No questions', said Mr Griffith-Jones.

*

Then came Professor KENNETH MUIR, who holds the chair of English Literature in the University of Liverpool, and is also Dean of the Faculty of Arts. He had published a large number of books – on Shakespeare, Milton, and Wyatt – and he had frequently lectured on D. H. Lawrence.

Mr Gardiner asked him what he thought was the essential theme of *Lady Chatterley's Lover*. 'I should say the redemption of the individual, and hence of society, by what Lawrence calls "reciprocity of tenderness", and that is why I feel that the expurgated version is a travesty of the original and ought never to have been published.'

'What do you say as to the literary merits of the unexpurgated edition in relation to novels of this century?' – 'I think it stands fairly high. I do not think it is one of Lawrence's very greatest novels, but I should say it is much better than nine-tenths of the novels that come out year by year.'

'How does it compare, as a whole, with the presentation of sexual intercourse in other novels published?' – 'In my opinion, it is very much healthier. The descriptions of sexual intercourse are poetical rather than physiological, and they are never sadistic or perverted. For that reason I regard it as a much healthier book than many which are now available.'

'Is Lawrence studied at many British Universities?' – 'Yes, at many, including my own.'

'And are his works the subject of doctoral theses and of articles in learned journals, and so on?' – 'Yes, and a number have been written by graduates at Liverpool.'

'Is this book a significant part of his work?' – 'A very signi-

SIR STANLEY UNWIN

ficant part of his work, and I think it is impossible to understand any one book of Lawrence's without having read all; this is very fundamental to the understanding of the whole.'

'I suppose it would be quite possible to publish an edition of Shakespeare leaving out the sonnets?' – 'Yes, it would be possible though undesirable, even though some people object to the tone of the sonnets.' – 'Thank you, Professor Muir', said Mr Gardiner.

'No questions', said Mr Griffith-Jones.

*

The doyen of the publishing world, as Mr Gardiner later called him, then came into the witness box – Sir STANLEY UNWIN, chairman and managing director of Allen & Unwin, and a publisher for fifty-six years. He was introduced by Mr Hutchinson as a long-established member of the Executive of the British Council and of the Royal Institute of International Affairs, a Fellow of the Royal Society of Literature, the recipient of numerous honours, and a man with ten grandchildren.

He began his evidence with a glowing tribute to Penguin Books. After that he said that he had read *Lady Chatterley's Lover*.

'What view do you take as to its literary merit in relation to the broad number of books that are published?' asked Mr Hutchinson. – 'D. H. Lawrence is certainly one of the first dozen amongst novelists of this century.'

'And this book?' – 'I do not say it is his best, but it is a book of undoubted importance.'

Mr Hutchinson sat down; and to the great disappointment of all, especially no doubt Sir Stanley himself, Mr Griffith-Jones again said 'No questions.'

*

Miss DILYS POWELL (Mrs Russell) of the *Sunday Times,* a reviewer of poetry, general books, and films on that paper for longer than looked remotely possible, then came into the witness box and said that among her critical essays on contemporary poets there was one on D. H. Lawrence. She said she thought that *Lady Chatterley's Lover* was 'in parts a very great book: it is not, in my opinion, a completely successful book, but it has extraordinary qualities of genius. It has an extraordinary organic unity, and although one does see certain faults in it, to extract anything from it would be to destroy a remarkable artistic unity.'

'It has been said that it places promiscuous intercourse on a pedestal.' (This phrase had now been used thirty-two times, and each time people looked at Mr Griffith-Jones.) 'Do you agree with that?' – 'Certainly not. On the contrary, it is an attack on promiscuity and a defence of clinging to one person.'

'Do you see every film that is issued?' – 'Nearly every film.'

'And you read large numbers of novels?' – 'Yes, I read novels extensively.'

'And watch television?' – 'Yes.'

'How do the literary merits of this book in relation to sexual relationships compare with the general climate of literature of its kind?' – 'It is on a very much higher moral plane. I regard it as an extremely moral book. A great proportion of the books I read and the films I see and the television I watch seems to have a degrading influence, and a great deal of the contemporary cinema seems to degrade the whole sanctity of sex, treating it as something trivial. But in Lawrence's book, which has great elements of sacredness, sex is taken as being something to be taken seriously and as a basis for a holy life.'

Mr Griffith-Jones cross-examined. 'Did I hear you aright', he said very slowly, 'that sex is treated on a holy basis in this book?' – 'Yes', said Miss Powell very firmly.

Mr Griffith-Jones sat down.

*

Author, poet, schoolmaster, publisher, reviewer, Cambridge lecturer, Professor of Poetry at Oxford, vice-president of the Royal Society of Literature – Mr CECIL DAY LEWIS stirred the Jury to movement when he admitted to Mr Hutchinson that he was also the Nicholas Blake who wrote detective novels. He said that *Lady Chatterley*, not one of Lawrence's greatest novels, was in a higher class than the average proficient novel or the average best-seller. Then Mr Hutchinson asked him: 'Does the fact that the heroine of a book or novel is an adulteress mean that the author is extolling adultery?' – 'No, most certainly not. Lady Chatterley is certainly an adulteress; she has committed adultery. I would not call her an immoral woman. She does certain things which one can call acts of weakness; but, as a whole, taking her character as a whole, I think there is more good in her than bad. There are, after all, a very great number of bad characters in literature, in novels, and in drama, and I think that they teach us as much about human behaviour and about morality as we can learn from the good ones. It would be impossible for literature to be conducted if one only brought the good people into it, and by bringing the bad people into a novel a novelist is surely not recommending wickedness or dissoluteness or any kind of vice.'

'Do you find that this book recommends wickedness and vice?' – 'No, I find it very much the reverse. I find it is recommending a right and full relationship between a man and a woman.'

Mr Griffith-Jones this time cross-examined at some length. 'It is really recommending a right and full relationship between a man and a woman who are virtually unknown to one another, is it not?' – 'They are unknown to one another at the beginning of their relationship, yes.'

'And even at the end they have had virtually no conversation about any topic at all, have they, except sexual intercourse?' – 'No, I would not agree with that.'

'Well, just take the book, would you, sir. Tell me if there is anything in that book which indicates, for example, con-

versation between the two which is about anything other than
sexual intercourse?' – 'There is a great deal of conversation,
I would say, between Lady Chatterley and the gamekeeper
which is not a conversation about the sexual side of love
alone.'

'Well, we won't occupy too long a time. What else did
they know of one another? Let me preface it by saying that,
of course, he tells her about his early love affairs and unsatisfactory sexual intercourse with other women, but, apart from
that, what does he tell her about himself?' – 'He tells her
about his time in the Army in India as an officer, for instance.'

'Well, that doesn't take her very far in getting to know this
man. What else?' – 'I can remember nothing else.'

'And what did she tell him of herself?' – 'She told him about
her life with her husband.' – 'Did she?' – 'I think so.'

'Did she? Can you point to any passage where she tells
Mellors about her life with her husband?' – 'No, I can't
point to it now without looking at the book again.'

'You see, this book is put forward as a tender book, and a
book teaching the lesson of true tenderness and understanding, fulfilment and happiness. Is it possible that any two
human beings can really love one another when they have
said practically not a word to one another about any subject at
all except copulation?' – 'Yes, because we cannot assume that
the dialogue in the novel is the only conversation between them.'

'The only occasions when they have any opportunity of any
conversation is either just before, during, or immediately
after the act of copulation. Those are the only occasions, in
the circumstances, when any conversation can occur, are
they not?' – 'That is so, yes. That is because . . .' But Mr
Day Lewis was not allowed to say why it was so.

'Apart from meeting him in the park, I think, when she is
out with her husband, can you point to any other occasion
when these two people meet, other than when they have
copulation?' – 'No. After their first meetings they do in fact
copulate on each occasion. They are lovers and it seems to be
perfectly natural they should.' – '"Perfectly natural"?' (incredulously.) – 'Yes.'

'"Perfectly natural" that Lady Chatterley should run off to the hut in the forest on every occasion to copulate with her husband's gamekeeper? Not "perfectly natural", sir!' – 'Yes; it is in her nature.'

'It is in her nature because she is an oversexed and adulterous woman; that is why it is in her nature, is it not?' – 'No, I entirely disagree.' – 'Why?' – 'I think it is in her nature because she is an averagely sexed woman, I would say. We have no particular evidence about her one way or the other, but she is a lonely woman who is not getting the affection and love that she needs and her nature sends her to the man who can give it to her.'

'Just one matter', said Mr Gerald Gardiner, rising to re-examine. 'If you would open your book at page 224, at the bottom: "She sat and talked to the keeper of her going abroad. 'And then when I come back,' she said, 'I can tell Clifford I must leave him. And you and I can go away. They never need even know it is you. We can go to another country, shall we? To Africa or Australia. Shall we?'" And then it goes on all down that page, I think, about the army and the colonies, and so on. "'You've never been to the Colonies, have you?' he asked her. 'No! Have you?' 'I've been in India, and South Africa, and Egypt.' 'Why shouldn't we go to South Africa?' 'We might!' he said slowly. 'Or don't you want to?' she asked. 'I don't care. I don't much care what I do.'" And so on. And then, having discussed their plans: "'And weren't you happy, when you were a lieutenant and an officer and a gentleman?' 'Happy? All right. I liked my Colonel.' 'Did you love him?' 'Yes! I loved him.' 'And did he love you?' 'Yes. In a way, he loved me.' 'Tell me about him.' 'What is there to tell? He had risen from the ranks. He loved the army. And he had never married. He was twenty years older than me. He was a very intelligent man . . .'" And so on. And if you go to page 228, half-way down, they are together and he says: "'Let's live for summat else. Let's not live ter make money, neither for us-selves nor for anybody else. Now we're forced to. We're forced to make a bit for us-selves, an' a fair lot for th' bosses. Let's stop it! Bit by bit, let's stop it. We needn't rant an' rave. Bit by bit, let's drop the whole industrial life an' go back. The least little bit o' money'll do. For everybody, me an' you, bosses an' masters, even th' king. The least little bit o' money'll really do. Just make up your mind to it, an' you've got out o' th' mess.' He paused, then went on " And then we go to page 289: "He was silent for a time, thinking. Then he resumed: 'They used to say I had too much of the woman in me. But it's not that. I'm not a woman not because I don't want to shoot birds, neither because I don't want to make money, or get on. I could have got on in the army, easily, but I didn't like the army. Though I could manage the men all right: they liked me and they had a bit of a holy fear of me when I got mad.'" And so on. Were those some of the passages you had in mind?' – 'Yes. I could not remember where the points come in the book, but I think I did say that he talked to her about his life in the army and about the state of the society they were living in, and it was two or three such passages I had in mind.'

'Having regard to the theme of this book about those two people, does it seem to you extraordinary, or does it seem to prove that the book has no literary merit, that there are not a great many long conversations about other things than their relationship together?' – 'I don't think so. The novelist must select his material to fit his theme, and his theme in this book, or one of the two main themes, was the theme of the relationship between men and women as shown particularly in the act of love. And it seems to me not unreasonable that a novelist should not bring in a lot of very irrelevant material for the sake of making them talk about other things.'

'What would you say was the other theme?' – 'His general theme which goes through nearly all his novels and short stories, and his poetry, that there is something wrong with our civilization. That the brain has moved too far ahead of the heart, of the instinctual part of man, and we must try to correct that.' – 'Thank you', said Mr Gardiner.

*

Mr Hutchinson then called for Mr STEPHEN POTTER, whose first book of literary criticism was on D. H. Lawrence and was written while Lawrence was still alive. Mr Potter said that he was for twelve years Lecturer in English Literature at London University, that while on the staff of the B.B.C. he had edited the 'New Judgement' series – criticisms of famous authors by famous authors – that he had for eight years been a member of the B.B.C. 'Critics' panel, and (with a wide but deprecating smile) that he was the author of the 'Lifemanship' books.

'What was your view when you *first* read *Lady Chatterley* as regards its literary merit?' – 'I thought that, in the whole cycle of Lawrence's novels, it was not the most successful. I thought also that he was perhaps using it too much as a pamphlet, although, of course, all his novels were written with a purpose – this, perhaps, rather more than the others. When I read it again I was surprised at its power and sometimes its great qualities. I read it last month and it was better than I had remembered.'

'What would you say as to its literary merit?' – 'In general Lawrence seemed to me then, and seems to me now, one of the greatest writers in a decade of giants. He made a great difference to me, and I owe a great debt to him. If it was not very high in his own works, by the standard of the novels of the times, which included Galsworthy and Arnold Bennett, I thought it stood very high.'

'Do you find the use of the four-letter words in the book valid?' – 'I think Lawrence was trying to do something very difficult and very courageous there. I think it is impossible to print the book without them. I think, I know indeed, what he was trying to do was to take these words out of what you may call the context of the lavatory wall and give them back a dignity and meaning, away from the context of obscenity and of the swear-word. A very difficult thing to do. I personally found, and I think Lawrence says in the book somewhere, the words shocked me, but, as he says, shocked the eye only, so the shock soon goes because it doesn't shock the brain. It shocks the eye because of the context in which we usually see those words.' – 'Thank you, Mr Potter', said Mr Hutchinson.

'No questions', said Mr Griffith-Jones.

*

Miss JANET ADAM SMITH, until recently literary editor of the *New Statesman* and one-time assistant editor of the *Listener,* was the next witness. She said she was the widow of the poet Michael Roberts, that she was educated at Cheltenham Ladies' College and Somerville College, Oxford, that she was Trustee of the National Library of Scotland, and that she was shortly leaving for America as Visiting Professor in English Literature at Columbia University.

She told Mr Gerald Gardiner that she had read *Lady Chatterley's Lover* as Lawrence intended it to be published, but not in an expurgated edition. 'I didn't want to read the work of a writer I greatly admired in an expurgated edition,' she said, 'and I didn't want to set about getting a copy of a work by an author I greatly admired as if it were a dirty book, so I didn't read it until September of this year.'

'What do you take to be the theme or meaning of the book?' – 'I thought the theme of the book was the deadness and sterility of England after the First World War, where nobody seemed to care about anything, and where mean houses were allowed to sprawl over beautiful countryside, where beauty was constantly being destroyed and nobody seemed to mind; and the necessity for counteracting this deadness and sterility by a new awareness of life and what life means, and what life's possibilities are, and the importance, as a source of this awareness and this caring for life and human beings, of right sexual relations; how they can be a source of vitality and energy which is carried far beyond the immediate relationship into the activities of men generally.'

'In your view, how far are the descriptions of intercourse relevant or necessary to the theme of the book?' – 'I think they are very relevant and necessary to the theme. They show the two characters having an increasing awareness of each other as fully human beings, and not just on the one side the gamekeeper and on the other side the lady up at the big house. I think that their importance is cumulative as showing how from such a beginning a deep relationship can arise.'

'It has been suggested' (general glances at Mr Griffith-Jones) 'that it sets upon a pedestal promiscuous and adulterous intercourse?' – 'I should have said it definitely did no such thing, and that promiscuity and philanderers are expressly condemned.'

'Reading a great deal of the literature which is available, how would you say this book, dealing as it does with human relations, including sexual relations, compares with the general climate of such literature?' – 'I find it difficult to think of another book with which to compare it properly, because other books that I know of which deal as fully with sexual relations are on an entirely different plane, it seems to me. There is a great gulf between the two, because of the sensitiveness and humanity with which Lawrence explores the situation, in which it seems to me there is nothing suggestive. It is never suggested that the action is trivial or degrading in the way in which sex is presented in so many popular books today. It is associated with tenderness, with thought for the other person, with the creation of new life, with regard for the consequences, and not with the mere satisfaction of the animal body. Compared with so many books today it does not associate sex with violence or cruelty or perversion.' – 'Thank you, Mrs Roberts', said Mr Gardiner.

'No questions', said Mr Griffith-Jones.

*

When Mr NOEL ANNAN, Provost of King's College, Cambridge, was called, once again the power of television was abroad in the courtroom. Mr Annan was introduced by Mr Gerald Gardiner as a University Lecturer in Politics. Politics? What was Mr Annan here to say?

'Did you lecture for seven or eight years at Cambridge on

the English Moralists? Mr Gardiner asked him. He replied that he did. (Moralists? Then he was a witness as to moral message.) 'Would you just tell us what you mean by that, whom they included, and what was the purpose of this?' – 'The English Moralists is a paper which is taken by students who read English Literature in their third and last year at Cambridge. It is a paper which deals with certain English writers, and, indeed, ancient writers such as Plato and Aristotle. The English writers with whom I was primarily concerned were those in the nineteenth and twentieth centuries, such as Carlisle, John Stuart Mill, George Eliot, Matthew Arnold, and D. H. Lawrence.'

'It goes without saying that at the University, with reference to this particular subject, Lawrence is a prescribed author?' – 'Yes.'

'He would be included with the other names you have mentioned?' – 'I agree.'

'Apart from what you have already said, what view do you put forward as to Lawrence's standing as a writer?' Was this a Machiavellian subtlety? Did 'standing as a writer' mean something different from 'literary merit'? Or was it a question about Lawrence's standing as a moralist who wrote books? 'He is the greatest imaginative writer in this century in English literature', was Mr Annan's answer. 'He stands I would say with Virginia Woolf, James Joyce, Conrad, and Mr E. M. Forster, who I think was a witness here, as among the major novelists in this century.'

The next two questions suggested that it might have meant something other than literary merit. 'You have read *Lady Chatterley*, have you?' – 'I have.'

'What do you say about its literary merit?' – 'I do not think it is the greatest of Lawrence's novels. On the other hand I think it is a very important novel, and one which Lawrence thought important.'

'Is it a book which you feel should be read and discussed from the literary point of view at the University where you hold this position?' – 'I do.'

'By the students who come up there?' – 'Certainly.' – 'Thank you, Mr Annan', said Mr Gardiner.

'No questions', said Mr Griffith-Jones – not even about the relationship between politics, the moralists, literature, and *Lady Chatterley*.

*

After lunch, the Director of Religious Education in Birmingham Diocese, the Rev. DONALD TYTLER, was called. He spoke of the book's moral and educational value. He was qualified to do so as former Chaplain to Birmingham University and Precentor of Birmingham Cathedral, by his contact with the young and his vocational concern with morality.

Mr Gardiner asked him whether *Lady Chatterley's Lover* had any educational merits. 'I think its educational merit is', he said, 'that by reading it young people will be helped to grow up as mature and responsible people.'

'Have you a general responsibility in working with people of all ages in the Diocese?' – 'Yes.'

'Will you tell us what you have in mind when you say that young people would be helped by reading it?' – 'Yes. I think one of the most important factors in respect of young people growing up is as to their physical and emotional powers, and I think they are often encouraged by the kind of society we live in to believe that sex is either shameful or unimportant and, therefore, promiscuity is the normal course. I think this book makes it quite clear that Lawrence was against irresponsibility in matters of sex and that by reading it, young people, even those who are potentially promiscuous, will be hauled up short and made to think again. People having a responsibility towards those growing up will hold the view that that is worthwhile.'

'If people read it in the ordinary way, that is to say in private, would it be a suitable subject for discussion in Youth Clubs?' – 'Yes, I think so.'

'I just want to ask your view of Lawrence's books. Have you read *A propos of Lady Chatterley* by Lawrence?' – 'Yes.'

Mr Gardiner then asked what must be the longest question ever put in examination to a witness. It comprised extracts from Lawrence's famous, superb, and impassioned championship of Christian marriage as every man's 'little kingdom'. Because it was crucial to the Defence, the question and its quotations are given here in full.

'Will you look at page 246, about ten lines from the bottom, where he says: "Make marriage in any serious degree unstable, dissoluble, destroy the permanency of marriage, and the Church falls. Witness the enormous decline of the Church of England. The reason being that the Church is established upon the element of union in mankind. And the first element of union in the Christian world is the marriage-tie. The marriage-tie, the marriage bond, take it which way you like, is the fundamental connecting link in Christian society. Break it, and you will have to go back to the overwhelming dominance of the State, which existed before the Christian era. The Roman State was all-powerful."

'Then he deals with the Roman State, the Soviet State, and Egypt. Then on page 247 he says: "Do we want to be bullied by a Soviet? For my part, I have to say NO! every time. And having said it, we have to come back and consider the famous saying, that perhaps the greatest contribution to the social life of man made by Christianity is – marriage. Christianity brought marriage into the world: marriage as we know it. Christianity established the little autonomy of the family within the greater rule of the State. Christianity made marriage in some respects inviolate, not to be violated by the State. It is marriage, perhaps, which has given man the best of his freedom, given him his little kingdom of his own within the big kingdom of the State, given him his foothold of independence on which to stand and resist an unjust State. Man and wife, a king and queen with one or two subjects, and a few square yards of territory of their own: this, really, is marriage. It is a true freedom because it is a true fulfilment, for man, woman, and children.

'"Do we, then, want to break marriage? If we do break it, it means we all fall to a far greater extent under the direct sway of the State. Do we want to fall under the direct sway of the State, any State? For my part, I don't.

'"And the Church created marriage by making it a sacrament, a sacrament of man and woman united in the sex communion, and never to be separated, except by death. And even when separated by death, still not freed from the marriage. Marriage, as far as the individual went, eternal. Marriage, making one complete body out of two incomplete ones, and providing for the complex development of the man's soul and the woman's soul in unison, throughout a life-time. Marriage sacred and inviolable, the great way of earthly fulfilment for man and woman, in unison, under the spiritual rule of the Church.

'"This is Christianity's great contribution to the life of man, and it is only too easily overlooked. Is it, or is it not, a great step in the direction of life-fulfilment, for men and women? Is it, or is it not? Is marriage a great help to the fulfilment of man and woman, or is it a frustration? It is a very important question indeed, and every man and woman must answer it."

'Then towards the bottom of the page, in the penultimate paragraph, he says: "Then I realize that marriage, or something like it, is essential, and that the old Church knew best the enduring needs of man, beyond the spasmodic needs of today and yesterday. The Church established marriage for life, for the fulfilment of the soul's living life, not postponing it till the after-death."

'Then, if you just look at the bottom of page 250, he says: "Sex is the balance of male and female in the universe, the attraction, the repulsion, the transit of neutrality, the new attraction, the new repulsion, always different, always new. The long neuter spell of Lent, when the blood is low, and the delight of the Easter kiss, the sexual revel of spring, the passion of midsummer, the slow recoil, revolt, and grief of autumn, greyness again, then the sharp stimulus of winter of the long nights."

'Then at the bottom of the page he says: "And is it not so throughout life? A man is different at thirty, at forty, at fifty, at sixty, at seventy: and the woman at his side is different. But is there not some strange conjunction in their differences? Is there not some peculiar harmony, through youth, the period of childbirth, the period of florescence and young children, the period of the woman's change of life, painful yet also a renewal, the period of waning passion but mellowing delight of affection, the dim, unequal period of the approach of death, when the man and woman look at one another with the dim apprehension of separation that is not really a separation: is there not, throughout it all, some unseen, unknown interplay of balance, harmony, completion, like some soundless symphony which moves with a rhythm from phase to phase, so different, so very different in the various movements, and yet one symphony, made out of the soundless singing of two strange and incompatible lives, a man's and a woman's?"

'Then, lastly, at the bottom: "But – and this 'but' crashes through our heart like a bullet – marriage is no marriage that is not basically and permanently phallic, and that is not linked up with the sun and the earth, the moon and the fixed stars and the planets, in the rhythm of days, in the rhythm of months, in the rhythm of quarters, of years, of decades, and of centuries."

'Has the word "phallic" always had a sacred connotation?' asked Mr Gardiner at the end of this profoundly illuminating reading. – 'I don't know that it has *always* had a sacred connotation,' said Mr Tytler, 'but, like many words taken over from a pagan world, it has been baptized by Christians and made into a sacred word.'

'Is there anything in what I have read about the institution of marriage, although he was not a Christian, which is inconsistent with the Christian religion?' – 'Not at all. I should have thought this was a most impressive statement of the Christian view of marriage.' – 'Thank you, Mr Tytler', said Mr Gardiner.

Mr Griffith-Jones could hardly allow all this to go by. 'Mr Tytler,' he began, 'you have just had some passages read to you from another book. Presumably you understand that this trial is concerned not with that book, but with *Lady Chatterley's Lover*?' – 'Yes'.

Once again the cross-examination showed Mr Griffith-Jones to be concerned not with Lawrence's obscenity but with the marital status of Lady Chatterley and her lover. 'It was put to you that Lawrence's views about marriage were that it was sacred and inviolable. Is there anything in *Lady Chatterley's Lover* which suggests that marriage is sacred and inviolable?' – '*Lady Chatterley's Lover* is a novel; it is not a tract.'

'Never mind whether it is a novel or tract. Is there anything in *Lady Chatterley's Lover* which suggests that marriage is sacred and inviolable?' – 'I think there is a very great deal to suggest that the union between a man and a woman is sacred.'

'I must invite you to answer my question. Is there anything in this book which suggests that marriage is sacred and inviolable?' – 'I think it is taken for granted throughout.'

'Let us see. Mellors did not regard marriage as sacred and inviolable, did he?' – 'He is very much attracted by Lady Chatterley.'

'Of course he is. Everybody who commits adultery is presumably very much attracted by the man or woman with whom they do it. Just answer my question, please. There is nothing in Mellors's history which suggests that he regards marriage as sacred and inviolable?' – 'That may well be.'

'And not only was he committing adultery, but he was committing adultery with somebody else who was committing adultery?' – 'Yes.'

'There is nothing, is there, to suggest that Lady Chatterley regarded her marriage as being particularly sacred or inviolable?' – 'That I am less sure about. I should have thought there was conversation between Lady Chatterley and Sir Clifford in the book which suggests that marriage was something of importance.'

'Do you – I don't know – in your experience of life find that people who are committing adultery behind their husbands' or wives' backs sometimes do talk to their husbands or wives as though nothing wrong was happening?' – 'Certainly.'

'It doesn't really indicate very much, does it, that she regarded marriage as sacred and inviolable when at the same

time she was having her husband's guests up to her boudoir?'
– 'I think so far as the individual characters found in this
book are concerned, that is perfectly correct; but the question
is whether Lawrence's view of marriage was that borne out
by these individual characters precisely.'

'That is where, with all this extraneous matter, we are perhaps in danger of losing sight of what we are considering
here. We are not considering Lawrence's views except as
they are reflected in this book . . .'

But this was too much, in view of the Judge's ruling (see
page 127) that other books might be referred to for specific
purposes. 'My Lord,' interposed Mr Gardiner, 'it would not
be right that I should let that pass without a challenge. When
my learned friend has asked witnesses questions, "Isn't this
what Lawrence did? Did he not run away with another man's
wife?", it is somewhat inconsistent, I suggest, at the same
time to assert that *all* we are concerned with is what is in *this*
book.'

'Yes, I agree to some extent, Mr Gardiner; but I think what
Mr Griffith-Jones is trying to indicate is that the Jury are not
trying the book which is called *A propos of Lady Chatterley's
Lover*, they are considering a book called *Lady Chatterley's
Lover*, and I think so long as that is the plain issue . . .' – 'Yes,
my Lord, I agree.'

'If I ask questions like that, my Lord,' said Mr Griffith-
Jones, 'it is only because Lawrence's intention has been
introduced.' – 'Yes', said the Judge noncommittally. And Mr
Griffith-Jones put one more question.

'There was nothing, I think, in Lady Chatterley's history,
or what we have heard of it, that leads us to believe that she
regarded marriage as sacred and inviolable?' – 'I think that is
a fair assumption', replied Mr Tytler.

Mr Gardiner decided to prompt the witness's memory
about Lady Chatterley's attitude to marriage. 'Would you
mind looking at page 81?' he asked (referring to *Lady Chatterley's Lover*). 'You see Michaelis is suggesting she should
break off the marriage. "But Connie's heart simply stood still

at the thought of abandoning Clifford there and then. She couldn't do it. No ... no! She just couldn't. She had to go back to Wragby." This, you may remember, is after her own husband has suggested that she should go and have a child by another man. Does that seem to you to be the attitude of a woman who has no regard of any kind to her marriage vows?' – 'No.'

'Is the book from which I was quoting to you, *A propos of Lady Chatterley*, written by Lawrence, dealing with his intentions in writing *Lady Chatterley's Lover*?' – 'Yes, it seems to me that it is.'

'Is there anything in the book which appears to advocate adultery, whether or not it is dealing with such a situation?' – 'No, I do not think there is any advocating of adultery at all.'

'But', said Mr Justice Byrne inexorably, 'does it really deal with anything other than adultery?' – 'I think it deals with the whole complex of human relationships, of which adultery is one part – an important part, admittedly.'

'If you cut adultery out of this book would there be very much left?' – 'I think you would still get the drama of an extraordinarily difficult marriage with a husband who is crippled by a war wound and impotent, and a passionate woman; the interplay between those two characters in that situation.' – 'Very well', said the Judge.

*

Then came a literary critic and reviewer, Mr JOHN CONNELL. He was the author of seven novels and a number of biographies, he said; as a journalist he was on the staff of the *Evening News* for twenty-six years. For nine years he was on the Education Committee of the L.C.C. He was now on the Executive Committees of the National Book League and the P.E.N. Club. He read something like 250 books a year.

'I read *Lady Chatterley's Lover* first when I was an undergraduate and a smuggled copy of it came to my university', said Mr Connell. 'I did not read it again until about three months ago, when I got, as a reviewer, an expurgated version, and I have since read the full version which is the subject of the case today,' he told Mr Hutchinson.

'With regard to the proper book as Lawrence wrote it, what is your view of its literary merit?' – 'I would put it, sir, as a very important and indeed an essential book in the whole corpus of D. H. Lawrence's work. By that I mean that you cannot understand or appreciate D. H. Lawrence as a writer in full without reading this book.'

'How high do you place it in the background of your own reading over the years, as regards its literary merit?' – 'I would put it very high indeed because, on its own, as well as within the corpus of Lawrence's work, it is a book of considerable literary merit, indeed very high literary merit, written with total honesty of purpose.'

'It has been described as a book which is only concerned with vicious sexual indulgence. Would you say that that was a valid account of it?' – 'I would disagree with that utterly and totally.' – 'Because?' – 'Because it is concerned with two very important themes in human life and in English society at the time that Lawrence was writing. It is concerned with the two interlinked themes in his mind of sex and class; and to suggest that it is a book – I can't quite remember your phrase, but to put these very pejorative terms on it seems to me to be extremely bad criticism.'

'Perhaps everybody has forgotten it now, but the first line in the book is, "Ours is essentially a tragic age, so we refuse to take it tragically." Is this a book, in your view, which is about a tragic situation?' – 'It is of course about a tragic situation, and the idea that it is about anything else would seem to me so perverse, and so to denigrate the novelist's purpose, that I would really rather not go much further in case I get angry!'

'As you did say that you had read the original a long time ago, then an expurgated edition, then this edition, what do you say about the expurgated edition from the point of view of literary merit compared with the book as Lawrence wrote it?' – 'Sir, I was fortunate enough – or unfortunate enough! – the other day to be sent for review the expurgated, paper-

backed edition. I found it (a) trivial, (b) furtive, (c) obscene.'
– 'Thank you, Mr Connell', said Mr Hutchinson.

'I don't want to make Mr Connell angry', said Mr Griffith-Jones, and the temperature fell to normal again.

*

Mr C. K. Young had just been appointed editor of the *Yorkshire Post,* having been with the *Daily Telegraph* since 1951, as well as reviewing novels and broadcasting on literary subjects. He had written a number of biographies, including a book on D. H. Lawrence which had since been twice revised. He was brought up in a family of Yorkshire mine-owners, in country very close to that depicted in *Lady Chatterley's Lover.* He thought the book 'a very important one in Lawrence's corpus of work', not his best novel but 'one of the next best'.

'Do you find the part of the book which deals with the mining country is convincing?' – 'It is convincing as it was then. Of course, the mining situation and community have changed a good deal since the war, but it is very convincing as I knew it in those days.'

'This book has been described as being really only about sexual intercourse, and the rest of the book, outside the descriptions of sexual intercourse, is mere padding. Would you say that was a valid criticism of it?' – 'No, I should have thought that totally untrue.'

'I think you are a married man with five children?' Mr Young said that he was; and since he was not cross-examined, the implication remained that he would let all the children read the book.

*

The Editor of the *Guardian,* Mr Hector Hetherington, then told Mr Gardiner that he graduated in English at Corpus Christi, Oxford, served with the Royal Armoured Corps in Northern Europe during the war, and thereafter was reporter, sub-editor, and leader-writer on the *Glasgow Herald* until 1953, when he went to the *Guardian*. He was a member of the Royal Commission on the Police, then still pursuing its inquiries.

Mr Gardiner asked him what he thought was the theme or meaning of *Lady Chatterley's Lover*. 'Well,' Mr Hetherington answered, 'the importance of the book to me was as an exposition of the beauty and goodness of physical love at its best, of the redeeming power of sex, and of the importance of tenderness. These are not the only themes, but these are the ones most important to me.'

'The one thing I wanted particularly to ask you about was this: this being a book which deals with relationships between human beings, including sex relationships, how does it compare with the literary climate of similar books on the market, or books dealing with these matters?' – 'There are many good books and many bad books on the market. We have had occasion recently, twice recently, to send out reporters to buy books within half a mile of our office, because I have heard there were books on sale openly dealing with sadism, lesbianism, incest, sexual perversions, and various forms of sex with violence, all of a disagreeable character. We have in the past fortnight checked again on this and found there are indeed a number of books of that character on sale.'

'Without mentioning the names of any particular ones, how does Lawrence's book compare with that type of book?' – 'It is in a wholly different class.'

'From the point of view of literary merit?' asked Mr Justice Byrne cautiously. 'It is in a wholly different class', Mr Hetherington repeated.

'In what way?' Mr Gardiner then asked. – 'Well, it is both better written, easier to follow in a way, with a more precise use of words, more factually descriptive. It is also imbued with a different feeling. Most of the books to which I referred earlier are pretty hard and brutal in their theme. I certainly found nothing of that in *Lady Chatterley's Lover*.'

'Are these other books books of any real literary merit?' – 'No, sir. I would say not.' – 'Thank you, Mr Hetherington', said Mr Gardiner.

'No questions', said Mr Griffith-Jones, without looking up.

Mr Justice Byrne then said that some members of the Jury had been asking whether they could have any indication as to the probable length of the trial; and he looked inquiringly at both leading Counsel. Mr Griffith-Jones now made the surprising announcement that he was calling no witnesses (he said 'no *further* witnesses', which cast minds back to the C.I.D. Inspector who had said, in the historic past, that he had collected the twelve copies of *Lady Chatterley* from Mr Schmoller). The gasp of surprise in Court was reprehensibly audible. All eyes then turned upon Mr Gardiner.

'My Lord,' he said, with a faint smile, 'I have been considering the position in this case, particularly as my learned friend indicates that the Prosecution do not propose to call any evidence. I have another thirty-six witnesses of the same character, but in view of the actual decrease in the amount of cross-examination, I propose to call only one further witness. Subject to this, I understood your Lordship on Friday to rule that expert evidence on the class of literature which may deprave and corrupt or may not, and expert evidence as to whether this book falls in one class or the other, would not be admissible, and I have thought in those circumstances no advantage would be gained by tendering witnesses to that end. In that case I will call my last witness.'

*

And the last witness, who made a deep impression on the Court, was Miss BERNARDINE WALL. She told Mr Gardiner that she was 21 years old, that she was educated at the Convent of Our Lady of Sion in Bayswater, and that she belonged to a Roman Catholic family.

'Since you came down from Cambridge', said Mr Gardiner, 'have you started to write your first novel?' – 'Yes.'

'Have you also assisted in editing the November issue of *The Twentieth Century*, which is devoted, is it not, to the writings of those under 25?' – 'Yes, that is right.'

BERNARDINE WALL

'Have you contributed an article to that issue?' – 'Yes.'

'When you were doing Part One of the Tripos at Cambridge did you have to read the works of D. H. Lawrence?' – 'Yes, I did.'

'When you were 17 did you read an expurgated version of Lawrence's *Lady Chatterley's Lover*?' – 'Yes, I did.'

'You now have an Honours Degree in English. Will you tell us what in your view was the literary merit of the expurgated version?' – 'I think it had very little literary merit because – well, it was not a book which Lawrence had written, and it was very difficult to assess it in a critical way at all.'

'Does there appear to be any difference in the relationship between Connie and Mellors, and the earlier relationships in the expurgated version?' – 'The relationships all seem to be trivial, promiscuous, and sensuous in the expurgated version, especially the love affair with Michaelis.'

'About a year ago did you read *Lady Chatterley's Lover* as Lawrence wrote it?' – 'Yes, I did, and I have read it once since.'

'What was your opinion of the literary merit of the unexpurgated book, particularly in comparison with the expurgated version?' – 'It gave the balance which I found lacking in the expurgated version, because it showed there was the contrast. Lawrence was presenting a positive contrast with the deadness of the industrial civilization that he was indicting. The novel, as Lawrence wrote it, held out a hope that this was not all, that there was some way out of this drab daily existence.'

'It has been suggested that it puts promiscuity on a pedestal. Have you any opinion about that?' – 'I think it is completely untrue. It precisely does *not* put promiscuity on a pedestal. Connie's and Michaelis's affair was most unsatisfactory, but her affair with Mellors was a serious, responsible affair, even if it was not within wedlock.'

'As far as the four-letter words in this book are concerned, had you known them when you read the book?' – 'Yes, I knew all of them by that time.'

'From what sort of age?' – 'Well, I do not think one can . . .'
Neither did Mr Griffith-Jones, but his doubts (which he had

stilled when other witnesses had spoken of their childhood vocabulary) concerned relevance. 'Does this go to the *literary* merit of the book,' he asked, 'or any other merit of the book?' – 'I am not quite sure', Mr Justice Byrne admitted.

'While I am on my feet', Mr Griffith-Jones went on, 'may I say that this witness is tendered as an expert on literary merit. She has a First Class Honours Degree, and that appears to be her only qualification?' – 'Not a First', smiled Miss Bernardine Wall.

'Does that mean that anybody with an Honours Degree is qualified to speak as an expert?' – 'She *has* started to write a novel', said the Judge, and everyone smiled with him. – 'We have all got to start', conceded Mr Griffith-Jones.

They were getting away from the question: the age at which Miss Wall first knew the four-letter words. 'I will leave that', said Mr Gardiner. 'Well,' Mr Griffith-Jones explained, 'when she is asked the *age* at which she knew, surely we are straying beyond any limit?' – 'She might think they were of literary merit. You never can tell', said Mr Justice Byrne, with the air of a man seeing new horizons. 'Mr Gardiner has not explored that.'

Nor did Mr Gardiner explore it. 'From the point of view of literary merit,' he said, 'in your view how did this book compare with any other books dealing with human relations, including sexual relations?' – 'Well, it treated that very important human relationship with great dignity.'

'And in comparison with other books, whether technical books or novels dealing with the subject?' Miss Wall pondered this for a full minute. 'Well,' she said, 'the relationship was made a very, very serious, important, and valuable one, which I think I have very rarely read in any other novel.' – 'Thank you, Miss Wall', said Mr Gardiner.

'No questions', said Mr Griffith-Jones.

*

'My Lord, that is the case for the Defence', said Mr Gardiner.

The Judge glanced at the clock: it was ten minutes to three. 'Would you like to begin your speech this afternoon,' he asked, 'or would you prefer to start tomorrow morning?'

'If it is of equal convenience to the Jury, my Lord, and they don't mind having a short day, I would prefer to begin tomorrow morning.' – 'Yes, you have called a lot of evidence. If you would like to begin tomorrow morning, it is only right that you should not start until then. Very well.'

And on the last day of October 1960, the trial of Lady Chatterley thus ended its fourth day.

'*Lady Chatterley's Lover*? Listen, mate, if that's the book that's so pure
and decent it's even fit for schoolgirls to read then we don't stock it.'

Sprod in PUNCH, *9 November 1960*

THE FIFTH DAY

At half past ten on Tuesday, 1 November 1960, Mr Gerald Gardiner began a speech for the Defence that was unique in legal and literary history. Recollecting how such an opportunity would have seduced some of the Old Bailey ranters of past years, it will be of interest to study Mr Gardiner's cogency and his freedom from empty rhetoric.

'Members of the Jury,' he began, 'this case has lasted some days, and if you will permit me to say so, nobody, whether concerned with the Prosecution or with the Defence, can have failed to observe the patience with which you have borne your duties and the close attention which you have paid to the evidence. It may not seem so, but it is a fact, that all those who work in these Courts have very much in mind the real hardship which jury service may sometimes impose. Unfortunately, particularly in a case of this kind, we have no substitute for the representatives of the public. You may perhaps console yourselves with the reflection that if you had been here for three weeks on some complicated financial fraud it might well have been a case of rather less human interest than this.

'I don't know whether any of you have at any time been involved in a civil action. If you have you will have noticed that the plaintiff, the person who brings the action, has this great advantage under our procedure, that he has both the first word and the last word. The last word, I think, is usually said to be the prerogative of the feminine sex, but I think even they don't claim the first word as well. Whether the tribunal is a Judge or Jury, what is always of importance is the first impression produced; but it is also a great advantage to have the last word, when, whatever you say, no one can contradict it. The same is true in criminal proceedings, inevitably, because the Prosecution bring the case. That means, you see, that at this point of the case I have to address you not knowing at all what the Prosecution are going to say when they reply. In a sense I am trying to guess what they are likely to say and to deal with it before they say it.

'It is very difficult for Counsel to say anything to a Jury in a case of this kind without dealing with the law at all. But if either my friend or I say anything which is not accurate on the law, then my Lord will direct you as to what the law is, and you will, of course, accept his direction. On the other hand the facts are entirely for you, and are not for my Lord at all. Just as you have no responsibility at all for any decisions of law, so my Lord has no responsibility at all for decisions of fact. They are entirely for you and each one of you.

'The reason why I say this is that, in every criminal case, before a Jury can convict anyone of a criminal offence, they must be unanimous.* Therefore there is a special responsibility on each one of you, so that if you are satisfied that your view is right, it is not only your right but your duty to maintain it. You may remember in a traditionally great summing-up, Mr Justice Stable in the case of Martin Secker & Warburg [the *Philanderer* case] said: "You in arriving at your verdict must arrive at a unanimous verdict. If you can all agree so much the better, but if there is any one of you, or more, who honestly cannot share the view of the others, then it is your duty so to say."

'And the last preliminary observation I would like to make is this: this is not a prosecution of pornographic booksellers. This is a prosecution of Penguin Books, whose directors thought, as they still think, that there is nothing in this book which in truth and in fact would deprave or corrupt anyone. They were of course conscious that, owing to its history, they might risk a prosecution. They were not concerned with the

---

* It is surprising how seldom this vital point is so much as mentioned to juries. I myself have served on a London Sessions jury which included two Scottish members; they both thought that, as in Scotland, we could return a majority verdict. No one had told them otherwise in Court. – Ed.

financial aspect of it. They could have published an expurgated edition in this country and the unexpurgated edition abroad and sold it elsewhere. They are concerned with the question of principle. They have at all times cooperated with the Prosecution.

'It will be quite plain to you, from the evidence which you have heard, that there is a vast amount of pornography about today – "dirt for dirt's sake". Equally clearly the proportion of that which anybody could by any stretch of the imagination describe as literature is minute. It is clear also that what Parliament is doing by the Act is making it easier to prosecute pornography, yet at the same time protecting that which can be called literature. The Act is an act to amend the law relating to the publishing of obscene matter, to provide for the protection of literature, and to strengthen the law concerning pornography.

'Another thing which Parliament has done is this. What used to be said was: "The better written the thing is, the more harm it does." That is an argument which obviously cannot apply now, for Parliament has gone out of its way to say that even if a thing appears to be obscene, nevertheless if it can be fairly described as literature its publication may be justified as being for the public good.

'You have had to read this book sitting together: you have not been able to take it home or refer to it after hearing the evidence which has been called. You presumably still have it, and while it is in my mind might I just say that perhaps the two best expressions of what Lawrence was really after are to be found on pages 292 and 317, and if you have an opportunity of considering his intention again you may turn to those pages.

'From certain questions asked by the Prosecution – or perhaps they would be not unfairly described as insults rather than questions – observations such as "You are not giving a lecture now" – it sounded as if it was going to be suggested to you that you should ignore the evidence which has been called, on the ground that these are professors of literature and people who are living rarefied lives, people who would not

know what the effect of a book like this, whether conscious or
unconscious, would be on ordinary people who read it. Of
course, it was precisely for that reason that, when I called each
witness, I didn't merely ask him whether he was a professor of
literature. It seemed to me only right that you should know
what these men and women had done in life, so that you could
judge for yourselves whether it was true to say they were men
and women living a rarefied life, and not really knowing what
goes on in the world. I cannot, of course, remind you of what
they all said, but many of them had had extremely varied
careers. I take as an example Mr Francis Williams, who after
being brought up in an industrial community in the North of
England was at a Grammar School in Lancashire, then a reporter on the staffs of various papers, the *Daily Express*, the
Daily Herald, and the *Evening Standard*. He was Controller of
News and Censorship at the Ministry of Information. He was
the Principal Press Adviser to the British Delegation to the
United Nations Conference at San Francisco. He was the
Chairman of the International Committee of Public Informa-

tion Policies for the United Nations. He was Adviser on Public Relations to the Prime Minister. He was the British represent-ative on the United Nations Commission on the Freedom of the Press. He was also an adviser to UNESCO on international press communications, and during the years 1949 and 1950 he was chief American correspondent to the *Observer* in the United States; and he was a Governor of the B.B.C. He held various honours. He has appeared regularly as a commentator on radio and television and has been Chairman of the B.B.C. television Press Conference. He has himself published a num-ber of books, including three novels, published not only here but in the United States and translated into many European languages. He is shortly to take up an appointment as Regents' Professor at the University of California.

'It was for the same reason that I called a man like Mr Cammaerts, who said he was headmaster of a grammar school. He was a teacher in ordinary schools; he had worked as an agricultural worker when he was a conscientious objector for two years; he then changed his mind and was parachuted into France and received various medals – the D.S.O., the Légion d'Honneur, Croix de Guerre, and American Medal of Free-dom. He was on the Military Government in Berlin, and after that has taken part in many other activities. He is now the headmaster of a school of over 500 boys, and is about to take up an appointment as the head of a teachers' training college.

'And, you see, the witnesses I have called include professors of English literature, like Professor Pinto and Professor Muir; a number of readers and lecturers, some of whom have been professors at English universities or visiting professors at other universities: Miss Gardner (Oxford), Mr Hough (Cambridge), Mr Raymond Williams (Oxford) – perhaps a particularly important witness because he deals not only with those who are members of the university but also extra-mural students, the general public. As no one knows better than Penguin Books, students of literature come from all classes of the community, and this was the witness, you may remember, who was used to taking classes of the Workers'

Educational Association. Then there was Mr Stephen Potter, formerly of London University, chairman of the Literature Committee of the B.B.C.; and Mrs Bennett (Cambridge), and Mr Hoggart (Leicester).

'Then we had the authors, and I am sure I will offend no one if I suggest that the witness who stands highest of all those called as a creative artist is, of course, Mr E. M. Forster. Then Dame Rebecca West, Mr Day Lewis, who was Professor of Poetry at Oxford, and Mr John Connell; and, of course many of the critics and reviewers who are also authors in their own right: Dr Veronica Wedgwood, Mr Walter Allen, Miss Janet Adam Smith, Miss Dilys Powell.

'Teachers, those connected with education, like Mr Annan, the Provost of King's College, Cambridge; Mr Cammaerts; Miss Jones, concerned with teaching girls all her life; Dr Hemming, occupying a rather special position in view of his work in the psychology of education and in educational research; Mr Hetherington, editor of the *Guardian*, and Mr Young, editor of the *Yorkshire Post*. Representatives of the Church: the Bishop of Woolwich; Prebendary Hopkinson, Director-General of the Industrial Christian Fellowship, who was used to dealing with ordinary people; Mr Tytler, Director of Religious Education in the Diocese of Birmingham; and Canon Milford; as well as Mr St John-Stevas, who, as a legal adviser, had a special experience in pornographic works. There was Miss Anne Scott-James – she is not leading any rarefied life but is dealing with women's and children's problems. Then there was a Member of Parliament; and Sir Stanley Unwin, the doyen of the publishers' world; and, of course, the directors of the defendant company, Sir Allen Lane, and Sir William Emrys Williams, very highly qualified in literature in his own right.

'I would suggest that no higher class of experts could have been called in any similar case, and I am sorry now that I ever suggested that they should remain in court while some of them gave their evidence. Of course it would have made it more interesting for them, but their evidence, you may think, gained from the fact that as each witness went into the witness box he had not the slightest idea what the previous witness had been asked or what answer he had given; and the fact that they were kept out of court you may think tended considerably to stress the evidence which they gave.

'And now, if I may come to what is the most important single fact in the whole of this case, it is that Parliament has expressly provided that evidence on this may be called both by the Defence and by the Prosecution. You have seen how, when the first few witnesses were called, they were attacked by the Prosecution (very properly), and they were asked: "Do you really say . . ." so-and-so? And then, gradually, the Prosecution plainly got overwhelmed by the evidence; gradually, more and more, they accepted the evidence; gradually, more and more, they asked no questions; *and then, when their turn came to call evidence, they called no evidence at all.*

'May I remind you, briefly, of what the witnesses you have heard have said. First of all, as to the author. Now, this is obviously of great importance when one is considering relative questions of literary merit. Obviously, if there were a prosecution for publishing Chaucer's *Canterbury Tales*, the first thing which the Defence would want to do would be to explain to the Jury in some detail Chaucer's standing in the history of English literature. It might be difficult to deny that some of the tales are obscene, but that obviously would be their defence. Now, Lawrence, you see, has been dead for thirty years. He was a highly controversial figure in his lifetime, and it may not be at all easy to judge. Indeed, any survey of the history of art and literature in this country makes it plain, does it not, that in the past we have not found it easy to judge the true merits of a highly controversial figure while he is living? But Lawrence has now been dead thirty years. There are apparently about 800 books all over the world written about him, and people just don't go on reading all the novels of a particular author long after his death unless in fact they are good literature. That really is the test, is it not, when a man has been dead for that length of time?'

Mr Gardiner quoted from the evidence of Dame Rebecca

West, Mr E. M. Forster, Mr Noel Annan, and Mr Hoggart as to the status of D. H. Lawrence in Western literature – and their differing treatment at the hands of the Prosecution.

'Mr Forster's evidence, you may remember, was quite un-challenged by the Prosecution. They had not accepted it from Mr Hoggart, but the moment Mr Forster said the same thing they accepted it and asked no questions. Miss Helen Gardner expressed her opinion, and that also was accepted by the Prosecution; it was not challenged. What she said was this: "I think in discussing literary merit one has to give weight to two things. One is, I think, what the writer is trying to say, and the other is his success in saying it. These two are not always commensurate. One can find great literary merit in a piece of writing of a trivial experience, because it is so fully and truthfully expressed. Equally one can find great literary merit in a piece of writing of an experience of great import-ance and great value, although one may feel at times the writer has not wholly succeeded in communicating what he wishes to communicate."'

Professor Pinto had referred to the double theme – the mechanization of humanity and the happiness to be found in tenderness. Dr C. V. Wedgwood had said that the expur-gated version left out Lawrence's central idea – the association of sex and tenderness – and Mr Hetherington that the import-ance of the book was 'the beauty and goodness of physical love at its best'. Mr Raymond Williams had quoted with approval the famous passage on page 277: 'It's the one thing they won't let you be, straight and open in your sex. In fact the more dirt you do on sex the better they like it. But if you do believe in your own sex, and won't have it done dirt to: they'll down you. It's the one insane taboo left: sex as a natural and vital thing.' Miss Helen Gardner, Canon Milford, and others were quoted by Mr Gardiner as in broad agreement with this, and he then went on to draw upon the evidence for a vindication of Lawrence's integrity of purpose.

'So much, then, for the general theme or meaning of the book. No one, of course, suggests that it is a perfect book or even Lawrence's best book. As we know, it was written three times, because that was Lawrence's practice. Most authors, I suppose, having written a book, alter it and take things out or put things in, but that was never Lawrence's method. He always did a complete rewrite. Having done the outline of the plot he then rewrote it and then rewrote it again.

'Although not his best book, since it is his last novel it is in a sense the crux of his work. Witness after witness has told you that it is not possible to judge Lawrence if one cannot read this book. It has faults: he was always a most uneven writer with very little sense of humour, and not always easy to read. There is one absolutely shocking passage in the book, and when I say "shocking", I don't mean because of words in it, but shocking because it is completely untrue. That is the conversation between Constance's father and Mellors. Passionately devoted to England as Lawrence was, it was not the England of the public schools and the West End clubs, but the England of the provinces, and having spent so much time out of England he just didn't know how a member of the aristocracy would talk in those particular circumstances.

'It is, of course, a book with sociological merits. The majority of the book has nothing to do with sexual relations at all. It is a description of life as it was at a particular time in the Midlands, the beauty of the countryside, the extraordinary sympathy which he has for nature and for all living things. He contrasts the unsatisfactory and futile nature of promiscuous relations with the normal and healthy relationship between people in love which should combine a man and a woman perfectly together.

'In answer to what these witnesses have said, hardly any question has been put to them by the Prosecution about the book as a whole. The technique has been just as it used to be before the Act: to read out particular passages and say "Now do you call that moral?", or "Do you think that is a good bit of writing?" The one thing which this Act has made plain is that in future, in fairness to the author, the book must be judged as a whole. And even in the case of these particular passages, even though they were read out making fun of the dialect and so on, you may have thought the ultimate effect, *even though so read,* was only to underline the sensitiveness and beauty of it. Because there is, is there not, a high breathlessness about beauty which cancels lust?

'One has to see, of course, what the Prosecution have to say about it. *Not one single witness* has been found to come into the witness box and say anything against Lawrence or this book. Of course, one can judge by what my learned friend said to you in opening this case: he suggested that sex was dragged in at every conceivable opportunity, and that the story was little more than padding. Really the episodes of sexual intercourse were the first things to which he took exception. He suggested that the only variations in the descriptions of sexual intercourse were in where they took place. Of course, his suggestion that sex was dragged in at every conceivable opportunity and that the story was little more than padding is the exact opposite of another suggestion which he made to you, namely *that the first draft was a very good story in itself and could quite well have been published by itself,* which is quite inconsistent with the suggestion that the whole of the rest of the story apart from the sexual parts in it was mere padding.

'You heard what the witnesses said about this. None of them would have it for a moment. Mr Hough was asked: "How far are the descriptions of sexual intercourse relevant or necessary to the theme or meaning of the book?", and he said: "In my view they are entirely necessary. Lawrence is making, admittedly, a bold experiment here. He is trying to study the sexual situation more clearly and more openly than is usually done in fiction, and to do that he must describe that which he purports to represent." The suggestion that they were all the same can be seen to be wrong by anyone who has read the book. It is perfectly plain, first of all, that the promiscuous sexual relations were entirely unsatisfactory, and that the situation with Mellors was a very slow development from beginning to end. He starts out, having been unhappily married, and having lived alone for some time, wanting to go on living alone, realizing the emotional entanglement if a woman comes into his life again, and fighting against it. And it is a slow and steady development of that situation. Nothing is more striking than the unanimity among all the witnesses as to Lawrence's integrity of purpose.

'Sir William Emrys Williams said: "But the whole point, I think, that he was determined to impress on us was that love can be a failure, love can be dirty, love can be clean; and these two people go through the whole cycle until they do discover the wholesome fulfilment, and I think that without the contours and the colours which distinguish these episodes that point would not have been made." He was asked: "Do you think the book would have been Lawrence's, a book of perhaps equal literary merit, if you had put a row of asterisks in every time these two people meet in the way we have seen?" He said: "I think that would make the thing just a dirty book."

'Mr Hough was asked: "Does it appear from the book whether sex was a thing which Lawrence treated with reverence or not?" and he said: "With the greatest reverence and the greatest tenderness." It is remarkable, is it not, how many of these witnesses, all choosing their own language and all putting it differently, have stressed Lawrence's integrity of purpose, his reverence for physical relations between men and women in love in a permanent relationship, and their effect as something sacred?

'Mrs Bennett, you may remember, said: "What appears very clearly in the book is that he believes that marriage – not in the legal sense – that the union between two people for a lifetime and with the possibility of childbearing included, marriage in that sense is of the highest importance, of almost *sacred* importance."

'The Rev. Mr Hopkinson said: "All life comes through sex itself, and believing that all life comes from God I would believe therefore that God himself created these functions, and we ought therefore to learn to regard them with respect and reverence, which does *not* mean with timidity."

'Mr Hoggart said of one passage of the book: "It is highly virtuous and, if anything, puritanical. He is interested in a relationship between people which is in the deepest sense spiritual. This includes a due and proper regard for our sexual and physical side. I believe that in this book what he said is 'I must face this problem head on, even at the risk of having people think I am obsessed by sex'. But one realizes from that last letter from Mellors that between him and Lady Chatterley there will be periods of extraordinary chasteness. There will be moments of coming together in love which will be all the better because they are not using one another like creatures for enjoyment. It is a kind of *sacrament* for him."

'Mr Stevas said: "It does seem to me this is undoubtedly a moral book." He did not suggest it was written from an orthodox Christian point of view, because Lawrence was not a Christian. "A great proportion of the books I read and the films I see and the television I watch seems to have a degrading influence, and a great deal of the contemporary cinema seems to degrade the whole sanctity of sex, treating it as something trivial; but in Lawrence's book, which has great elements of *sacredness,* sex is taken as being something to be taken seriously and as a basis for a holy life."

'The Bishop of Woolwich said: "Clearly, Lawrence did not have a Christian valuation of sex, and the kind of sexual relationship depicted in the book is not one that I would necessarily regard as ideal, but what I think is clear is that what Lawrence is trying to do is to portray the sex relationship as something essentially *sacred*." Mr Tytler, the director of religious education, used similar wording. He said: "I think there is a very great deal to suggest that the union between a man and a woman is *sacred*."

'You may think it is significant that the word "sacred" should, quite independently and in a different context, have been used by so many of these witnesses.

'The next thing which we know from my learned friend's opening is that the Prosecution challenge the use of the four-letter words. You have heard from the witnesses called here for the Defence why in their view this use was legitimate in this particular book by this particular author.

'Mr Hough said this: "In Lawrence's view there is no proper language in which to talk about sexual matters. They are either discussed in clinical terms, which deprive them of all emotional content, or they are discussed in words that are normally thought to be obscene and coarse. He thinks that this results in a secretive and morbid attitude towards sex, and he wishes to find the language in which it can be discussed openly and not irreverently; and to do this he tries to redeem the normally obscene words. He tries to use them in contexts that are entirely serious, and to make use seriously of words that are generally used in contexts of mockery or abuse. I do not myself think this is successful, but that is what he is trying to do."

'I put this myself to Miss Helen Gardner (whose evidence, you remember, was not challenged at all by the Prosecution) when making this point. I said this to her: "It has been said that the four-letter words form the whole subject matter of the Prosecution – that is the phrase you may remember which my learned friend used in opening this case to you – and that the word 'fuck' or 'fucking' occurs not less than thirty times. What, in your view, is the relation of the four-letter words in this book to its literary merits?" She said this: "I would like to begin by saying that I do not think any words are brutal and disgusting in themselves. They are brutal and disgusting if they are used in a brutal and disgusting sense or a brutal and disgusting context. I think that because this word is used so frequently in the book, with every subsequent use the original shock is diminished; and I would say that by the end of the book Lawrence has gone very far, within the context of this book, to redeem this word from low and vulgar associations, and make one feel it is the only word the character in the book could use. If one attempts to find any substitute I think it is impossible. By the time one reads the last page, Mellors's letter, this word has taken on great depth of meaning, has become related to natural processes and is wholly justified in the context of this book. I do not mean I think Lawrence was able to redeem the word in usage, I am talking about its usage within the book itself."

'Only yesterday Mr Potter, in answer to the question, "Do you find the use of the four-letter words in the book valid?", said this: "I think Lawrence was trying to do something very difficult and very courageous there. I think it is impossible to print the book without them. I think, I know indeed, that what he was trying to do was to take these words out of what you may call the context of the lavatory wall and give them back a dignity and meaning, away from the context of obscenity and of the swear-word."

'Members of the Jury, there is one thing about which I want to be quite plain, because in my submission it is of some importance not only that you should realize this but that everybody should realize it. It is this: that no one should think that, if the use of these words for this special purpose by this particular author in this particular book is legitimate, it will follow that these words can be used by any scribbler writing any kind of novel. It is perhaps important that this should be realized.* Here again, there is no answer by the Prosecution. We have not had any witness called to say, "For the following reasons I do not consider that the use of these words is either relevant or necessary to the purpose of the author."

'There has been talk, although the Prosecution have not put it in, of an expurgated edition. It has been suggested that it would be much better if there was a whole lot of asterisks. On the *un*expurgated edition, Professor Muir was asked "What do you take to be the theme of the unexpurgated edition?", and he said, "I should say the redemption of the individual, and hence of society, by what Lawrence calls 'reciprocity of tenderness', and that is why I feel that the expurgated edition is a travesty of the original and ought never to have been published." Mr Connell, when sent an expurgated edition for review, said he found it "(a) trivial, (b) furtive, (c) obscene."

'It was then suggested that perhaps it would have been nice to have published, instead of this book, what has been called

* Subsequent comment in letters to the newspapers showed that this warning, designed perhaps to limit the Jury's feeling of responsibility, went largely unnoticed elsewhere. A group of M.P.s actually drafted and presented a Parliamentary Bill to punish bad language, not knowing, perhaps, that the Profane Oaths Act, 1745, was still good law. This Act prescribes penalties for those who 'profanely curse or swear': one shilling for a day-labourer or common soldier, two shillings for anyone else 'under the degree of a gentleman', and five shillings for gents and upwards, or ten days if you don't pay.

the first version, which, apparently many years after Lawrence's death, was published (I think in America) under the title *The First Lady Chatterley*. It is not a "version", properly called, at all. I suppose it might be interesting to students of literature to see the first rough draft of *Sons and Lovers* so as to see how Lawrence's mind progressed and how he carried out his creative function, but the first draft of any of his books is not really a "version" at all; it is merely what he says it was, a first rough draft. It is said that to publish that would be quite all right because that version contains the letters "f . . k" and "c . . t". Have we really descended to this? Are we so frightened of words that while it is perfectly all right to publish a book with "f . . k" it is all wrong to publish a book with the word in its full form? This would in fact have destroyed the whole purpose with which Lawrence was using the words. People in real life do not say "f . . k". After all, these words have been part of spoken English for hundreds and hundreds of years. They are apparently known not only to boys but also to girls at school age.

'Then it is said, and a great deal was made of this, that the book set promiscuous relations on a pedestal. There again, if I may just remind you of what the actual evidence was, there was the evidence of Mr Hough. He said, "I think that is not true either. Promiscuity hardly comes in question here. It is very much condemned by Lawrence. It is true that at the centre of the book there is an adulterous situation. That is true of a good deal of fiction in Europe from the Iliad on." Mrs Bennett, when it was put to her, said: "But the very reverse, I would have thought. In so far as any promiscuous intercourse is shown in the book it is shown as unsatisfactory, giving no fulfilment, no joy, and as really rather disgusting."

'This was put to Mr Hoggart: "It is said that there are descriptions in this book of promiscuity and of talk about sex amongst numbers of the characters, particularly at the beginning of the book. What do you say about the purpose of those descriptions?" Mr Hoggart answered, "I think they do underline the description of Lawrence's book as moral. There is talk of promiscuity there – his description of promiscuity in

Constance Chatterley's affairs in Germany and her affair with Michaelis early in the book – and I think Lawrence made it clear in the book that the relationship between Constance Chatterley and the gamekeeper was not conceived as a promiscuous relationship, but as really moral. The other affairs of Constance, with the German student and with Michaelis – I think he means us to read them as promiscuous, and both of them are barren of satisfaction."

'When it was put to Dame Rebecca West, she said, ". . . it is not a recommendation of such intercourse. It shows a broken life, and what somebody did with it, but it certainly doesn't suggest adultery because it *couldn't*. Lawrence was a man who spent all of his life working out the problem of how to make a good marriage, because he thought a good marriage was perhaps the most important thing in the world."'

Mr Young, Miss Dilys Powell, Miss Janet Adam Smith, Mr Tytler, Mr J. W. Lambert, were all cited to the same effect. 'There is no answer to this evidence', said Mr. Gardiner. 'Not one single man can be found to go into the witness box to point to any passage in the book which seems to condone or advocate promiscuous relations.

'The witnesses differ, as those giving evidence of opinion may well do, as to the degree to which the book was an accurate mirror of our age. Mr Hough I think expressed the opinion that in some passages Mellors would not have talked as he does in the book. On the other hand Mr Hoggart, who came from that class – he was, you may remember, at an elementary school, and orphaned at the age of eight – apparently disagrees with that. He said, "This is just the language which Mellors would have used." So did Mr Williams, the man who had been brought up in an industrial community in the North of England.

'Then it has been suggested that this is a book about adultery. It is necessary in my submission to be clear about this. In the first place Lawrence was not a Christian, and he was not seeking to deal here with any ecclesiastical situation. I suppose it is true to say that to a Catholic the only right use of sex is in Christian marriage; in the Church of England, on the other hand, divorce is permissible. But he is not dealing with matters of that kind. In literature a writer puts his characters in a situation which is likely to give rise to some question of human behaviour which he is seeking to consider; and of course a large proportion of novels do include adultery. They may or may not – it depends on the context of the book – advocate adultery. This is a moral book because the message, the meaning, the outcome is that two people find an aspect of truth. It is said that they discuss nothing but sex. That is not literally true. As relations between different human beings – an echo of the age around us – right relationships, including sexual relations, are the theme of the book one would not expect to find long conversations between the characters about the weather. It is just not true to say that this is a book *all* about sex.

'There is one true marriage in the book which is clearly held up for esteem – Mrs Bolton's marriage. The setting is one in which adultery takes place, but the book is a book by a pagan and not a Christian, by one who clearly felt that for his purposes a permanent union was of very great importance indeed, and who was writing this at the end of his life. No opportunity has been lost to attack Lawrence, and it has been said that he himself ran off with someone else's wife. That is true, but Lawrence was only married once in his life and that marriage lasted until his death. Whatever his view may have been ten or twenty years before, the only view with which we are concerned is the view expressed in this book written not long before his death.

'It is, as we all know, a book about human beings. It was St Augustine who said: "Man being sinful: a book about sinless man would be a contradiction in terms." It is a book about real people, and for my part I respectfully protest at the sort of statements which have been made about the character of Constance. There is this love affair in Germany. She marries. There she is all through the war, and at the end of the war her husband comes back unable to take further part in the physical side of marriage. When Michaelis suggests that she should go off with him, her regard for the marriage tie is perfectly clear;

she says she can't possibly do that. There is no further incon-
stancy on her part until her husband suggests that she should
have a child by another man so that there can be an heir to
inherit Wragby. Nobody would suggest on a specifically
Christian standard that what she did in committing adultery
was right, but that is not the subject of the book. That is merely
the position in which the characters are situated. And even
so it is not really right, is it, to convict Constance as if she were
some kind of nymphomaniac?

'Lawrence very much stacked the cards against himself. He
could quite easily have made Clifford a husband with very
little need for sexual expression with his wife at all, the sort of
man who believed that really a woman ought not to have any
say in those matters. But he stacks the cards against himself by
having Clifford, through no fault of his own, condemned to a
wheelchair existence for the rest of his life so that anybody who
reads the book cannot fail to have sympathy with that
character.

'When it is said that this is a book about adultery, one
wonders how there can be things which people do not see. I
suppose it is possible that somewhere there might be a mind
which would describe *Antony and Cleopatra* as "a tale about
adultery". Antony had a wife in Rome, and I suppose there
might be a mind somewhere which would describe this play of
Shakespeare's as "the story of a sex-starved man copulating
with an Egyptian queen", a parallel with the way this book
has been put before you on behalf of the Prosecution. Thus
there are minds which are unable to see beauty where it exists,
and doubt the integrity of purpose in an author where it is
obvious.

'Witnesses were very properly asked whether they agreed or
did not agree with the views expressed about Lawrence and
about this book by other eminent authorities. It was first put
to Mr Hough who was asked this by the Prosecution: "You
told us that others do not agree with you; I just want to see
to what extent certain other eminent literary people do not
agree with the views which you hold about this book." That
was a perfectly proper course to take. It turned out that the

first of them was a lady who had written a preface, but unfortunately nobody had ever heard of her. Mr Hough was asked and he had never heard of her; Mr Hoggart had never heard of her; Professor Pinto described her as not a critic of any importance.

'The second was a rather remarkable lady who had written an article in *Encounter*, which, so far from telling against Lawrence, merely stressed the fact that everybody, except this lady, who I think wrote short stories, thought the exact opposite. Indeed, she herself quotes them in that article. She quotes Archibald MacLeish, the poet and former Librarian of Congress, as saying that the work was "'pure' and a work of high literary merit". She says "he dares us at our own risk to deny that the book is 'one of the most important works of the century, or to express an opinion about the literature of our own time, or about the spiritual history that literature expresses without making his peace in one way or another with D. H. Lawrence and with this work'". She then quotes Harvey Breit: "The language and the incidents or scenes in question are deeply moving and very beautiful. Lawrence was concerned how love, how a relationship between a man and a woman, can be most touching and beautiful, but only when uninhibited and total." Then there was Mr Edmund Wilson, who we were told by the witness was perhaps the foremost living American critic, and who had referred to this book as "the most inspiriting book I have seen in a long time". Then there was Professor Schorer, who referred to what Yeats had said, and what he said was this: "These two lovers, the gamekeeper and his employer's wife, each separated from their class by their love and fate, are poignant in their loneliness; the coarse language of the one accepted by both becomes a forlorn poetry, uniting their solitudes, something ancient, humble, and terrible." Professor Schorer was writing the preface to the American edition.

'The lady disagrees with everybody else; that is all it comes to. You may think she was a curious authority for the Prosecution to rely on, not only because she appears to be unknown as a critic but known as a short-story writer, but also because in this article she quotes from Jacques Barzun who says this: "I have no hesitation in saying that I do not consider Lawrence's novel pornographic." Then this lady, whom the Prosecution hold up as being a critic of the sort of standard they would ask you to accept, says: "I agree with this admirably prudent statement"; and again, when Mr Barzun notes Lawrence's ruling passion for reforming everything and everybody in sight: "My quarrel with the book" – now we know what the lady's real quarrel with the book is – "is that it really is *not* pornographic." This is the woman on whom the Prosecution rely.

'The only other one they produced was Mr Middleton Murry, who at one time was a personal friend of Lawrence. They had quarrelled, and he had then criticized Lawrence. You may remember that I read in re-examination from a paper written by Murry about the book before the quarrel. Although they have very properly put to witnesses any opinions which might seem to support the case for the Prosecution, it is a very strong point, is it not, that a man whose works include this book should have been commented on by about 800 subsequent authors who have written books about him, and yet, you will notice, with all the world of literature commenting on Lawrence, these, and these alone, are the only critical comments which the Prosecution have been able to find to put to the witnesses called for the Defence, while not at the same time calling any evidence whatever themselves?

'I must deal with what no doubt will be a point sought to be made by the Prosecution. "This is in a book published at 3s. 6d. It will be available to the general public." Of course, that is perfectly true and perfectly obvious. It may well be said that everybody will rush to buy it. You may well think *that* is perfectly true and perfectly obvious, because it happens in every case. Whether it is *The Philanderer* or any other book which is wrongly prosecuted, inevitably people go and buy it. It would be idle to deny it. But whose fault is that? It is always the fact that there has been a wrong prosecution of a book that leads a large number of people to buy it. What was said on this aspect of the case was this. I am most anxious not to do my learned friend any injustice, and so may I quote exactly what he said? He invited you to consider this question after you had read it. "Is it a book that you would even wish your wife or your servants to read?" I cannot help thinking that this was, consciously or unconsciously, an echo from an observation which had fallen from the Bench in an earlier case: "It would never do to let members of the working class read this." I do not want to upset the Prosecution by suggesting that there are a certain number of people nowadays who as a matter of fact don't *have* servants. But of course that whole attitude is one which Penguin Books was formed to fight against, which they always have fought against, and which they will go on fighting against – the attitude that it is all right to publish a special edition at five or ten guineas so that people who are less well off cannot read what other people read. Isn't everybody, whether earning £10 a week or £20 a week, equally interested in the society in which we live, in the problems of human relationships including sexual relationships? In view of the reference made to wives, aren't women equally interested in human relations, including sexual relationships?

'The book has to be judged as a whole, in relation to the general public as a whole, and not to some particular section of the public. You see, there are students of literature in all walks of life, and the sale of 250 million books shows, does it not, that Mr Lane (as he then was) was right in thinking that there are. If it is right that this book should be read, it should be available to the man who is working in the factory or to the teacher who is working in the school. It is rather extraordinary on the face of it, is it not, that, when a visiting professor goes from this country to other countries to lecture on Lawrence, he is not supposed, really, to know anything about this book at all.

'You have been told that, quite apart from the literary merit of this book, it also has sociological and educational merits, and I would like, if I may, to say a word about that. Of course, as always where merits are discussed, whether literary or educational, they must be comparative and must be judged against the climate of existing educational literature in the field of human relations, including sexual relations. Mr Cammaerts, you may remember – *I stress this because his evidence was not challenged by the Prosecution at all* – said this: "I would say it is the only book I know that treats the sexual relationships between human beings in a really serious way, and would have the effect on most young people who are interested in this problem of giving them a serious approach to it."

'And you may remember that Miss Jones, who deals with girls and has had a lifetime of experience of what girls read, said this: "I think that this book has a considerable educational merit if taken at the proper time, which I would say is normally after 17 years old, because it deals openly and honestly with the problems of sex which are very real to the girls themselves." She went on to explain that in her view children did not read books before they were ready to come to them.

'Mr Hemming, from a slightly different point of view, said: "Today young people are subjected to a constant titillation and insinuation of what I would describe as shallow and corrupting values with regard to sex and the relationships between the sexes. For example, the picture is put before the young girl that if she has the right proportions, wears the right clothes, uses the right cosmetics, she will become irresistible to men and that that is the supreme achievement of a woman, to become irresistible to men. On the other hand, the general effect of this titillation and insinuation so far as the young man is concerned is to suggest that sex is little more than a physical thrill, that to have a pretty woman in their arms is the supreme ecstasy of life, and that to seduce a woman is manly and something to be attempted for yourself and to be envied in others. In fact, if I may add this point, very often young people today, were they to read *Lady Chatterley's Lover*, would for the first time be brought into touch with a concept of sex which includes tenderness, compassion, sensitivity, and all that makes sex human."

'And lastly Mr Tytler, a Director of Religious Education, was asked about it, and he said: "I think this book makes it quite clear that Lawrence was against irresponsibility in matters of sex and that therefore, by reading it, young people, even those who are potentially promiscuous, will be hauled up short and made to think again, and those having a responsibility towards those growing up will hold the view that that is worthwhile."

'Now, members of the Jury, it has not been possible for the defendants to call before you specific evidence of what I might call the comparative literature available, but I have already reminded you of what Miss Dilys Powell says about that, seeing that she does television and novel reviewing. Mr St John-Stevas is in a somewhat special position, having been for four years legal adviser to a committee which has considered these matters, and he said: "I have certainly read a great many books of a pornographic and obscene nature in connexion with a study which I did, and my judgement is, with regard to literary merit, that, of course, *Lady Chatterley's Lover* has nothing in common with those books. And I would use 'literary merit' there not only in the sense of the language but – I do not think this can be separated – the theme and method and the underlying morality of the book. These books which I have studied have nothing to be said for them at all, and I find it difficult to make a comparison with *Lady Chatterley's Lover* because the gulf between them is so great." Miss Janet Adam Smith referred to "the sensitiveness and humanity with which Lawrence explores the situation, in which it seems to me there is nothing suggestive. It is never suggested that the action is trivial or degrading in the way in which sex is presented in so many popular books today. It is associated with tenderness, with thought for the other person, with the creation of new life, with regard for the consequences, and not with the mere satisfaction of the animal body. Compared with so many books today it does not associate sex with violence or cruelty or perversion." Mr Hetherington, of the *Guardian*, said: "We have had occasion recently, twice recently, to send out reporters to buy books within half a mile of our office, because I had heard there were books on sale openly dealing with sadism, lesbianism, incest, sexual

perversion, and various forms of sex with violence, all o[f]
a disagreeable character. We have in the past fortnigh[t]
checked again on this and found there are indeed a numbe[r]
of books of that character on sale." He said this was a boo[k]
in an entirely different class: "Most of the books to which [I]
referred earlier are pretty hard and brutal in their theme[.]
I certainly found nothing of that in *Lady Chatterley'[s]
Lover.*"

'Now, here again, you see, no evidence, no answer. An[d]
if it is suggested to you, members of the Jury, that really yo[u]
ought not to pay any attention to the evidence, that "you an[d]
I are ordinary people, we understand these things; don't le[t]
us pay any attention to these people who have spent thei[r]
lives among young people; don't let us pay any attention t[o]
these men and women who have reached various positions o[f]
some eminence in our society; don't let us pay any attentio[n]
because you and I are ordinary people and we understand" -
well, of course, Lawrence himself wa[s] precisely that, was h[e]
not, a man of the people. And, of course, it is very eas[y]
for Counsel for the Prosecution, at the end of a case when h[e]
has not called any evidence at all, to make any suggestions h[e]
likes. How far the Prosecution lawyers are in contact wit[h]
real life we do not know. My learned friend does not go int[o]
the witness box and I cannot cross-examine him. Indeed [I]
have not been allowed to cross-examine anybody, because, o[f]
course, it would be quite obvious to you that the moment the[y]
called *one* expert I would be entitled to put it to him that the
evidence which I had called was consistent with the whole o[f]
the run of those who had ever studied Lawrence or studied this
book. I could produce to him, and ask him whether he agreed
with, all the 800 works which from time to time have bee[n]
written about Lawrence. It is very easy to adopt the line,
"You and I are ordinary chaps, and don't you bother about
these experts, because they are teachers who live in their books
and they don't really know what goes on in the world: you
have seen them in the witness box, they don't do shopping and
washing up and get married and have children, they don't
really know what goes on at all"; but, you know, any sugges-

tion of that kind will not be founded on evidence, because none of the submissions which he makes to you will be founded on any evidence.

'And you may not have forgotten that when you started this case you took an oath fairly to try the issue joined between our Sovereign Lady the Queen and the prisoner at the bar and a true verdict give *according to the evidence*. It is very easy in a final speech to make this or that suggestion which is not founded on any evidence at all at a time when there is no right of reply. The truth is, is it not, that we have unhappily done this in England before, and during a man's lifetime. It may be justified in the sense that, particularly if he is a very controversial figure, it may not be easy to recognize whether it is real literature or not, and so we ban him. Hardy, Shaw, Ibsen, Wilde, Joyce! Epstein's statues were tarred and feathered and now they are in cathedrals. Is Lawrence always to be confined to dirty bookshops – the greatest irony, perhaps, in literary history, in view of his passionate concern for the purity of sex?

'In my submission to you the defendants have shown, on a balance of probabilities, that it would be for the public good that this book should be generally available. I say on a balance of probabilities because – this is entirely a matter for my Lord – where the Prosecution has to establish something in a criminal case the burden which rests on them is to satisfy a Jury beyond reasonable doubt; *where the Defence have to discharge some burden of proof it is a lesser burden, it is the burden of satisfying a Jury on a mere balance of probabilities*. It is not a question of whether it is good for the public. That is not the question. The question is whether its publication would be justified for the public good because, first, of the standing of the author and of the fact (of which Miss Helen Gardner gave evidence that was not challenged) that in the whole of our literature this is now the only book written for publication by an author of anything remotely like Lawrence's standing which has not been published. Secondly, because this is a book written with great integrity by an author who passionately believed that he had a message for us, and who deals with the relations between Mellors and Connie with great reverence and as something sacred. Thirdly, because the physical descriptions and the words used are relevant and necessary to his purpose, which is a legitimate one. Fourthly, because the work has beauty, and both the passages dealing with sexual relations and those dealing with other matters contain, we have been told, some of his finest writing. And lastly because, judging the book as a whole, it is for the public good that this work of literature by this great writer should be available to the public. If this is not a case to which Section 4 applies, is it not difficult to conceive of any book written for publication by an author of this kind to which the section does apply?

'Members of the Jury, the test is not whether this is suitable for a young person to read: though it is a part of the strength of the defendants' case that they need not run away even from the consideration of a particular section of the community. Young people who were not ready for this book would never get through the first twenty pages. It is not the sort of book to be read by juvenile delinquents who can only read picture comics. But one has to consider the general public as a whole, and, so considered, this is a book, in my submission, and for the reasons I have ventured to give, which in the public interest should be published.

'On Section 2 which defines obscenity, I propose to deal with this quite briefly. As you know, Penguin Books have always thought and said that in real life there is nothing in this book which would in fact tend to deprave or corrupt anyone. But when you consider this there are various questions which I would ask you to bear in mind. You have heard my submission to my Lord, that among the statements of law by learned Judges, read out by my learned friend in opening this case, were statements which were not only *not* the law but the exact opposite of what the law directs. My Lord, of course, will direct you as to that.

'First, we are particularly told by Parliament to regard the book as a whole and not particular passages of it. I stress that because, almost as if the Act had not been passed, so much or the relatively little cross-examination there has been was directed, not to the effect of the book as a whole, but to particular passages. The words are "tending to deprave and corrupt". I don't know if there is a lot of difference between the two dictionaries used – mine is the *Oxford Dictionary* – but the words "deprave" and "corrupt", according to the ordinary dictionary meaning, mean in ordinary life, do they not, "effect a change of character for the worse". That is really what it comes to. There are various things which it does *not* mean, and various things which it is not your function to consider. It is *not* a question of whether you think the book is shocking. It is *not* a question of whether you think the book is disgusting or whether it is in good taste.

'Secondly, in a work published at 3s. 6d., you are to consider the question in relation to the general public and not some particular section. It is of importance that you should remember the former definition – and I mention this because again this is one of the things read out to you in opening – the former definition which in addition to the words "deprave or corrupt those into whose hands the work may fall", used the words "and whose minds are open to such immoral influences". *Those words have been expressly and carefully omitted by Parliament from the new Statutory definition, so we are not to consider some particular type of person or particular group, but the general public.**

'Thirdly, a book is not obscene merely because part of its subject matter is the relationship between people who are not married, or are married to someone else. If that made a book obscene I suppose ninety per cent of English literature would be obscene.

'Fourthly, it is not the law that the question you have to decide is whether the book may tend to corrupt or deprave. I mention this because this again was something said to you

---

* Neither the Judge nor Mr Griffith-Jones made any reference to this ingenious interpretation, which, by logical extension, would enable all the more esoteric obscenities to be sold at the lowest possible prices. But in *his* final speech (see pages 209–10) Mr Griffith-Jones offered precisely the opposite view of what the Act had done.

in opening. My learned friend used the expression "may tend", and then repeatedly said, "might tend". Let us see what the Section actually says: "If its effect, if taken as a whole, is such as to tend to deprave and corrupt persons who are likely to read it." So it is not "may tend" or "might tend".

'Fifthly, it is not the law, subject to my Lord's ruling, that a book which has a tendency to suggest impure thoughts is a book which has a tendency to deprave and corrupt. This again I mention because some observation by a Judge in a very old case was read out to you, and you were invited to consider whether the book had a tendency to suggest impure thoughts. What is the meaning of "impure thoughts"? It is evil thoughts, impure and lascivious thoughts; and if one looks at the dictionary under "l", one could add lecherous and lustful. What it means no one has the foggiest idea. If it means thoughts of sexual intercourse, then the whole population has been corrupted and depraved from a very early age. It can only mean this on the assumption that sexual intercourse is unclean and impure, and therefore thoughts about it are unclean and impure. This is obviously something quite different from the sole definition in the Act, which is whether the effect of the book if taken as a whole is such as would tend to deprave and corrupt persons who are likely to read it.

'You appreciate that you are *seriously* being asked to say by the Prosecution that this book would tend to deprave and corrupt people. To some it might seem an astonishing suggestion from the point of view of real life. Take the four-letter words. Do you really suppose anyone would be depraved by reading words they know very well? However high the purpose of this author, you might entirely disagree with what he was trying to do, but that again, of course, is not the question, is it? Because what freedom means is freedom for other people to say that with which we violently disagree. So it is not a question of whether you agree with what the author is trying to do or not.

'It is not an answer to say that if this book is obscene there are other obscene books on the market, because if that is so the answer is that they ought to be prosecuted. At the same time, when one is considering whether this has a tendency to deprave and corrupt one cannot divorce the question altogether from the climate of literature, in the sense that times change. We all know that subjects are discussed openly today which would never have been discussed only a short time ago. There are books banned at the time they were published which are now no longer banned and which no one would suggest ought not to be published today.

'Nothing, members of the Jury, will ever prevent young people from looking up certain words in the dictionary, or Shakespeare, or the Old Testament, and as long as there are medical books in the secondhand bookshops, some young people who may look at a particular diagram may not be solely influenced by a desire for medical education. We do not say for that reason that medical books should not be sold. Society cannot fix its standards by what is suitable for a young person of 14.

'My submission is that this book would not deprave or corrupt anyone in real life, young people included; with deference to my friend I should add, not even your wives or servants.' (And the Jury smiled.)

'It is not the fault of the Defence that I have not been able to assist you more under this Section. As the law is even now, the Defence has to fight this issue very largely with its hands tied behind its back. You might have thought it would assist you to hear the evidence of doctors, and of people who have to deal with those who are sexually depraved or corrupted. But as you have heard, the Defence are not allowed to call such witnesses. They are not allowed to call expert evidence as to what the tendency of this book might be for the ordinary reader. They are not allowed, on the climate of literature, to put any specific books before you. They are allowed only to give you a hazy and very general description of the sort of things which are published. They are not allowed to tell you in how many novels these four-letter words appear. You have to decide this in the air without the Defence being able to call any evidence at all under this particular head.* All you can do is to judge it as a whole in the existing climate of literature and with your own knowledge of human life.

'You see, we are a country known throughout the world for two things in particular: our literature and our democratic institutions, Parliament, trial by Jury, and so forth. Strange indeed if this were the only country where this man's work, an Englishman's work, could not be read.

'I would ask you to bear in mind that the decision is entirely your responsibility on all questions of fact. It may have seemed to you that my learned friend was reading out differing passages from the summings-up of different judges. Judges have approached this question from rather different points of view, and I suppose as long as human nature is human nature this is the sort of case in which judges may hold personal views, one judge taking one view and one another. That makes it all the more important, does it not, that you and you alone, the representatives of the public, should decide that which is your responsibility.

'In my submission the decision of the Board of Penguin Books to include this book in the publication of Lawrence's seven remaining novels which they had not already published, a decision taken responsibly and after taking into account the fact that this is, after all, Lawrence's own country, was a right decision. Lawrence lived and died suffering from a public opinion, caused by the banning of this book, that he had

* All these might have been points to be taken to the Court of Criminal Appeal, in the event of a conviction.

written a piece of pornography called *Lady Chatterley's Lover,*
and if this case has done nothing else it has for the first time
enabled this book to be dragged out into the light of day so
that we can see what it really is, and so that those who are
qualified to judge can express their opinion about it. As you
have seen in the witness box, those who have been able to
read it didn't think that it was anything like the public reputation which it has always had. But because it was banned,
students of literature among the general public had had no
opportunity of judging for themselves. The slur was never
justified. All the time, this book was the passionately sincere
book of a moralist in the puritan tradition, who believed he
had a message for us and the society in which we live, whether
we agree with this message or not. Is it not time that we
rescued Lawrence's name from the quite unjust reputation
which, because of this book, it has always had, and allowed our
people, his people, to judge for themselves its high purpose?
Members of the Jury, I leave Lawrence's reputation, and the
reputation of Penguin Books, with confidence in your hands.'

Mr Gardiner's had been a long speech – this version of it is
condensed – delivered with great fluency and disregard for the
shorthand writers; but every word carried its due weight, and
the Jury were visibly impressed.

*

Mr Griffith-Jones, for the Crown, spoke (as always) with
far greater deliberation, sometimes feeling for his words as if
in doubt as to the value of words as a vehicle of communica-
tion; a doubt which, in this trial, may well have been intensi-
fied by the Lawrentian glimpses of a new level of language.

'Members of the Jury, you can have no doubt left in your
minds now that this case, both from the point of view of
Penguins, and you may think of the literary profession and of
the public, is one of immense importance, the effect of which
will go far beyond the actual question which you have to
decide. On an issue in a matter of such gravity I am not going

to occupy, and indeed waste, your time by answering debating points which have been made against me. It is easy enough, particularly in a case of this kind, to poke fun at the Prosecution, to draw laughs as to the conduct and the observations which have passed. That can easily be done on both sides. I am not going to refer to any such matters, save two. There are two matters which have fallen from my learned friend, one in opening and one in his closing address to you, which I feel ought not to be left unchallenged or without comment.

'The first was in his opening. You may remember he mentioned the fact that in every prosecution of this kind which had taken place a director or someone connected with the company has also been charged in person, but that in this case the company alone were charged. He then went on to make this observation: "It is not for us to inquire whether in this particular case the Prosecution thought the Jury might give a verdict of 'Guilty' rather more readily if the dock were empty than if they saw an individual director sitting there, but there is nothing to stop them doing that; there is nothing to stop them doing it next time. This is a serious offence." Members of the Jury, to those whose responsibility it is to institute criminal proceedings, be they of this nature or of any other, part of their duty is to decide which of those who are connected with the transaction in question ought to be charged. That duty is undertaken, I hope, with a sense of responsibility and fairness. As in this particular case you have a firm of the highest repute, whose directors one and all have acted from the moment their attention was drawn to these possible proceedings with the utmost propriety, who have withheld the release of this book, who in order to save proceedings being taken against their retailers afforded the Prosecution evidence in order that the matter should be tested, do you think that it would be right to put Sir Allen Lane in the dock, to charge him personally? Can you imagine the comments which my learned friend would have had to make if that had been done? Members of the Jury, nobody – and he, I hope, knows it – at the Bar is held in higher respect than he, and nobody at the Bar holds him in higher respect than I. I leave that matter, I

hope without presumption, by saying it was a comment which was wholly unworthy of him.*

'The other matter is this. It has been emphasized to you in his closing address again, again, and again that you have heard no witnesses called by the Prosecution to answer the witnesses called by the Defence. Members of the Jury, this Act is perfectly clear, that expert witnesses are confined in their evidence to the literary, artistic, or other merit of the book. As to the merit of this book as literature, from the very first I have conceded – you will remember I conceded this in practically the first words I uttered in this case – that Lawrence is a great writer. I never challenged his honesty of purpose. I

* Mr Gardiner's comment had, in fact, offended the Prosecution rather badly. But in all the 1954 prosecutions except one, the publishers, authors, and printers had looked so very respectable sitting in the dock, that it *might* have been harder for the Jury to think of them as depravers and corrupters. The exception was Mr Fredric Warburg in the *Philanderer* case: he looked equally respectable, but Mr Justice Stable brought him out of the dock and gave him a seat at the solicitors' table.

never challenged that this book was a book of some merit; and you may think that, in view of the evidence which you have heard from the experts who have been called on that aspect of it, it was about right. If I understated it a little, then you will have taken note. But those were matters upon which the Prosecution never sought to argue. They were matters, therefore, upon which it would have been wholly irrelevant and redundant to call evidence for the Prosecution.

'Members of the Jury, it has been put now – it may well be that the Act perhaps has been stretched a little – that this work is a work of educational and sociological value. Upon that it may be that the Prosecution could have called witnesses. I am quite happy to leave that aspect to the book itself, to give its own evidence. I cannot believe, although it is not for me, that you or any other Jury would wish evidence called to utter such words as: "This book is not a great educational document, nor is it of any great sociological value." Goodness alone knows, you have had enough of your time occupied with a sufficient number of witnesses already in this case without hearing me ask leave to call further witnesses to say only that. Upon the question of whether this book is obscene, members of the Jury, I am barred from calling any evidence because the Act restricts me to calling evidence only as to the literary and other merits of the book.

'Although it may sound a good point to reiterate again and again that there is no evidence called to challenge this, and that much of the evidence which the witnesses gave I never challenged in cross-examination, I venture to suggest to you that it is an empty point and not the kind of point or argument upon which you are going to decide this case. You are going to decide this case, are you not, on the book, on the document itself, in accordance with what my Lord will lay down to you as being the principles of law which you are to apply.'

This might have been described as the end of the defence of the Prosecution. Criticism of the way in which the Prosecution was mounted still goes on, and will go on desultorily in legal circles for years to come. For use in argument the foregoing is the Prosecution's answer.

'There are in my submission, as I told you when I started, and indeed I do not think my learned friend quarrels with me, two questions. The first is: is this obscene? The second, arising only if you should answer the first question in the affirmative is: is its publication justified as being for the public good because it is in the interests of literature? Members of the Jury, my Lord will no doubt direct you as to the way in which you should approach those two questions. Perhaps it is not entirely easy to divorce the one from the other. The truer approach, the approach which is indicated by Parliament, is that you should weigh in the balance on the one hand the obscenity (and remember that it is the tendency to deprave and corrupt, and of course with it the possible evils which might follow) and on the other the literary merit and the other merits, any merit you can find, and say, does that weigh it down in the interests of the public? That is the way in which, I venture to suggest, (and indeed the only way) this Act, the two Sections together, can be treated for your purpose in that jury box. I say it is not very easy to divorce the two questions, but so far as we can it is convenient perhaps to deal with them under their respective headings – the obscenity question and the justification question.

'Upon the question of the meaning of obscenity my learned friend has suggested to you that the old words which are now adopted in this Act "deprave and corrupt" no longer mean, as judges have regarded them as meaning over the years, raising impure thoughts in the minds of those who now read the book. Members of the Jury, why that should have been changed, or what ground there is for suggesting that there is any change in the law in that respect, I know not. It is true that the old definition is now altered, and the words "those whose minds are open to such influences", are changed to "those who may in all the circumstances read the book". You may think that places rather a less burden upon the Prosecution than hitherto, that it rather widens the scope of this Act than otherwise, for now, irrespective of whether the person reading the book is one of a rather dull or perhaps retarded or stupid intellect, one whose mind may be open to such influences, there is not any such restricted class. It is *anyone who may read the book* in all the circumstances. In all the circumstances of this case there is no limit, is there, to the number and the kind of people who may read this book which would be on sale at every bookstall, paperstall, and bookshop, all for the price of 3s. 6d.?

'While I am dealing with this question of what the words "deprave and corrupt" mean, Mr Gardiner suggested that they entail, and must entail, a change of character. Surely that cannot be right. One can deprave and corrupt, can one not, debase, lower the minds and thoughts, the general code of behaviour and the conduct, without pointing to someone who immediately goes off and has sexual intercourse after reading the book.

'Members of the Jury, there must be standards, must there not – I say this in all seriousness, and no doubt it is a matter which you will consider as serious – which we are to maintain, some standards of morality, some standards of language and conversation, some standards of conduct which are essential to the well-being of our society. There must be, must there not, instilled in all of us, and at the earliest possible age, standards of respect, respect for the conventions of society, for the kind of conduct of which society approves, respect for other people's feeling, respect, you may think too, for the intimacy, the privacy, of relations between people. There must be instilled in all of us, must there not, standards of restraint. And when one sees what is happening today and has been happening, perhaps all the more since the war, restraint becomes all the more essential, does it not, in the education of the youth of our country, and an understanding that restraint is essential.

'Members of the Jury, you have only to read your papers to see, day by day, the results of unbridled sex. I have in fact here a document which is issued by Her Majesty's Stationery Office called *Criminal Statistics*, and I have looked through that document for 1959, last year, just to try and see what kind of picture it shows of cases which can be said to result from unrestrained sex. There were . . .' But Mr Gardiner was on his feet by this time; the *Criminal Statistics* had made no appearance before.

'With great respect, this can't be right', he said. 'This is a piece of evidence which has not been put to any witness: there is no opportunity of answering it at all, and it is not, in my respectful submission, proper that Counsel in a final speech should read something from a document, or still less tell a Jury the conclusions which he has formed from the document, when the document has not been put in.' – 'I think that is right, Mr Griffith-Jones', said the Judge inevitably.

'My Lord, if it be so, I will leave it. It is a document...' – 'It has not been referred to in the course of the case.'

'My Lord, I will leave it. One can make the comments from one's general knowledge, and, I hope your Lordship will think, make the comment properly without perhaps giving the statistics. As I say, one has only got to read one's daily papers to see the kind of thing that is happening, and it is all that type of offence,* it is all through lack of standards, lack of restraint, lack of discipline – mental, moral discipline. And why? It is because, is it not, of the lack of discipline imposed upon so many of the younger generation and the influences to which they are open: the Sunday papers, it may be, as Mr Gardiner has already suggested, the cinema, it may be, and, members of the Jury, literature, it may be. How necessary, therefore, it is to bear in mind these considerations when the decision which you have to take is whether or not a book of this kind, this book in particular, has a tendency to deprave and corrupt.

'Members of the Jury, my learned friend has anticipated – as I certainly had anticipated that he would anticipate – the comments, or some of the comments, that I was going to make to you, or rather the arguments that I was going to put before you. It is perfectly true that I am going to urge upon you that it is *you* who have to decide this case; it is not the various witnesses whose views you have heard; it is you, and you alone. You may think – I do not say this in any sense as

---

* This seems to have meant not that the *Criminal Statistics* are all about sex offences, but that the daily papers are. No objection was taken that sex offences sell more papers than larceny and shopbreaking.

criticism, for perhaps a little more latitude, and quite rightly so, is allowed to the Defence than the Prosecution in all criminal cases – that while witnesses are called as experts to give their views upon the literary merits and the sociological merits and the educational merits, no effort has been spared to impress upon you what also is in fact the view they take as to whether this book is obscene or not.

'Whom have we had? Bishops, prebendaries, other clergymen, the Master of the Temple, schoolteachers and a fashion page editor, a young girl who has just started her first novel, all under the guise of literary experts or sociological experts or educational experts; and there has not been one that has not been asked whether he has got children.' (In fact, Mr Gardiner had been rather more discriminating than this.) 'What possible relevance, members of the Jury, has that question, unless it be to suggest that, since he is there giving this evidence, having children indicates that he does not think there is anything wrong in the book? "Are you a Roman Catholic?" or "Are you a Presbyterian?" What possible relevance, I ask you? What possible relevance unless it be to ram down your throats that here again is a Presbyterian who does not, apparently, think that this book is obscene? And then, to one of them, "Would you feel any embarrassment in discussing this book in your class?" That, under the guise of educational value! Members of the Jury, you will not be brow-beaten by evidence given by these people upon this question, in effect given as to what they think of this book on the question of whether it is obscene or not. You will judge this as ordinary men and women, with your feet, I trust, firmly planted upon the ground.

'And I do say to you – as my learned friend anticipated that I would – I do say to you, are these views that you have heard from these most eminent and academic ladies and gentlemen, are they really of such value as the views which you (perhaps, if I may say so, without the eminence and without the academic learning that they possess) hold and can see from the ordinary life in which you live?

'Members of the Jury, what is said of this book by these witnesses and by the Defence as a whole? It is said to be in support of marriage. If you accept that, if you think that that is a realistic view of this book, so be it, members of the Jury. Then it is not obscene and I suppose its publication will be justified on educational grounds, or perhaps religious grounds, I know not. But I do not seek to draw fun simply for the fun of drawing fun at their expense by such comments as I make, because let it not be thought for one moment that I question their absolute integrity; I do not. But I do suggest that they have got what in Scotland I think is said to be a bee in their bonnet about this matter, and indeed, when one sees and hears some of them launching themselves at the first opportunity, with the first question that is asked of them, into a sermon or a lecture, according to their vocations in this world, with apostolic fervour, as they did, one cannot help feeling that, sincerely and honestly as they feel, they feel in such a way that common sense perhaps has gone by the board. You have this reverend gentleman regarding this book as a most impressive statement of the Christian view of marriage. Well, there it is.

'It is said that this book condemns promiscuity. Does it? We have dealt with this matter in cross-examination. He said I have not cross-examined everybody. You may feel thankful I have not repeated the points I had to make by putting them to everybody who suggested that this book did not condone promiscuity. But it does, doesn't it? The earlier sexual experiences of both parties, then Michaelis, then Mellors – it is said that this is only showing how perfect sexual intercourse can lead to ultimate happiness. Members of the Jury, the short answer to that view of the matter is this, which I think I put to one witness: what is there in this book to suggest that if the sexual intercourse between Lady Chatterley and Mellors had not eventually turned out to be successful she would not have gone on and on and on elsewhere until she did find it? Indeed it follows, does it not, from what is said to be the main theme of the book – the search and the importance of finding somebody with whom you can have satisfactory sexual intercourse – that until you do find that person you go on looking for him, married or unmarried?

'It was put forward during the course of the evidence, when we had the Bishop of Woolwich here, that this was a book of ethical value! The bishop himself, however, knocked that argument upon the head when he said, "I would not say it was of instructional value upon the subject of ethics." Members of the Jury, I do not suppose that there will be any of you who will disagree with him upon that point.

'"Treatment of sex on a holy basis", said Mrs Russell' (Miss Dilys Powell). 'Can *that* be a realistic view? Is *that* the kind of way in which the young boys and men leaving school, thousands of them, tens of thousands every year, I suppose, leaving school at the age of 15, going into their first jobs this last September, is *that* how they are going to read this book – as a treatment of sex on a holy basis – or is it wholly unrealistic to think that they are?

'Then the bishop again – to return to him – goes one better than Mrs Russell. "Something sacred," he said, "in a real sense as an act of holy communion." Do you think that that is how the girls working in the factory are going to read this book – as something sacred, in a real sense as an act of holy communion – or does it put my Lord Bishop, with all respect to him, wholly out of touch with a very large percentage of the number of people who are going to buy this book at 3s. 6d.?

'"A book of moral purpose", said the Rev. Mr Hopkinson. What moral purpose do you read into this book, I wonder? What moral purpose do you think that all the young people who are going to read this book are going to see in it?

'"An antidote", said Mr Hemming, the psychologist. Let me quote: "It is an antidote, a positive antidote to the shallow, superficial values of sex which are widely current today and which are now corrupting the attitude of young people towards sex." I do not know – let us be serious – but as I say, no doubt it was honest. But *can* it be said that this book offers "an antidote to the shallow and superficial values of sex which are widely current today and corrupting the attitude of young people"?

'Miss Rebecca West, for whom, I am quite sure, we all

have the highest respect and regard, was asked about this book and gave, you remember, a number of rather long answers to the questions that were put to her.' Mr Griffith-Jones quoted one of them – 'perhaps not *too* long a one', was his subtle disparagement.'"The idea that the story is padding cannot be true; as a matter of fact the book has that story because it was designed from the first as an allegory. Behind the book the allegory which he intended was that here was a culture that had become sterile and unhelpful to man's deepest needs, and he wanted to have the whole of civilization realizing that it was not living fully enough, that it would be exploited in various ways if it did not try to get down to the springs of its being and live more fully, and bring its spiritual gifts into play. The baronet and his impotence are a symbol of the impotent culture of his time, and the love affair with the gamekeeper was a calling, a return of the soul to the more intense life that he felt when people had had a different culture, such as the cultural basis of religious faith." I have no doubt that with the learning and reading that lies behind Miss Rebecca West she is capable of reading all that into this book, but I ask you, is that typical of the effect that this book will have upon the average reader, and all the more, the average young reader? Are they really going to see an allegory in the thing? Is the baronet in his impotence going to be read by them as a symbol of the impotent culture of that time, the 1920s? Or the love affair with the gamekeeper a calling, a return of the soul, to the more intense life that he felt when people had had a different culture? Is that how they are going to read it?

'Members of the Jury, surely if you, as Parliament has decided, are to judge this issue, you have got to approach the question from some quite different viewpoint if you are going to be anything approaching realistic. One wonders perhaps, reading, or listening to, that evidence, and all the more when one reads through some of the transcript, whether one is talking the same language, whether these words are being used by these ladies and gentlemen in the same sense as by the ordinary man and woman. Mrs Bennett – we had a long discussion, she and I, about marriage, before it turned out she did not mean marriage in the ordinary way of wedlock at all. No, I venture to submit to you that the reality of this position is really quite different. The effect this book will have upon those who read it and the way it will be understood by those who read it is quite different.

'One has a glimpse, perhaps, of the reality in some of the evidence which was given. Mr Hoggart was asked: "As far as the young people under your care are concerned, would you think, having regard to what you said about this book, that this was a proper book for them to read?" His answer was: "Viewed purely in the abstract, I would think it proper, if they came to me to ask me if they could read it, to tell them to ask their parents, and probably I should give them a note to their parents asking them if they could read it, but I would not take that responsibility upon myself." Why not? *Why not?* If this book has no tendency to deprave and corrupt, why shouldn't Mr Hoggart take the responsibility of telling them to read it? What responsibility had he?

'The Master of the Temple too: "I think it would be indecent to show scenes such as described in this book on the cinema, still more to do them in public." *Why?* He said this book did not make the reader an onlooker but rather brought the reader into the position of one of the parties taking part in the bout. Doesn't that make it all the worse? [*Sic.*] What is the logic in it? If this book is all right to read why should not the same thing be seen? And if what is seen is obscene, how comes it that what is written, and written in this way, is harmless?' To many in Court it seemed at this moment that words could not indeed have the same meaning for Mr Griffith-Jones as for ordinary men and women.

'Mr Lambert, the Assistant [Literary] Editor of the *Sunday Times,* perhaps gave the answer which was more fatal to my learned friend's case than any other answer. I asked him: "Tell me, Mr Lambert: when the boy brought it back to school, why did he bring it back?" Answer: "I don't remember, but it was a book we had all heard of when he brought it back." I asked: "Did he bring it back because it was of such high literary merit that he thought his companions at school ought to read it?" Answer: "I doubt that." Question: "He brought it back because it was regarded as a dirty book?" Answer: "I expect so." Question: "And that is the kind of book boys like to read?" Answer: "No, I would not have said that." Question: "Would I be doing you an injustice if I suggested that that was the reason why you read it?" Answer: "Undoubtedly it was one of the reasons; but I had already read many others of Lawrence's books." Question: "That may well be so, but for those perhaps who had not read Lawrence's books do you think that that was the main reason for their reading it?" And he said: "The main reason why they first looked into it, certainly, yes." There we are getting, are we not, at least a touch of realism in this evidence that we have heard so much of.

'Members of the Jury, you have this book. You have its effect, as I suggest it must be, on the mind of those, or many of those, reading it. Sometimes it is said of a book, "Ah well, that may be so, but look at the book as a whole, as you have to, and you see the bad things are condemned. It carries in it a plain lesson. What you might suggest is depraving is not put in that way at all. Here there is real moral virtue in a book." Do we find anything of that kind in this book? Again I am asking you to look at it not from the Olympian heights, but as the ordinary man in the street. Do you think when you read that book that, generally speaking, its emphasis is upon the thrill and the sensation of these two persons having sexual intercourse together? Is there really anything other of any weight that this book contains? Is there any moral teaching in it at all? Promiscuity I have dealt with. Adultery the whole way through.' (Mr Griffith-Jones was back on his main theme: the greater offence of human biology when it is adulterous.) 'Never a word to suggest really it is wrong, save that before the lady went with Michaelis for the first time there were apparently some doubts as to whether she should leave her husband or not.

'There is no basis for any real love. Talk of "lasting communion" between these two people, a "lasting partnership" –

how *can* there be when we have not a word spoken between them until right at the end of the book when they have decided to get their respective divorces and are planning the future? Up to that time, during the time they were having their thirteen first bouts, there is not a single word spoken between them at any other time than just before, during, or afterwards, or about anything other than sex. Not only is there not a word spoken, but you know there is not an occasion when such a word *could* be spoken. Is that a book which suggests a permanent and satisfactory union of love between man and woman, when all they have done before they decide to run away and get married and get their respective divorces is to copulate thirteen times, and say nothing else to one another at all, save that he has told her very briefly in about half a page of his previous history and she may have uttered one or two sentences. One talks of educational value. Is that the way to suggest to young people that they can find permanent happiness in marriage, that they have only got to find somebody with whom they can copulate satisfactorily and all will be well, and there is no need to know anything more about them whatsoever?

'Members of the Jury, in this book it may be, and I don't dissent from it, there is much that is beautifully written. Some is less well written. But what is the general background against which we see these so-called lessons? It is the foul language, isn't it, as I said to you when I opened, and other little matters of sex drawn in on every conceivable opportunity like the gondolier and Mrs Bolton's breasts.

'Then the language. Miss Helen Gardner said: "I think by the very fact that this **word is** used so frequently in the book, that with every subse**quent use the** original shock is diminished ..." I suppose that is **put as** mitigation for the use of this language. Is it? Or, if it be right, is it not a terrible thing to say, "It's all right; if we forget about the shock of using this language, if we use it sufficient times, no one will be shocked, everybody will be using it and it will all be all right"? Can you not apply the same test to everything? Filthy pictures – if you look at them a number of times, the shock, the effect, will die out and so we can have everything flooded with filthy pictures? Cinemas, even the Sunday papers again: read them enough times and it does not matter what is printed because we get used to it and the shock disappears? Members of the Jury, that is not an argument, is it, that can seriously be put forward as an argument why books should contain language such as this. One gentleman comes and says: "I heard a man say 'fuck' three times running as I came into court this morning.' Is there any relationship at all between the use of the word in that sense, and the sense in which it is used in the conversation which appears in the book? This book is by every means drawing the reader's attention to the satisfaction of the acts of sexual intercourse.

'I do not desire to repeat what I have already said. It may be that I have said enough. But I have a little more to say upon the justification aspect. I venture to suggest to you that, read not as lecturers, bishops, and so on would read it, but read as ordinary, common men and women would read it – and by the word "common" I include all of us, that is to say, those who are not of great literary or other academic qualifications – is it likely to deprave and corrupt? Will it suggest impure thoughts? Do you think it will have a tendency to lead to a wholly false conception of what proper thought and conduct ought to be in times when some proper conception is so vitally needed? I submit to you that there can be but one answer.

'Members of the Jury, may I say a few words about the defence? The real defence, as I understand it (although I don't know that I am justified in saying that because it has been said equally strongly that it is not obscene) is the justification. Its literary merit, its educational merit, and its sociological merit, with possibly ethics thrown in. You see, you have to ask yourselves here, if you come to the conclusion that there *is* a tendency to deprave and corrupt: what is the justification? What good, what public good, is being done by this book to offset, to outweigh, the harm? It is said that the literary merit depends not only upon the actual writing of the book, but quite naturally upon its theme, and we have heard a great deal of evidence about the author's intention. I submit to you again, the author's intention is irrelevant as such; it only becomes relevant as it shows itself through this book.

'Its themes are threefold, as they are put before you: the need for perfect sexual relationships, to be put under the heading of "tenderness"; secondly, that sex should be discussed without shame; and, thirdly, a treatise on the effects, the harmful effects, of the industrialization of the country. One can discount the third because one can almost add up the number of words which are devoted to that particular theme. What about tenderness? is that a theme which it is in the public good to read as expressed in this book? I will tell you how it is expressed in this book, in the words of the book itself: "Tenderness, really – cunt tenderness. Sex is really the closest touch of all. Cunt tenderness." That is the tenderness that this book is advocating through the mouth of one of its chief characters. And again may I quote from my note: "I believe in something" – this is Mellors speaking – "I believe in being warm-hearted. I believe especially in being warm-hearted in love. I believe that if men could fuck with warm hearts and women took it warm-heartedly, everything would come all right." That is put before you as a theme which justifies this book for the public good, the theme advocating to the young of this country who are going to read the book. "Fuck warm-heartedly and everything will come all right." Does it justify it?

Counsel then poured scorn on Mr Graham Hough's belief that Lawrence had sought 'language in which sex could be discussed openly and not irreverently'. As 'examples of sex being discussed not irreverently' he read passages from pages 219 and 232.

'Members of the Jury, let me in conclusion come back to the summing-up of Mr Justice Stable, upon which Mr Gardiner has so much relied in this case: "It is the business of the parents and teachers", he said, "and the environment of society to see, so far as possible, that those ideas" – he is talking about the adolescent ideas of young people – "that those ideas are wisely and naturally directed to the fulfilment of a balanced life." Are the ideas, the theme, the language which this book contains directed to the fulfilment of a balanced life? Are authors exempt from those obligations which lie upon society – because books surely are as much a part of the environment of society as anything else, books which are now being read by everybody? Just let us see. I ask your forgiveness, if it be necessary, for referring to just two other passages in the book because it may have been noticed that in my learned friend's address to you the one thing which he never referred you to at all was the contents of this book; and, after all, it is this book that you are trying and it is this book which constitutes the evidence upon which I rely.

'Would you look at page 258. It is a passage which I have not – and I do not think anybody has – referred to during the course of cross-examination, or indeed at any time during this trial. It is that passage which describes what is called the "night of sensual passion".

' "It was a night of sensual passion, in which she was a little startled and almost unwilling: yet it pierced again with piercing thrills of sensuality, different, sharper, more terrible than the thrills of tenderness, but, at the moment, more desirable. Though a little frightened, she let him have his way . . ." Not very easy, sometimes, not very easy, you know, to know what in fact he is driving at in that passage.' This unexpected and totally unheralded innuendo visibly shocked some members of the Jury. ' "Though a little frightened, she let him have his way, and the reckless, shameless sensuality shook her to her foundations, stripped her to the very last, and made a different woman of her. It was not really love. It was not voluptuousness. It was sensuality sharp and searing as fire, burning the soul to tinder." I don't know: is this stuff having a good influence on the young reader? "Burning out the shames, the deepest, oldest shames, in the most secret places. It cost her an effort to let him have his way and his will of her." One wonders why, with all the experiences that had gone before!' Again the innuendo, again the shock.

Mr Griffith-Jones then went on to the passage where Constance was thinking about the story of Abélard and

Héloïse. '"She had to be a passive, consenting thing, like a slave, a physical slave. Yet the passion licked round her, consuming, and when the sensual flame of it pressed through her bowels and breast, she really thought she was dying: yet a poignant, marvellous death. She had often wondered what Abélard meant, when he said that in their year of love he and Héloïse had passed through all the stages and refinements of passion." Members of the Jury, you may wonder what Abélard meant. You may wonder who Abélard was. Abélard was a man . . .'

But Mr Gardiner decided that Mr Griffith-Jones, again, was giving evidence – and evidence that no witness had been asked to give. 'With the greatest respect, I have called, I think, thirty-five witnesses. This passage was not read in opening; it was not put to a single one of those witnesses; apparently it has been saved up for the final speech. My learned friend is now telling the Jury his view of who Abélard was. There is no evidence about it at all.' – 'I will leave out who Abélard was', said Mr Griffith-Jones.

But Mr Justice Byrne thought that Abélard should be kept in. 'Certainly I think you are quite entitled to deal with this passage in your final speech', said the Judge. 'On the question of obscenity the book is the only evidence before the Jury.'

'Indeed, members of the Jury,' said Mr Griffith-Jones gratefully, 'unless I was so entitled I should have had to have read the whole book to you. I do read this passage, and you will read it, and, if you can, try to understand it. "She had often wondered what Abélard meant, when he said that in their year of love he and Héloïse had passed through all the stages and refinements of passion. The same thing, a thousand years ago: ten thousand years ago! The same on the Greek vases, everywhere! The refinements of passion, the extravagance of sensuality! And necessary, forever necessary, to burn out false shames and smelt out the heaviest ore of the body into purity. With the fire of sheer sensuality." Forever necessary, this conduct, whatever it was, between, incidentally, quite incidentally, a married woman and a married man.

'"In the short summer night she learnt so much. She would

have thought a woman would have died of shame. Instead of which the shame died. Shame, which is fear; the deep organic shame, the old, old physical fear which crouches in the bodily roots of us, and can only be chased away by the sensual fire, at last it was roused up and routed by the phallic hunt of the man, . . ." Perhaps it will not have escaped you what Mr Gardiner had invited you to remember, that "phallic" is a holy word, a religious word, always used in connexion with holiness. Read it, and see whether it is used in that sense here. ". . . at last it was roused up and routed by the phallic hunt of the man, and she came to the very heart of the jungle of her-self. She felt, now, she had come to the real bedrock of her nature, and was essentially shameless. She was her sensual self, naked and unashamed." I do not know what it means; you will have to think. "She felt a triumph, almost a vain-glory. So! That was how it was! That was life! That was how oneself really was! There was nothing left to disguise or be ashamed of. She shared her ultimate nakedness with a man, another being. And what a reckless devil the man was! really like a devil! One had to be strong to bear him. But it took some getting at, the core of the physical jungle, the last and deepest recess of organic shame.'' What does it mean?' asked Mr Griffith-Jones, on this fifth day of the trial.

'"The phallus alone could explore it. And how he had pressed in on her! And how, in fear, she had hated it. But how she had really wanted it! She knew now. At the bottom of her soul, fundamentally, she had needed this phallic hunting out, she had secretly wanted it, and she had believed that she would never get it. Now suddenly there it was, and a man was sharing her last and final nakedness, she was shameless.

'"What liars the poets and everybody were! They made one think one wanted sentiment. When what one supremely wan-ted was this piercing, consuming, rather awful sensuality. To find a man who dared do it, without shame or sin or final misgiving! If he had been ashamed afterwards, and made one feel ashamed, how awful! What a pity most men are so doggy, a bit shameful, like Clifford! Like Michaelis even! Both sensu-ally a bit doggy and humiliating. The supreme pleasure of the mind! And what is that to a woman? What is it, really, to the man either! He becomes merely messy and doggy, even in his mind. It needs sheer sensuality even to purify and quicken the mind. Sheer fiery sensuality, not messiness.

'"Ah, God, how rare a thing a man is! They are all dogs that trot and sniff and copulate. To have found a man who was not afraid and not ashamed! She looked at him now, sleeping so like a wild animal asleep, gone, gone in the remoteness of it. She nestled down, not to be away from him."

'I do not know, I do not suggest. There is more than one meaning which you can put to those two pages, if you want to take offence. Who knows what is the effect on the young man or woman reading those two pages? What is he or she going to think? Is it going to be a good influence, or can it only corrupt and deprave? What is the tendency of it? Where is the justification contained? Where again is the good that a book can do, any book which contains a passage such as that?

'Will you turn to page 217? We will read from the bottom of the page. "'Fancy that we are here!' she said, looking down at him. He was lying watching her, stroking her breasts with his fingers, under the thin nightdress. When he was warm and smoothed out, he looked young and handsome. His eyes could look so warm. And she was fresh and young like a flower. 'I want to take this off!' she said, gathering the thin batiste nightdress and pulling it over her head. She sat there with bare shoulders and longish breasts faintly golden. He loved to make her breasts swing softly, like bells." I do not know, members of the Jury, but is this a passage which gives a theme? Why introduce a little striptease into it at all? What is the point of taking off the nightdress?

'What a passage!' said Mr Griffith-Jones after reading on. 'Is *that* the kind of thing that qualifies a book as great literature? You would have to go, would you not, some way in the Charing Cross Road, in the back streets of Paris, even Port Said, to find a description of sexual intercourse which is perhaps as lurid as that one. And yet one is told here, and told again by the reverend gentleman, Mr Tytler, "this book is a suitable subject for discussion in youth clubs". I don't know whether any of you have had any experience of youth clubs. Can you imagine the bawdiness of what would follow, however seriously the discussion might be conducted, a discussion of that passage and similar passages in this book, in any youth club?

'Members of the Jury, this book has been likened to *Antony and Cleopatra*. Is it really possible to compare the two? Is it possible to bracket them in the same way, as literature? Is it possible to compare the difference in the effect that the one will have and the other will have?

'Let all these witnesses hold their views, and hold them sincerely, as they no doubt do. It is not they who are deciding this case. Parliament has said that you, twelve men and women of the community, the ordinary community if you will forgive me for saying so, the ordinary run of life, must decide, just in the same way as twelve men and women decide all the cases in this Court – not the so-called experts, not the experts on anything. I ask you to bring to bear upon this matter your knowledge of the world and of the life which the average person leads. I respectfully submit to you that the effect upon that average person must be to deprave and corrupt, must be to lower the general standards of thought, conduct, and decency, and must be the very opposite to encouraging that restraint in sexual matters which is so all-important at the present time.

'I submit to you further that there is nothing in this document which is of such great value as literature, from an educational point of view, or from a sociological point of view, nothing in this book of such value, as can justify its publication for the public good.'

Having spoken his final words with studied emphasis, Mr Griffith-Jones sat down; and everyone in Court turned to Mr Justice Byrne, who was assembling his notes for the final act in a drama that was nearing the end of its fifth day.

*

'Members of the Jury,' his Lordship began, 'you have listened with the greatest care and attention to this case, and you have read this book. Now the time is rapidly approaching when you will have to return a verdict. It is just as well, in case you have not served on a jury before, that I should say a few words to you with regard to the function of the Judge and the function of the Jury. As Mr Gardiner told you, quite rightly, questions of law are my province. You have to accept the law from me as what I tell you it is, having the consolation of knowing that if my law is wrong it can be corrected elsewhere.

'Then you are the sole judges of the facts. They are nothing to do with me. They are your province, and your province alone. If during the course of the observations which I shall have to make to you I express any opinion, or I appear to express any opinion, you will pay not the slightest attention to it, unless it happens to coincide with your own opinion. You are the judges of fact. As we all know, in these days the world seems to be full of experts. There is not a subject you can think of where there is not to be found an expert who will be able, or says he will be able, to deal with the situation; but *our criminal law in this country is based upon the view that a jury takes of the facts and not upon the view that experts may have*.*

'There are two limbs to this case, and they cannot be dealt with both at once. They must be taken separately in order that you shall see what the position is so far as the law is concerned. Before I tell you anything about the law let me say this to you. This case is quite plainly, is it not, an important case? Every criminal case is important to the defendant who is charged with the commission of an offence. Here it is quite true that the dock is empty, that a company is charged, and it is a company, as you know, that bears the highest reputation and a company that has acted with the utmost propriety in regard to this matter.

* In the event of a conviction and appeal, this would presumably have been pleaded as a misdirection. For if Parliament makes 'scientific merits' relevant, and provides for the calling of scientific experts, can a Judge properly tell a jury to ignore such evidence and form their own scientific views? If not, are literary merits subject to a different test?

'You will recollect that publication has to be proved; the offence is *publishing* an obscene article. All that is meant by publishing for the purpose of this case is handing a copy of this book to somebody. It was arranged, agreed, that the company, rather than distribute copies of this book to some bookseller so that he could publish it and could be prosecuted, said: "No, we won't allow anybody to take our place. We, the company, ourselves will publish it." You will recollect that it was arranged that a police officer should go to their office and be handed a copy or copies of the book. As I say, the company have acted with great propriety. It is an important case from their point of view. Two of the directors who have given evidence have told you that they have for some time desired to publish this novel by Lawrence, but they felt, and incidentally you may think that it is not without significance, that they were unable to publish it until 1959 when the Statute was passed under which this Prosecution is taking place, which gave them as defendants the right to call evidence with regard to literary or other merits connected with the publication.

'Now it is an important case from the point of view of the defendant company, but it is an equally important case from the point of view of the public which you represent. Because is it right or is it wrong to say that in these days our moral standards have reached a low ebb? And you, of course, will not exercise your minds about questions of taste or the functions of a censor, but you will decide whether it has been proved beyond reasonable doubt that this book is obscene. That is the first question.

'How the Statute puts the matter is this: it provides that an article shall be deemed to be obscene if its effect is, if taken as a whole, such as to tend to deprave and corrupt persons who are likely, having regard to all relevant circumstances, to read the matter contained in it. Of course, the first thing you would want to know is, what is meant by the words "to deprave and corrupt", and you have had those words defined from dictionaries. One was the Oxford Dictionary, and I think it would be quite fair to put it in this way, that to deprave means to make morally bad, to pervert, to debase, or corrupt morally. The words "to corrupt" mean to render morally unsound or rotten, to destroy the moral purity or chastity of, to pervert or ruin a good quality, to debase, to defile. Those are the meanings of those two words. And you will observe that no *intent* to deprave or corrupt need be proved in order that this offence shall be committed. It is an objective test. Having read the book the question is, does it tend to deprave or corrupt?

'Now what are the relevant circumstances? Who are the people, having regard to the relevant circumstances, who are likely to read the book? Well, what we know about it is this, it was to be put, or is to be put, according to the verdict you give, upon the market at a price of 3s. 6d. a copy, which is by no means, you may think, an excessive price for the book. In these days when not only high wages but shall I say high pocket-money to younger members of the community are the order of the day, 3s. 6d., you might think, would be putting this book within the grasp of a vast mass of the population. You must bear that in mind in deciding whether there is a tendency to deprave and corrupt persons who are likely, having regard to all the relevant circumstances, to read the matter contained in it.

'Well now, evidence has been given in this case by a number of witnesses called on behalf of the defendant company, and I am not prepared to say that some of the evidence that they gave was not relevant upon this first question that you have to decide, as to whether the book is obscene. But a good deal of the evidence that they gave was certainly not relevant to this issue of obscenity. The evidence that you have to consider with regard to whether this book is obscene, which is the first question you have to decide, is the evidence of the book itself.

'Now, how are you to do it? You must consider the book as a whole. You must not select a passage here and a passage there and say, for the sake of argument, "Well, we think *that* is obscene and we think *that* is obscene." You must take the book as a whole. Another thing you must not do is this: you must not regard yourselves as a board of censors with blue pencil in hand, saying to yourselves, "Well, I don't think it is very desirable that that piece should be put in and I think we will cut out that piece." You are not acting as a board of censors. You are deciding whether it has been proved that the offence of publishing an obscene publication has been committed.

'You will also bear in mind that it is not a question of taste. When Mr Gardiner opened this case on behalf of his clients before you read the book, you may remember that he said you would be shocked and that you might be disgusted when you read the book. Well now, of course, there is a considerable difference between that which shocks and disgusts and that which depraves and corrupts. Therefore the mere fact that you are shocked or disgusted, the mere fact that you hate the sight of the book when you have read it, does not solve the question as to whether you are satisfied beyond reasonable doubt that the tendency of the book is to deprave and corrupt. Many observations made by judges have been cited to you by learned Counsel. I have no doubt you will pay very great attention to them, but there is just one passage that I would like to draw your attention to simply for this reason, that it puts in words very much better than I could put it the view that I would like you to bear in mind in deciding this case. I refer to some observations by Mr Justice Devlin (as he then was) when he was engaged in trying a case* similar to this, which in those days was called Criminal Libel. What he is reported as having said is this: "Then there is obscene libel; and just as loyalty is one of the things which is essential to the well-being of a nation, so some sense of morality is something that is essential to the well-being of a nation, and to the healthy life of the community; and, accordingly, anyone who seeks, by his writing, to corrupt that fundamental sense of morality is guilty of obscene libel." I would only venture to make this difference in the words that he used: where he says, ". . . and accordingly, anyone who seeks by his writing to corrupt", I would prefer to say,

* *The Image and the Search.*

"... and accordingly, anyone who by his writing *tends* to corrupt that fundamental sense of morality is guilty of an obscene libel".

'And then he went on to say this. "Of course, there is a right to express oneself, either in pictures or in literature. People who hold strong political views are often anxious to say exactly what they think, irrespective of any restraint, and so too a creative writer or a creative artist, one can well understand, naturally desires complete freedom within which to express his talents or his genius. But he is a member of the community like any other member of the community. He is under the same obligation to other members of the community as any other is, not to do harm, either mentally or physically or spiritually, and if there is a conflict between an artist or writer in his desire for self-expression, and the sense that morality is fundamental to the well-being of the community, if there is such a conflict, then it is morality that must prevail."

'Well now, that is the duty that you have to perform. Having read that book, you must ask yourselves, as men and women of this world, not with prudish minds but with liberal minds, the question: is the tendency of that book to deprave and corrupt those who are likely to read it? Because, you know, once a book goes into circulation it does not spend its time in the rarefied atmosphere of some academic institution where the young mind will be perhaps directed to it and shown how to approach it and have indicated to it the real meaning of it, and so forth; it finds its way into the bookshops and on to bookstalls, at 3s. 6d. a time, into public libraries, where it is available for all and sundry to read. And you must ask yourselves, looking at that book, reading it dispassionately: are you satisfied beyond reasonable doubt that it has a tendency to deprave and corrupt?

'You have been told by some of the witnesses who gave evidence upon the other limbs of this case – with which I will deal in due course – you have been told by them all kinds of things about its meaning. Those witnesses, all of them, or nearly all of them, men or women of letters, some of them sociologists, some of them psychologists, came to tell you about the ethics of the matter. They, it may be (for many of them have been students of this author for many years) are able to read into that book some message or some meaning that they decide the author is trying to convey, and nobody, of course, for one moment questions the honesty of their opinions. You have got to look at that book as a book that you yourselves might have bought for 3s. 6d. at a bookstall and read, and you must ask yourselves the question: does it tend to deprave and corrupt?

'Now, what is the story that the book tells? You are the judges of that. You have had all kinds of opinions expressed with regard to it. It has been said to be a moral tract. It has been said to be a virtuous and puritanical production, and it was said to be a book that Christians should read. You had all those expressions of opinion about it. But what do *you* think about it? Whether some of you have a great knowledge of Lawrence as an author, I know not; but what do *you* think of that book, reading it for yourselves? What is the story? Is it right to say that the story is the story of a woman who first of all, before she is married, has sexual intercourse and then, after marriage, when her husband has met with disaster in the war and has become confined to a wheelchair, paralysed from the waist downwards, after marriage, she, living with her husband in this dreary place of Wragby (I think it was called), commits adultery on two occasions with somebody called Michaelis while her husband is downstairs in the same house, and then proceeds to have adulterous intercourse with her husband's gamekeeper? And that is described – it is for you to say; if you do not agree with what I am saying now you will pay no attention to it – that is described in the most lurid way, and the whole sensuality and passion of the various pieces of sexual intercourse is fully and completely described.

'If you have any reasonable doubt as to whether it has been proved to your satisfaction that the tendency of the book is to deprave and corrupt morals, of course you will acquit, and that will be an end of this case. But, on the other hand, if with your knowledge of the world and with your knowledge now of that book, having read it for yourselves, you are satisfied beyond reasonable doubt that that book has a tendency to deprave and corrupt those who might, in the circumstances, be expected to read it, you, of course, will not hesitate to say so.

'That really is the first limb of this case; and, as I said to you, before 1959, before the passing of the Obscene Publications Act of that year, the defendant company felt, although they wished to do so, that they could not publish that book because, prior to the passing of the Statute under which this charge is made, defendants were not allowed by law to call any evidence with regard to the literary or other merits of the book. Thus there was simply the book for the Jury to read, and it was for the Jury then to determine the question as to whether there was a tendency to deprave and corrupt the morals of persons who might read it and the morals, as the old law put it, "of persons whose minds might be affected by such matter" – or words to that effect.

'But Section 4 of the new Act – and it is only right that you should have this quite clearly before you – provides that a person shall not be convicted if it is proved that publication of the article in question is justified as being for the public good on the grounds that it is in the interests of science, literature, art, or learning, or other objects of general concern. By Sub-section (2) of the same Section it is provided "that the opinion of experts as to the literary, artistic, scientific, or other merits of an article may be admitted in any proceedings under this Act either to establish or to negative the said ground". It is by virtue of that Sub-section that the defendants have called this body of evidence before you.

'As I understand that Section, it was not the intention of Parliament to provide immunity to an author or publisher who published an obscene book *simply* because that work had literary or other merits. In my own view, and I am telling you this as a matter of law, the important words in that Section are the words that the publication "is justified as being for the public good"; and that being so I give you this direction as a matter of law. If you are not satisfied that the book is obscene, of course, as I have told you, that is an end of the case; you acquit. But if, on the other hand, you are satisfied that the book is an obscene book, then you must go on to consider this further question, and I give you this direction with regard to it. The question is: have the defendants established the probability that the merits of the book as a novel are so high that they outbalance the obscenity, so that its publication is for the public good? In other words, in my view, it was not the intention of Parliament by that Section to say, "Well, if somebody who is a skilful author is prepared to write filth, and write it very well, he will escape conviction." What has to be established, that is to say the probability of the matter has to be established, is that the merits of the book are so high that they outbalance the obscenity so that its publication is for the public good.

'The burden of proof, as lawyers call it, is in this Section put upon the defendants. Whether the book is obscene or not – there the onus of proof is put upon the Prosecution. The Prosecution, as you know, have to prove "beyond reasonable doubt". If there is a reasonable doubt, the Jury acquit. In *this* Section the *defendants* had to prove these matters, and that means they had *not* got to prove beyond reasonable doubt; all they have to do is to satisfy you as to the probability of the matter which they are called upon to establish. Thus, if you come to the conclusion that this book is obscene, you must ask yourselves this further question. I will repeat it once again so that you shall have it in mind. Have the defendants established the probability that the merits of the book as a novel are so high that they outbalance the obscenity, so that its publication is for the public good?

'As I say, a vast number of witnesses have been called. It is conceded by the Prosecution that this is a book of some literary merit. You observed that many of the witnesses were in fact not cross-examined. Indeed, it would be very difficult for the Prosecution to adopt any other attitude, you may think, because, after all, the evidence – which is undisputed – is that D. H. Lawrence is one of the great authors of the twentieth century.' (It may be observed here, with respect, that the

Prosecution had frequently found it possible to cross-examine in a way that presented Lawrence as a semi-literate pornographer – 'Is *that* good writing?' and so on.) 'Although many of the witnesses said that this was by no means his best book, nevertheless they all subscribed to the fact that it was a book of literary merit.

'It has also been said to be a book of other merit as well, and as I have told you the Statute speaks of literary merit and of "objects of general concern". It has been said by witnesses called on behalf of the defendants that it is a book of merit, not only literary merit, but also from a sociological point of view, from an ethical point of view, and from an educational point of view. That is what has been said.

'It will be necessary, therefore, for me to remind you of some of the evidence that has been given by those witnesses who were called before you on behalf of the defendants. You will recollect I told you that those witnesses were called in order to assist you. You are not governed by the opinions which they have expressed. You are the judges of the matter. You decide whether you accept their evidence, and what weight you will attach to it. They are all matters for you. Because you get a tremendous number of witnesses called it does not follow that you will be weighed down by the weight of the evidence. You will consider the evidence, and decide what view you take of it.

'There is only just one other matter I will mention before we adjourn this afternoon, and it is this. Just for a moment I am going back to obscenity because I omitted to mention this to you, and I want to make it complete. You are considering this book, and no other book. You, very likely, with your knowledge of this world, know perfectly well that there are a vast number of obscene books which can be bought. You will not judge this book by saying to yourselves, "Oh, this book is not as bad as that book", or "This book is worse than that book". Other books have got nothing at all to do with this case. You might just as well say that because somebody was not charged with some particular type of offence, nobody should be charged with it.'

It was four o'clock, and the proceedings had reached a 'natural break'. Mr Justice Byrne said that the remainder of his observations, which would not take very long, would be best reserved for the following morning; they would concern the Jury's task of balancing the book's obscenity (if they found it obscene) against the likelihood that its literary or other merits would redound to the public good. The Court adjourned.

'* * * * !'

David Langdon in PUNCH, *16 November 1960*

THE SIXTH DAY

'MEMBERS of the Jury,' resumed Mr Justice Byrne the next morning (Wednesday, 2 November), 'in considering this case I would repeat to you an observation that was made by Mr Griffith-Jones. He said, "Keep your feet on the ground". In other words, do not allow yourselves to get lost in the higher realms of literature, education, sociology, and ethics. I say that for this reason. I am going to refer in some little detail to the evidence of some of the witnesses who were called.

'There were two witnesses who were called on behalf of the defendants who made observations, expressed views, which lead me to make that observation to you for your consideration. Do not for one moment imagine I am asking you to take any particular views at all. I put these matters before you for your consideration. You are the judges of the matter.

'One of the witnesses you will recollect was Mrs Bennett. She said: "A reader who is capable of understanding him" – that is to say, Lawrence – "would learn much of what his view is." [Pause] Well, who are the people who are capable of understanding him? You have to think of the public at large. Another witness, Professor Muir, said: "I think it is impossible to understand any one book of Lawrence without having read all, and that this" – that is this book – "is very fundamental to the understanding of the whole."

'If a person is an authority on English literature as the vast bulk of these witnesses unquestionably are, if a person has been a student of this particular author as the great bulk of these witnesses have all been, then this book, you may think, might present a very different picture, so to speak, from what it would to a person with no literary background, no learning or little learning, and no knowledge or little knowledge of

Lawrence. Those are the considerations which in my view you must apply to this aspect of the case.

'Now just let me remind you of the evidence. I do not propose to remind you of the evidence of every one of these witnesses, but I will remind you of the more salient features of the evidence of a number of them.'

His Lordship then selected salient passages from the evidence of twenty-one of the witnesses, quoting from the type-written transcript of each day's proceedings, and rounding off each citation with a few words of studied disengagement.

Thus of Mr Graham Hough, who had said that Lawrence was concerned with 'the nature of proper marriage', he said 'You will have to ask yourselves what you understand him to mean when he speaks of "the nature of proper marriage". There was a proper marriage in this book, Lady Chatterley and her lawful husband. Another relationship, which it is suggested became a permanent relationship, was the relationship between Lady Chatterley and the gamekeeper, but there is nothing in the book to indicate that it was ever a marriage or ever would be. You have read the book, and you will know whether it is right or wrong to say that Lady Chatterley's husband had said that he would not divorce her. The gamekeeper, incidentally, had a wife also. Thus what the ultimate result there would be is a matter for you to consider.' And of Mr Hough's view that promiscuity was condemned by Lawrence, but that adultery figured in 'a great deal of fiction in Europe, from the Iliad on', the Judge said: 'Well, you have got to say what view *you* take of the matter. Of course, pay the greatest attention to the evidence of these witnesses, who no doubt have all expressed very sincere opinions with regard to this book, but you are the final judges of the matter whether there was promiscuity, whether promiscuity was condemned in this book by Lawrence.' Promiscuity and adultery had indeed, become major issues, obscenity and exculpatory merit being for that purpose irrelevant. Mr Hough had said that, in using the four-letter words, Lawrence was trying to redeem words which were 'normally obscene' and 'generally used in contexts of mockery or abuse'. 'Is that *your* view of it?' asked

he Judge. 'Is *that* what he is trying to do? You have read
he book. You must be careful not to be led away by what
ome people have decided is the real message and the real
hought which were operating so far as the author was con-
erned. *Is* he wishing to find language in which these sexual
matters can be discussed openly, or is he using those words, as
ou read the book, coarse words, the sort of words which
might be used by a man in the position of the gamekeeper? Are
hose words part of the general make-up of this book which
n the submission of the Prosecution is not justified as being
or the public good?'

Some of the witnesses, continued Mr Justice Byrne, had
aid: 'Well, the book really does not deal simply and solely
with sexual relationships; it deals with other matters as well –
he industrial state of the country, the hard lives that people
re living, the way it affects human relationships and so forth.'
The Judge compared this with Miss Helen Gardner's view
hat the descriptions of sexual intercourse were central to the
heme and meaning of the book. 'Whether you find there is
ery much of this book which deals with that aspect or not is
matter for you,' he said, 'but at any rate Miss Gardner said
hat the core and heart of the book's theme and meaning was
he description of sexual intercourse.' And of Miss Gardner's
vocation of Henry James and 'the bitch goddess success', the
emoteness of men from each other and from the sources of
appiness, his Lordship said: 'Well, as I say, these various
witnesses have purported to tell you what was in the mind of
he author, what the message was that he was proposing to
give or attempting to give by this book, and of course you
vill pay whatever attention you consider is right to their
vidence, and you will make your assessment of it. But you
vill no doubt ask yourselves whether, unless a person was a
tudent of literature, an authority on English literature, and a
tudent of Lawrence, he would be able to read into this book
he many different things that many of these witnesses have
aid he intended should be in the book.'

Mrs Joan Bennett had said, of the allegation that Lawrence
et adulterous intercourse on a pedestal, that he was 'obviously

set against promiscuity', and that 'by "adulterous" he mean
that a marriage can be broken when it is unfulfilled – the
book is not against divorce'. (Pause) 'Well,' said the Judge
'what on earth *that* answer means is a matter for you to con
sider, but she clarified it a little later on. She disagreed tha
sex is dragged in at every conceivable opportunity and that th
story is little more than padding. She was asked why she sai
that, and her answer was: "Well, for one thing, it is not wholl
about sex. I mean, Lawrence is also interested in, though
don't think he does this quite so well, he is clearly interested i
social questions in the book; and some part of the book i
concerned with upper classes, middle classes, working classes
and their relations to one another. But in any case I don'
think 'padding' is the right word, because you are al
through the story being led to the climaxes, which are,
suppose, what are objected to."

'Then Mr Gardiner put some more questions, one o
which was, "When you said that Lawrence's view on marriag
appeared from the book, what exactly did you mean by that?"
and she said "Well, I meant that what appears very clearl
in the book is that he believes that marriage – not in the lega
sense . . ." What *is* a marriage if it is not in a legal sense
[Pause] What *are* we talking about? This is a Christian country
and quite apart from Christianity there is a lawful marriage
even if it is only contracted before a registrar. What *are* w
talking about – "a marriage not in the legal sense"? Howeve
. . . he believes that marriage – not in the legal sense – that th
union between two people for a lifetime and with possibilit
for childbearing included, marriage in that sense is of th
highest importance, of almost sacred importance." Almos
sacred importance', repeated Mr Justice Byrne slowly.

And later, after a long dissection of Mrs Bennett's answer
in cross-examination on marriage and adultery, he came to th
point where he had intervened himself: 'Mr Griffith-Jone
said, "This book, my learned friend in his opening says tha
it clearly showed the author's very strong support for mar
riage; but this series of adulterous intercourses – you don'
suggest that that shows a very strong support for marriage, d

you, in the sense that I use the word marriage?" The answer was, "Well, *you* use the word – could you define the sense you use it in?". I intervened at that moment and said, "Lawful wedlock, madam. You know what that means, do you not?" She said, "Yes. Well, I am afraid I would have to repeat that the book shows that as to lawful wedlock Lawrence believes that it can be, as I believe the law allows, broken on certain conditions." Mr Griffith-Jones said, "I do not want to repeat it, but he shows the woman breaking it without any conditions at all, without even telling her husband, does he not?" The answer was, "Yes." Question: "And indeed one does not want to speak disrespectfully of the dead, but if one is talking about what the author's views were and what he was endeavouring to show, that is in fact, is it not, exactly what he himself had done? He had run off with his friend's wife, had he not?" The answer was, "Yes." Question: "And married her?" Answer: "Yes." Question: "And it is just that type of behaviour, is it not, that is depicted in this book?" To that the witness did not make a reply. The question was repeated, "Is it not?" Answer: "You mean that a woman is shown . . .", and she was interrupted by the question, "I mean a man running off with another man's wife. It is just that which is happening throughout this book? The whole book is about that subject, is it not?" The answer was, "Yes." [Pause] That was *her* evidence.' (It will not escape the reader's notice that, in a trial concerned with *obscenity* and its possible justification by literary merit, the whole of this colloquy had been concerned with the question, universal as it is in world literature, of adultery.)

His Lordship then turned to the evidence of Dame Rebecca West, who, on the literary merits of the book, had said that it was 'full of sentences of which any child could make a fool because they are badly written'. 'That', said Mr Justice Byrne, 'was *her* view, for what it is worth.' Dame Rebecca had said that although many pages in the book seemed to her ludicrous, a work of art was 'not an arbitrary thing', it was 'an analysis of an experience and a synthesis of the findings of the analysis that makes life a serious matter and makes the world seem beautiful; and though there are ugly things, though there is this unsuccessful attempt to handle the ugly words, this is still from that standard a good book, in my opinion.' 'Well,' said Mr Justice Byrne, 'you will decide the matter.'

Then, he said, they entered the world of ethics when the Bishop of Woolwich gave evidence. He said that what Lawrence was trying to do was to 'portray the sex relationship as something essentially sacred'. Mr Justice Byrne looked up from his notes. 'Something essentially sacred!' he said slowly. He recalled the Bishop's quotation of Archbishop William Temple, that 'Christians do not make jokes about sex for the same reason that they do not make jokes about Holy Communion, not because it is sordid, but because it is sacred, and I think Lawrence tried to portray this relation as in a real sense something sacred, in a real sense an act of holy communion.' It had seemed to many people in Court that this reference to an act of total communion between two persons might indeed, in the Lawrentian view of life, partake of the character of holiness. But – 'Where *are* we getting to?' said the Judge expressively. '*You* will consider. It is for *you* to decide. Reading that book, do *you* find that it is a book in which the author is trying to portray sex in a real sense as something sacred, as an act of holy communion?'

Coming to the Bishop's cross-examination about the ethical value of the book, the Judge came back also to adultery.

'Then', he said, 'I put the question: "As you read the book does it portray the life of an immoral woman?", and the answer was, "It portrays the love of a woman in an immoral relationship in so far as* adultery is an immoral relationship." Well,' said Mr Justice Byrne, nevertheless, '*is* adultery an immoral relationship? It is a matter for you to consider.'

Mr Gardiner had asked the Bishop whether *Lady Chatterley's Lover* was a book which, in his view, 'Christians ought to read'. (This was not generally understood to be a suggestion

---

* The phrase 'in so far as' was understood by most people in Court to mean 'inasmuch as'; accepting as a fact of social judgement that adultery is an immoral relationship, and that to that extent Lady Chatterley was an 'immoral woman'.

that it should be a set book for the faithful, but rather an inquiry whether they should be told not to read it at all. The
Bishop had seemed to say no more than that they might read it
with profit. He was going on to say why, when Mr Griffith-
Jones objected.) But 'at any rate,' said the Judge, 'there is the
Bishop saying that he thinks this is a book that Christians ought
to read. It is for you to say whether you are of opinion that
this is a book which is designed as being for the public good.

'And so one goes on through the evidence of these witnesses. Then we come to another clergyman, Prebendary
Hopkinson. He dealt with the ethical and sociological merits
of the book. He said it was a book of moral purpose. He
put it in this way (so that one shall not summarize his evidence
too much): "It seems to me to be a study in compassion and
human tenderness, not solely in relation to the two leading
characters but in relation to all the other persons of the book;
that, as part of this instrument of essential human relationships, it deals with a physical one, and he seems to me to deal
with it with respect and honesty and only in so far as it is

essential to the whole theme of human relationships. I think, therefore, that, judged as a whole, it is a book of moral purpose which does set out a picture of understanding and kindness, that nothing in it is out of key or keeping with that, and that in fact it emphasizes what is to me an important part of the Christian tradition: that God is himself a creator, that man shares in the responsibility for creation, and that that is directly expressed in the relationship of the sexes, particularly as regards the procreation of children."' Prebendary Hopkinson's cross-examination was reviewed. He had dealt with the ethical and sociological aspects of the book, and thus the *leitmotiv* of adultery was sustained. 'The whole book is about that?' he had been asked. He said it was about a marriage that went wrong, and that 'afterwards she takes what I would totally agree to be a wrong course, but the marriage had failed before this happened'. 'The marriage, of course, had failed', said his Lordship, 'in the sense that the unfortunate man had been wounded and had become paralysed from the waist down. But that was Prebendary Hopkinson's view of the matter.'

Even Mr Richard Hoggart, there to testify about literary merit, was kept largely to adultery. He had said that the relationship between Constance Chatterley and the gamekeeper was not conceived as a promiscuous relationship, but really moral. 'Does that agree with *your* reading of this book?' the Judge asked the Jury. 'Do *you* find that the relationship was really moral? Do *you* find that there was any spark of affection between these two people until quite late in the book? There were all the instances of sexual intercourse between them, to the accompaniment of these four-letter words, as they are called. Do *you* find – it is for you to say, and you, of course, will not pay the slightest attention to what I am saying unless you agree with it; I only put it forward for your consideration – do *you* find that in the earlier stages those people had a spark of affection for each other, or were they merely having sexual intercourse and enjoying it, and out of that sexual intercourse perhaps some affection ultimately sprang? It is for you to say. You have read the book. You are the judges. 'Mr Hoggart was eventually cross-examined, you will remember, about one of the passages in this book upon the question as to whether it was virtuous if not puritanical, and the passage was read to him, I think I am right in saying, beginning on about page 180 (I am not going to read it to you, you have read the book and you have heard passages read over and over again). Mr Griffith-Jones, having read that passage to Mr Hoggart, said: "That again, I assume you say, is puritanical?" And the answer was, "It is puritanical in its reverence." [Pause] Well, it is for *you* to say what weight you attach to *that* opinion.'

Mr Cammaerts, the headmaster of a Grammar School, had said that it was the only book he knew that treated the sexual relationships between human beings in a really serious way, and that it would have the effect on most young people interested in this problem of giving them a serious approach to it. 'Does *that* coincide with your view of the matter', asked the Judge, 'that this book has the effect, on most young people who are interested in the problem of sexual relationships between human beings, of giving a serious approach to it? [Pause] Well, there it is.'

His Lordship quoted without comment the evidence of Miss Beryl Jones, and of Miss C. V. Wedgwood ('she is an author, you will recollect, of some dozen books ...'). Mr Francis Williams was quoted at some length on Lawrence's belief that the intellectuals were an effete and doomed society, and on the justification of the use of four-letter words for Lawrence's artistic purpose. 'There again,' Mr Justice Byrne said, 'he, like a number of these witnesses, is looking into the mind of the author and saying what, in his opinion, the author was driving at. Whether that is apparent, or was apparent to you when you read this book is another matter. Whether it would be apparent to the public when they read this book is a question that you have to decide, because you have to decide whether the publication of this book is justified as being for the public good.

'Then Doctor Hemming,' he continued, 'who, you will recall, is a Doctor of Philosophy, and a consultant to publishers on psychological and educational matters – he said of this book that in his opinion it is an antidote to the idea that sex is nothing more than a physical thrill. You will, of course, make up your *own* minds about that. *You* will decide that and ask yourselves whether upon reading this book as ordinary persons, without great knowledge of literature, without a great knowledge of the author, whether you regard it as an antidote to the idea that sex is nothing more than a physical thrill, or whether it leads you to the conclusion that it is a book which indicates a *tremendous* amount of thrill in sexual intercourse. Those are entirely matters for you, and don't think for one moment I am asking you to take any particular view. It is entirely your province.

'I am not dealing with every witness who gave evidence, because I don't think it is necessary, but there was Mr Norman St John-Stevas, who is an author and a Barrister-at-Law, and he dealt with the literary merit of the book, and he said it was a moral book.' His Lordship did not remind the Jury that Mr St John-Stevas was a Roman Catholic, or that he was the author of the text book so much quoted during the trial, *Obscenity and the Law*. But in dealing with Mr St John-Stevas's opinion – a personal one, not advanced as being that of the Catholic hierarchy – that Catholics might profit by reading the book, his Lordship said: 'Well, that was *his* view. You may perhaps think it a little presumptuous for him to say every Catholic priest should read the book, because he would profit by reading it. But at any rate, he is entitled to express his opinion and he has expressed it and it is for you to say what you think of it.

'Then there was the Master of the Temple, who was full of praise for this book. There was Mrs Russell, an author, a book reviewer, and a critic [it was Miss Dilys Powell], and *she* said sex in this book is treated on a holy basis. Whether you agree with that is for you to determine. Sex is treated on a holy basis', his Lordship repeated carefully.

'And there was Mr Day Lewis, who is an author and poet and publisher. He said that in his view this was not one of Lawrence's greatest novels, "that it is too much affected in places by his wish to persuade the reader towards what he considered to be the right and wholesome view of sex. At the same time, I feel it to be in quite a different class, a higher class, than the average proficient novel or the average best seller." He was asked whether in fact the only relationship that existed between Lady Chatterley and Mellors was the sexual relationship and he said, "I would agree that most of their talk together is about the sexual side of their relationship, but, for all that, when I read the book I got the strong impression that they were getting to know each other better . . ." [Pause] well, probably they would, I suppose, ". . . they are coming to understand each other better, to feel greater tenderness and tolerance for each other, and this is conveyed to you in the way they talk."

'And there was another reverend gentleman who gave evidence, Mr Tytler, who was the Director of Religious Education in the Diocese of Birmingham, and he said he thought it was a suitable subject for discussion in youth clubs.

'There', said Mr Justice Byrne, 'is a summary of a good many of the witnesses who gave evidence, and I have not troubled you with the evidence of every witness.' (Among the witnesses with whose evidence he had not troubled the Jury, to the real surprise of many in Court, was Mr E. M. Forster.) 'It is conceded by the Prosecution that there is some literary merit in this book. Of course, you must ask yourselves whether some people who have given evidence on behalf of the defendants have approached their task upon the basis: "Lawrence is a good author, this is a book written by Lawrence, and therefore this is a good book." You must ask yourselves whether, as you have read the book, you find that you can agree with that, with all the things that they say Lawrence was saying, was trying to say, the things that they indicate were the message that he was trying to give his readers. You must ask yourselves whether you agree with these expressions of opinion or whether you disagree; because although these witnesses are called to assist you, you, of course, are not bound by their evidence; you are the judges; you make up your minds.'

He then briefly and very clearly restated the law as it

applied to the questions of fact and opinion they had to consider; and he concluded: 'Now, there is the case. You have listened to it, if you will permit me to say so, with the greatest attention. I have pointed out to you the importance of this case, from the public point of view as well as from the point of view of the defendants. The verdict must be the verdict of each one of you, and now will you be kind enough to retire and consider your verdict and tell me how you find.'

The Jury stood up, ready to move off: an usher restrained them while, with uplifted testament, he swore convincingly that he would keep them 'in some convenient place', allow no one to speak to them, and not even speak to them himself. And they filed out of Court at three minutes before midday. The Judge began disposing of some prisoners who were 'up for sentence' on less heinous indictments, and for the Penguin community there began a wait of three hours.

*

It was at 2.53 p.m. that the knell-like whisper swept the Old Bailey corridors: 'Jury coming back.' Court No. 1 quickly filled, the doorways silting up with those who had been too slow off their marks. The Jury came in with their usher, and the Clerk of the Court called their names over, to make certain (one supposed) that they were the same jury.

'Members of the Jury,' said the Clerk, 'are you agreed upon your verdict?' The usher motioned to the foreman to stand up. 'We are', said the foreman, standing up.

'Do you find that Penguin Books Ltd are guilty or not guilty of publishing an obscene article?' – 'NOT GUILTY', said the foreman loudly and firmly; and no one can ever know whether that meant 'not obscene', or 'obscene but justified'.

'And that', prompted the Clerk, traditionally, 'is the verdict of you all?' (It is a question that always raises the sudden fear that a foreman will begin saying 'Well, sir, there *are* two of us who . . .'.) 'Yes', answered the foreman, though his voice was drowned by an outburst of clapping and one or two noises

248

that sounded scandalously like cheers from among the elated *literati* at the back of the Court. This was sibilantly suppressed by the ushers, who, under genuine indignation, can produce the noise of escaping steam; and it was then found that Mr Gerald Gardiner was addressing the Judge.

'My Lord, I apply for costs, if your Lordship thinks it is a proper case, and I do so on the following grounds. In opening this case Mr Griffith-Jones said, no doubt accurately, that "the Company did, in effect, provide evidence of publication of the book, in order that it should be brought before the Jury really *as a test case*". I can understand the desire of the Director of Public Prosecutions to obtain a decision on the construction of this new Act and how it would work; but nobody appreciates being the vehicle for such a case.

'Perhaps your Lordship will allow me to say this. Penguin Books were hopeful that there would not be a prosecution, very largely because, while the form of the law in America is different, all the questions to be considered, such as the standing of the author, the descriptions of intercourse, the four-letter words, the integrity and purpose of the author, the literary merit, were considered in the American case by the American Court and before the Court of Appeal.' (This, properly enough, was the first clear indication in the trial of a fact which, even if it was unknown to the majority of the Jury, was known to almost everyone else in Court: the decision of a United States Federal Court, a year before, that *Lady Chatterley's Lover* was not an obscene book. If the Jury were surprised, no doubt they were also fortified.)

'As your Lordship will appreciate,' continued Mr Gardiner, 'the costs of a case of this kind have been very extensive.' (They were actually £13,000.) 'A number of witnesses and prospective witnesses have all had to be seen. As, therefore, the case was opened by the Prosecution *as a test case*, I would respectfully submit that it is a case in which a very substantial contribution ought to be made to the costs of the defendants.'

It seemed to most people present a reasonable enough

application. Costs in criminal cases may be recovered against the Crown through county funds in the event of an acquittal *if* the Judge makes the necessary order; the mere acquittal is not itself enough to justify this (says a Home Office ruling of 1948), and Lord Goddard laid down in 1952 that 'the power should be reserved for exceptional cases', but the Judges have in recent years been more generous than they were. Too much English case-law has been dearly bought, for the future benefit of all, by luckless litigants subsidizing the law's uncertainties. Mr Justice Byrne had decided that Penguin Books must buy some more. He seemed at first to be about to give some reasons for this; but at last he smiled, a little enigmatically, and pushed his chair back.

'I will say no more than this,' he said, 'that I will make no order as to costs.'

*

One important, final consideration was suggested in a letter written to Penguin's solicitors by Canon V. A. Demant of Christ Church, Oxford. He thought that publication as a Penguin was for the public good; but not, he said, 'in the sense that if no one had written this sort of thing, somebody should.'

And let Mr Gerald Gardiner, denied by the rules of procedure the last word to the Jury, have the last word here: 'There is one thing about which I want to be quite plain, because in my submission it is of some importance not only that you (the Jury) should realize this but that everybody should realize it. It is this: that no one should think that if the use of these words for this special purpose, by this particular author, in this particular book, is legitimate, it will follow that these words can be used by any scribbler writing any kind of novel.'

It was the words that caused all the trouble, putting her Ladyship on trial as an adulteress where a more conventionally spoken gamekeeper might have lent her the immunity of Emma Bovary and Anna Karenina. Two cheers, then for Constance Chatterley and the Act of 1959; but we have been warned.